IMAGES
of America

ARIZONA STATE MUSEUM

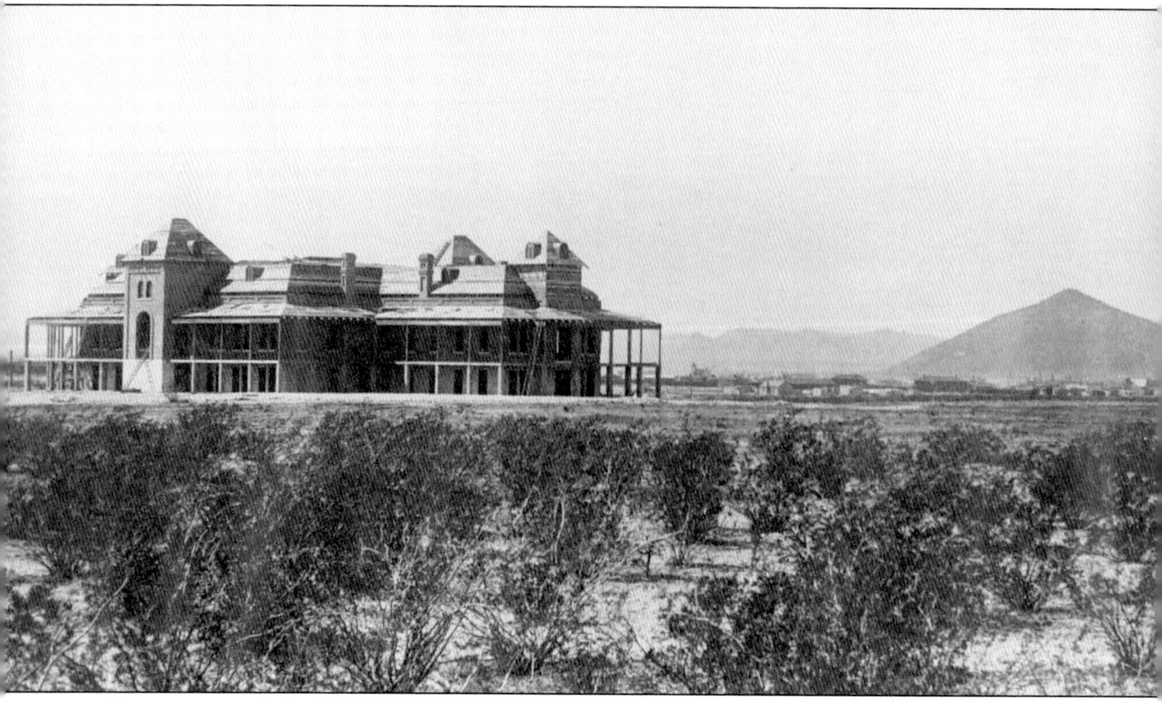

Construction of the first building on the University of Arizona campus lasted from 1887 to 1891. Built in a Territorial Queen Anne style, it was first known as the School of Mines Building, but, since 1927, it has been known as Old Main. Starting in 1893, it would be the first home of the Arizona Territorial Museum. This 1889 view looks southwest, with A Mountain in the distance and, on the far right, the scattered buildings of Tucson. (Photograph by W.P. Haynes, courtesy of University of Arizona Photograph Files, Special Collections, University of Arizona Libraries, Tucson, image no. N-114.)

On the Cover: The former basketry storage room in the Arizona State Museum's South Building is seen here in September 1968 (see page 24). Curator of collections Wilma Kaemlein is posed with historic Pima baskets on the left and Tohono O'odham baskets on the right. Both are Southern Arizona tribes that have always made baskets for their own use. Beginning in the 1800s, they began selling both functional forms and an ever-increasing variety of innovative decorative items to the Mexican and American communities around their reservations. Basketry continues into the present as a vibrant craft and art form for both tribes. (Photograph by H. Teiwes, courtesy of Arizona State Museum, University of Arizona, Tucson, image no. 18826.)

IMAGES
of America

ARIZONA STATE MUSEUM

Alan Ferg

ARCADIA
PUBLISHING

ISBN 978-1-4671-3162-9

Published by Arcadia Publishing
Charleston, South Carolina

Printed in the United States of America

Library of Congress Control Number: 2013952052

For all general information, please contact Arcadia Publishing:
Telephone 843-853-2070
Fax 843-853-0044
E-mail sales@arcadiapublishing.com
For customer service and orders:
Toll-Free 1-888-313-2665

Visit us on the Internet at www.arcadiapublishing.com

To all of the current and past Arizona State Museum archivists, collections curators, photographers, and registrars, who protect and document the objects and information that intrigue and inform us about our collective past

Contents

Acknowledgments

I owe many colleagues a huge debt of thanks for having tutored and entertained me in the history of all manner of people, places, and things. Three in particular need special mention. The first is Phyllis Ball (born 1920, died 1998), who graduated from the University of Arizona (UA) in 1943 with a BA in English and joined the UA Library in 1944, working in the University History, Manuscript and Archives section, the predecessor to UA Special Collections, which she helped create. In 1986, she privately published *A Photographic History of the University of Arizona, 1885–1985*, an astonishing synthesis of 100 years of specific details and dates.

Dr. Raymond H. Thompson, director emeritus of the Arizona State Museum (ASM) and former head of the Department of Anthropology, possesses the acme of institutional memories, apparently the happy combination of an ever-curious mind supported by sturdy synapses. At age 90, he happily answered all of my innumerable questions about topics big and small, and he would then tell me the really interesting part of the story that I had not thought to ask about.

Second only to Dr. Thompson in the prodigiousness of his ability to recall ASM particulars is George Michael Jacobs, who has always gone by Mike. (Mike's runner-up status is probably due to Dr. Thompson having gotten a 25-year head start.) In recognition of Mike's gifts, his coworkers rebranded him "Mikipedia" in 2012. Mike started graduate school at UA in 1968 and began working for ASM in 1970. In 1978, his job title changed, and he became the first and, so far, only curator of Archaeological Collections.

At UA Special Collections, Mona Ammon, Roger Myers, and Charles Wommack helped me find the items I needed. At the UA School of Law Library, Maureen Garmon and Jacquelyn Kasper answered the nagging (for me) question of what to call a territorial legislative bill when it became law. At the Arizona State Museum itself, director Patrick Lyons provided critical logistical support. Diane Dittemore, Beth DeWitt, Rich Lange, John Madsen, and Georgine Speranzo all plied me with information. Thanks to many contributors, but especially to webmaster Laura LePere, the ASM website (www.statemuseum.arizona.edu) is a font of information about ASM. Head of Photographic Collections Jannelle Weakly was crucial to the success of assembling this photographic history; I thank her for the considerable intellectual and technical expertise she cheerfully provided. Last, but hardly least, I would like to thank Tobi Lopez Taylor, whose help made my research on this book more enjoyable and whose skillful editing improved my prose.

Sources of images are indicated at the end of each caption, with the photographer's name (if known) listed first, followed by the image owner and identifying number (if it has one):

AHST: Arizona History Museum, Arizona Historical Society, Tucson.
ASL: Arizona State Library, Archives and Public Records, History and Archives Division, Phoenix.
ASM: Arizona State Museum, University of Arizona, Tucson.
UASC: UA Photograph Files, Special Collections, University of Arizona Libraries, Tucson.

INTRODUCTION

The Arizona State Museum at the University of Arizona, in Tucson, Arizona, was founded in 1893 as the Arizona Territorial Museum. The cast of characters and the mechanics of its establishment are recounted in chapter 1. The impetus for its creation came from territorial legislators' pragmatic concerns about getting Arizona admitted to the union, fortuitously coinciding with the interests and enthusiasms of a few inspired pioneers. Two birds were killed with one piece of legislation. The economic pursuit of statehood is easily understood, but it is less clear how territorial legislator George W.P. Hunt and first curator of the museum Herbert Brown came by their *Wissensdurst*—their "thirst for knowledge," as my high school German teacher liked to say. Hunt was a businessman from Globe whose wife, Helen Duett Ellison, came from a local ranching family. Both were smart, comfortable in this frontier setting, and familiar with their Apache neighbors living on the San Carlos and Fort Apache Indian Reservations. (The Hunts would later donate a major collection of Apache baskets to the fledgling museum; see page 42.) In Globe, Hunt had been the first town mayor, a justice of the peace, treasurer, and supervisor. He was president of the convention that drafted the Arizona state constitution, won seven terms as governor of Arizona, and was briefly US minister to Siam. Based on a lifetime of diverse experiences, Hunt seems to have genuinely believed that education was valuable, and he was a lifelong supporter of the university and museum. Brown, too, was a savvy businessman, a jack-of-all-trades, an editor of the *Arizona Daily Citizen* newspaper in Tucson, and a natural history researcher at heart. While warden of the Yuma Territorial Prison, Brown spent time collecting birds' eggs, nests, and specimens, along with a small, but important, collection of Quechan Indian artifacts. Both men's attitudes may have been formed, in part, by a growing sense in America of the value of museums as social institutions. On the East Coast, where the Smithsonian Institution had been founded in 1846, having a good museum became a point of pride. The Peabody Museum at Harvard was created in 1866, the American Museum of Natural History in New York in 1869, and the University of Pennsylvania Museum in 1887. In 1892, to commemorate the 400th anniversary of the discovery of America by Christopher Columbus, the Columbian Historical Exposition was held in Madrid, Spain, and featured exhibits of archaeological and ethnographic materials from the Southwest. The World's Columbian Exposition, or Chicago World's Fair, opened to the public in May 1893. The anthropological collections assembled for exhibits at this fair gave rise to the creation of the Field Museum of Natural History in 1893 (opened six months after the founding of ASM).

In the West, the University of Utah was founded in 1850. In 1864, the Arizona territorial legislature created what would become the Arizona Historical Society, Arizona's first cultural institution. All of these events, directly or indirectly, must have helped set the stage for the legislature to create a territorial museum once the idea was proposed. And the rest is the ongoing history of the Arizona State Museum. To the list of catchy C-words touted by Arizona politicians, tourism bureaus, and business leaders as the strengths and virtues of Arizona, we at ASM believe that another should be added so that the list reads: "Copper, Cattle, Cotton, Citrus, Climate, and *Culture*."

Important Dates in the History and Growth of the Arizona State Museum

1893: first curator, Herbert Brown
1915: first director, Byron Cummings
1937: locking bookcases for Cummings's library built by Emil W. Haury
1938: second director, Emil W. Haury
1941: first open house
1943: first curator of collections, E.B. Sayles
1943: first secretary, Frances T. Slutes
1948: Gladys Sayles Memorial Library collection established
1948: sales desk/gift shop established
1952: first exhibits preparator, Robert G. Baker
1957: library becomes an official entity as a result of Rev. Victor Stoner bequest
1962: first associate director, Edwin N. Ferdon
1963: first librarian, Beth C. Chery (Joan Evans as museum assistant since 1960)
1964: third director, Raymond H. Thompson
1964: ASM Archives established by John Baroco, Edward Spicer, and Edward Dozier
1964: first ethnologist, Bernard L. Fontana
1964–1981: Highway Salvage Program (in the works since 1955)
1965: first photographer, Helga Teiwes (started in 1964 on Snaketown project)
1968: Human Identification Laboratory established
1972–1990: Cultural Resource Management Section/Division (in the works since 1970)
1973: first bookkeeper, Martha B. Morrow
1973: Zooarchaeology Laboratory established with hiring of Stanley J. Olsen
1973: first curator of ethnohistory, Rev. Charles W. Polzer
1975: Office of Ethnohistorical Research established
1978: first head of collections, Jan Bell
1978: first curator of Archaeological Collections, Mike Jacobs
1978: first curator of Ethnological Collections, Seth Schindler
1978: first curator of Photographic Collections, Alice Holmes (started in 1972)
1980: first registrar, Steve Rogers
1981: first conservator, Barbara Pough Moore
1983: Conservation Laboratory established with hiring of Nancy Odegaard
1984: first archivist, Jeanne Armstrong
1990: first repatriation coordinator, Lynn S. Teague
1990: first curator of Archaeological Repository Collections, Arthur W. Vokes
1992: Native American Advisory Group established (in the works since 1980s)
1993: Southwest Indian Art Fair (SWIAF) founded by Jan Bell
1995: AZSITE Consortium founded by Beth Grindell and Rick Karl
1996: Human Identification Laboratory renamed Bioarchaeology Laboratory
1998: fourth director, George J. Gumerman
1998: first director of development, Miriam Nickerson
1998: first director of marketing, Darlene Lizarraga
1999–2011: ASM Advisory Board
1999: first curator of American Indian Programs, Alyce Sadongei
1999: Native American Advisory Group renamed Southwest Native Nations Advisory Board
2002: fifth director, Hartman H. Lomawaima
2005: Friends of ASM Collections established by Diane Dittemore
2008: sixth director, Beth Grindell
2012: first deputy director, Irene Romano
2013: seventh director, Patrick D. Lyons
2013: ASM Director's Council established by Patrick D. Lyons

The Arizona State Museum is the oldest and largest anthropology museum in the Southwest. (The American Southwest is largely the same as the Spanish Colonial and Mexican Northwest, taking in essentially all of the states of Arizona and New Mexico, much of Sonora and Chihuahua, and bits of California, Nevada, Utah, and Colorado. The mnemonic for remembering its rough boundaries is that it reaches from Durango, Mexico, to Durango, Colorado, and from Las Vegas, Nevada, to Las Vegas, New Mexico.) It is a rare hybrid in being both a state museum and a university museum in a land-grant institution. The three-fold land-grant mandate of teaching, research, and service is echoed in the museum's mission statement: "The Arizona State Museum promotes understanding of and respect for the peoples and cultures of Arizona and surrounding regions through research, stewardship of collections, and public outreach." Mandated responsibilities include administration of the Arizona Antiquities Act, state laws providing protection to human burials on state and private lands in Arizona, permitting all archaeological and paleontological work done on state lands in Arizona, and curating in perpetuity the materials and documentation resulting from those projects.

ASM's collections of Southwestern Native American materials, both prehistoric and historic, are among the world's largest. ASM cares for more than three million objects, including 500,000+ photographic negatives and prints, 300,000+ catalogued archaeological items, 40,000+ ethnographic items, 4,000+ animal skeletons, 90,000 library books and periodicals, 1,000+ sound recordings, 15,000+ linear feet of archival documents, and 6,000+ oversize maps.

On April 11, 2013, Dr. Raymond H. Thompson, the ASM director with the longest tenure (1964–1998) and perspective on the museum's history, spoke at ASM's 120th anniversary. His predecessor was Emil Haury (1938–1964), and *his* predecessor was Byron Cummings, the museum's first director (1915–1938). They directed the course of ASM for a combined 82 years, or 70 percent of its 120-year existence. Fortunately for ASM, all were exceptionally good directors, each able to build a bigger and better institution, thanks to the solid work of his predecessor. With the repeated use of the word *predecessor*, this all sounds like some sort of genealogical research, but, in a sense, that is what it is. Dr. Thompson noted that "for many of us who are interested in the story of the Museum, everything that happened before the arrival of Cummings was a prequel. In many ways that is a valid judgment because we have no real personal contact with the first forefathers. We have no one amongst us who knew them and can tell us stories about them. Moreover, while they took important actions that created the Museum, it never became the main focus of their lives. So, they emerge from the mist of our past as lonely patriarchs of almost biblical and, therefore, impersonal significance. In contrast, we have a rich body of recently remembered stories about Cummings, so that we can recognize and appreciate that it was his energy, enthusiasm, administrative talent, and sense of responsibility that started ASM on the road to excellence." Thompson touched upon this "ancestors" theme several times, and rightly so. People should know from whence they came. This volume is a family album for the Arizona State Museum, full of our relatives. Some we know, or knew, personally; others we have only heard stories about. Some are fading from memory, and a few are shirt-tail relatives we did not know existed. But all are part of an extended family going back quite a few generations. So we present them here that we might better know and remember how we came to be the institution we are today, over 120 years after being planted in Tucson, still growing, still flowering.

In a volume of photographs, it seems appropriate to say something about the photographers. Many of the earliest photographs of ASM were taken by faculty in other UA departments and reside in UA Special Collections or in the Arizona Historical Society in Tucson. James William Toumey (born 1865, died 1932) was one of the University of Arizona's six original faculty members and a botanist for the Agricultural Experiment Station. He planted the university's original cactus garden in 1891, and went to Yale University in 1899 to help establish its forestry program. Rubert Burley Streets Sr. (born 1895, died 1981) worked in various positions in the UA Department of Plant Pathology from 1924 to 1978, retiring only when a new UA policy required it. Edwin Francis Carpenter (born 1898, died 1963) joined the UA Department of Astronomy in 1925 and worked there until his death; along with A. E. Douglass and Emil W. Haury, he was a founder of the UA Laboratory of Tree-Ring Research.

Early field and studio photographs for ASM were, for many years, taken by directors Byron Cummings and Emil Haury themselves (there was no one else). After 1943, they were taken by museum curator E.B. Sayles. Other early photographers at ASM have proved difficult to document, and photographs *of* them are rare or nonexistent, as each was almost always behind the camera. In the late 1940s and throughout the 1950s, a Dr. L.F.H. Lowe put in a great deal of time as a volunteer photographer for ASM; the ASM annual report for 1951–1952 alone lists his donation as 500 hours, equivalent to a quarter-time position. More research will be necessary to identify Lowe, but he appears to have been a professor of French literature with a degree from, and retired from, Princeton. In the early 1960s, Gilbert Duke Bartell, Philip M. Hobler, and Bruce Douglas Lindsay may all have been student employees. At the start of 1963, Jim Tallen was apparently hired as a full-time photographer, but he departed after three months for reasons unknown. In 1964, Haury hired Helga Teiwes to photograph his excavations at Snaketown (see page 62). Teiwes was a professional photographer who had not worked in the Southwest or done archaeology before, but she quickly came to love both. After fieldwork ended, she was hired at the museum. Finally, ASM had a permanent photographer. Teiwes (1964–1993) was followed by Ken Matesich (1993–2000), who worked as a student at ASM from 1976 to 1978, and Geoffrey H. Ashley (2001). From 1981 to 1986, Jannelle Weakly worked for ASM's contract division doing fieldwork, laboratory work, and photography. After 10 years teaching school, she returned, was hired in 2001 as the ASM photographer, and continues in that position to the present.

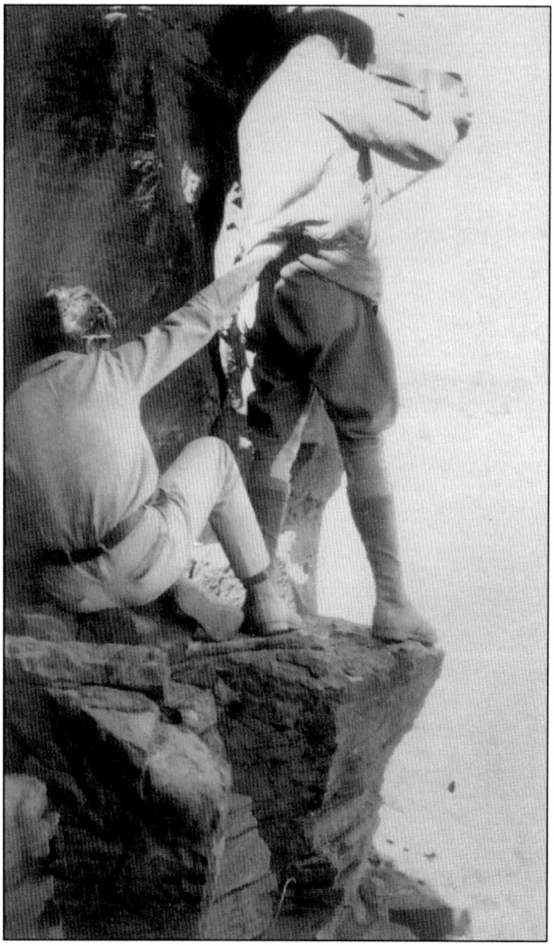

Future ASM director Emil W. Haury is photographing the Canyon Creek Ruin cliff dwelling in the Sierra Ancha Mountains, from across the canyon, in the summer of 1932. Solon T. Kimball steadies Haury on the ledge as small rocks fall into the abyss. (Russell Hastings, Gila Pueblo Archaeological Foundation negative 71184, courtesy of ASM.)

One

Anthropology for Arizona

Arizona is rich in living, vibrant Native American communities, with 22 federally recognized tribes, as well as in archaeological sites and artifacts created by their ancestors. The study of historic/modern peoples is ethnology, and the study of prehistoric (and abandoned historic) materials is archaeology, both of which are subdisciplines of anthropology. Everyone in Arizona is, to a greater or lesser degree, aware of both. The first Spanish explorers in what would become Arizona encountered Native American groups and ruins wherever they went. The massive prehistoric adobe structures at Casa Grande National Monument were first visited by Father Francisco Kino, a Jesuit, in 1694. And, before the federal Antiquities Act of 1906 gave protection to archaeological materials, Pres. Benjamin Harrison created the Casa Grande Reservation in 1892 to protect its buildings—the first national archaeological reservation in US history. In short, residents of the Arizona Territory were well aware of archaeology and ethnology, even if they had never heard the words.

They were also useful words for territorial legislators trying to get Arizona admitted to the union. To smooth the path toward statehood, they passed numerous pieces of legislation aimed at "civilizing" Arizona: a prison in Yuma, an insane asylum in Phoenix, and the University of Arizona in Tucson. It was doubtless hoped that creation of a territorial museum would be considered yet another promising sign of enlightenment in the territory. The 17th Arizona Territorial Legislature met in Phoenix from February 13 to April 13, 1893. Nathan Murphy, the acting territorial governor, opened the session with a call to have it be the last before statehood, a goal that would elude the territory for another 19 years. Rep. George W.P. Hunt sent a draft bill to Murphy proposing the creation of a museum. In an apparent act of bipartisan cooperation rarely seen in Arizona, or anywhere else, in recent years, Democrat Hunt and Republican Murphy exchanged revisions and got the bill passed. Ironically, Murphy's replacement had already been identified. Whether by an act of forbearance or a schedule that did not permit quicker action, President Cleveland did not replace Murphy until April 12, allowing him to essentially complete the work of the 17th Legislature, which ended the next day.

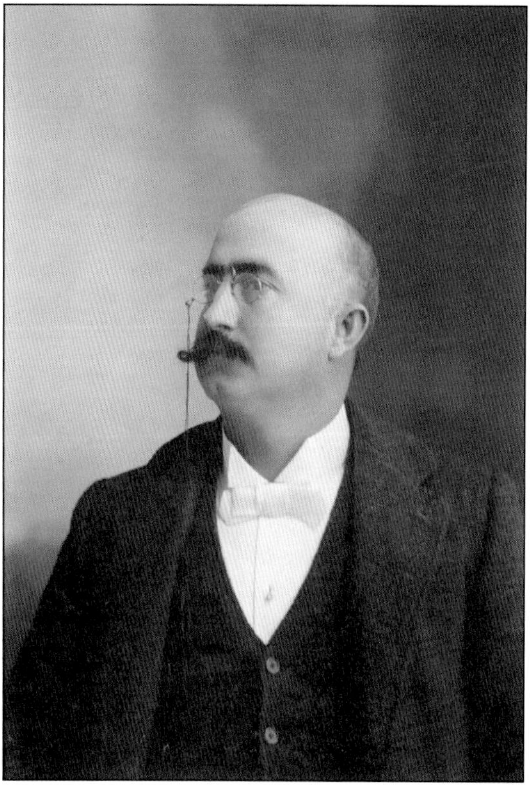

George Wylie Paul Hunt left Missouri at age 18, traveled in the West for three years, and arrived in Globe, Arizona Territory, in 1881. First employed in a restaurant, by 1900, about the time this portrait was taken, he was president of the Old Dominion Commercial (mercantile) Company. In the 1890s, his new career as a politician saw him elected to numerous offices in Gila County and to terms in both houses of the Arizona Territorial Legislature. Upon Arizona's admission to the union on February 14, 1912, he was elected its first governor. (ASL 01-3084.)

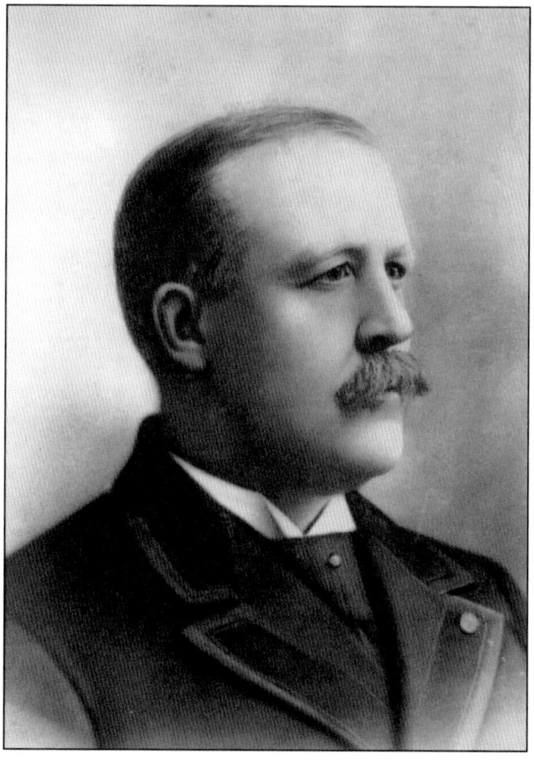

Nathan Oakes Murphy came to Prescott, Arizona Territory, in 1883 and worked in mining and real estate. He entered politics in 1885, and, upon the resignation of territorial governor John N. Irwin, Murphy, a Republican, became acting governor on May 11, 1892. With the election of Democrat Grover Cleveland as president in November 1892, Democratic candidates lined up to replace Murphy even as the 1893 legislative session began. Cleveland took office on March 4, 1893, and Murphy was replaced by Louis Cameron Hughes on April 12, 1893. (Henry Buehman, ASL 96-1389.)

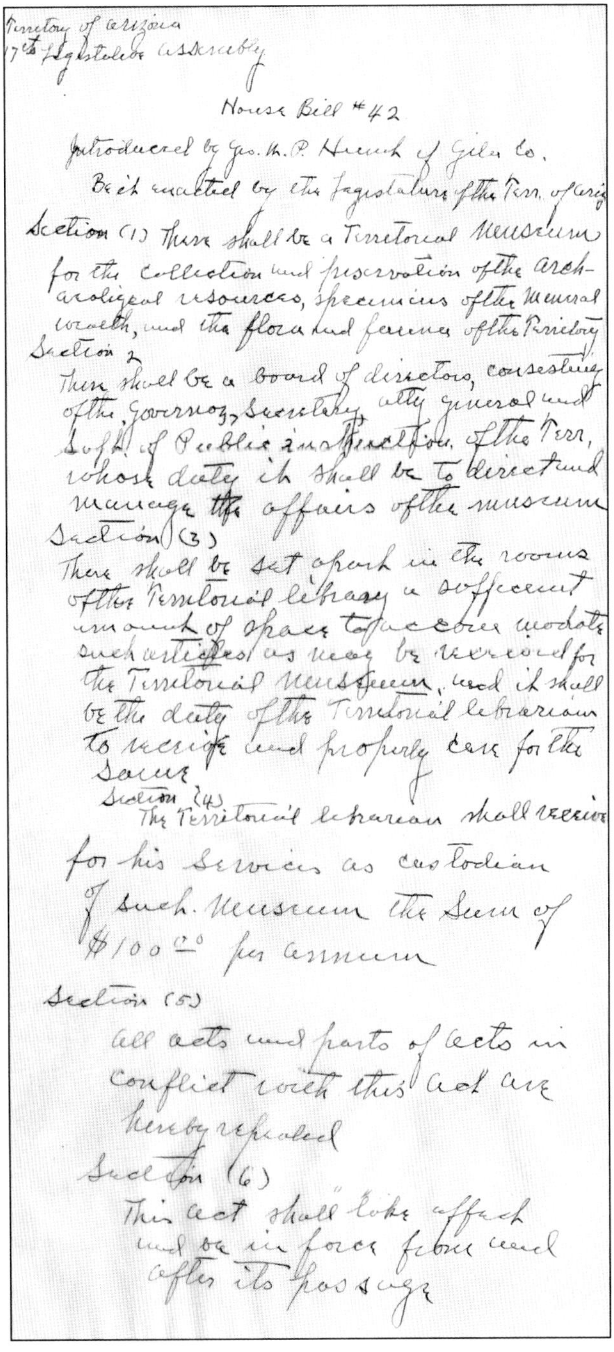

Territory of Arizona
17th Legislative Assembly

House Bill #42

Introduced by Geo. W. P. Hunt of Gila Co.

Be it enacted by the Legislature of the Terr. of Ariz

Section (1) There shall be a Territorial Museum for the collection and preservation of the archaeological resources, specimens of the mineral wealth, and the flora and fauna of the Territory

Section 2
There shall be a board of directors, consisting of the Governor, Secretary, atty general and Supt. of Public instruction of the Terr, whose duty it shall be to direct and manage the affairs of the museum

Section (3)
There shall be set apart in the rooms of the Territorial library a sufficient amount of space to accommodate such artifacts as may be received for the Territorial museum, and it shall be the duty of the Territorial librarian to receive and properly care for the same

Section (4)
The Territorial librarian shall receive for his services as custodian of such museum the sum of $100.00 per annum

Section (5)
All acts and parts of acts in conflict with this act are hereby repealed

Section (6)
This act shall take effect and be in force from and after its passage

During his first term as representative from Gila County to the Arizona Territorial House of Representatives, George W.P. Hunt drafted House Bill 42 to create a territorial museum. His undated, handwritten draft (pictured) proposes the creation of such a museum, to be governed by a board consisting of the governor, secretary, attorney general, and superintendent of public instruction. It was to be housed in the territorial library in Phoenix, with the librarian paid $100 per month to care for the archaeological, mineral, plant, and animal specimens received. On March 17, 1893, acting governor Nathan Murphy returned the draft to the house of representatives, recommending changes. He notes the library is not big enough to accommodate the museum, and, while he mentions the possibility of locating the museum in the territorial capitol building, he twice suggests placing it at the University of Arizona, in Tucson, noting the university has staff who could care for it, and he asks that the university board of regents have oversight of the museum, a seemingly strong endorsement for placing it in Tucson. The changes were adopted, the bill unanimously passed in the house on April 4, and Murphy signed it into law on April 7, 1893 (see page 14). Thus was created the Arizona Territorial Museum, later the Arizona State Museum. Both original documents are in the ASM Archives, a gift from Hunt. (J. Weakly, ASM.)

No. 53. AN ACT

To Create a Territorial Museum.

Be it Enacted by the Legislative Assembly of the Territory of Arizona:

SECTION 1. There shall be a Territorial Museum for the collection and preservation of the archæological resources, specimens of the mineral wealth and the flora and fauna of the Territory.

SEC. 2. There shall be a Board of Directors, consisting of the regents of the University, whose duty it shall be to direct and manage the affairs of the Museum.

SEC. 3. There shall be set apart in the rooms of the Territorial University a sufficient amount of space to accommodate such articles as may be received for the Territorial Museum, which shall be under the direct supervision of the Board of Regents of the University.

SEC. 4. The officer in charge shall receive for his services as custodian of such Museum, the sum of $100.00 per annum.

SEC. 5. All Acts and parts of Acts in conflict with this Act are hereby repealed.

SEC. 6. This Act shall take effect and be in force from and after its passage.

Approved April 7, 1893.

Once signed by acting governor Murphy, House Bill 42 became 1893 Arizona Session Law 53, the official wording of which appears here, reproduced from the printed 1893 *Laws of Arizona*. Lest anyone think that the creation of a territorial museum was the primary achievement or goal of this legislative session, it can be noted that this was the 53rd of 91 laws passed, including regulation of dentists, doctors, prostitutes, and slaughterhouses; prohibitions against carrying concealed weapons and cruelty to animals; the creation of a reform school; and the authorization for a $5,000 reward for the capture of the Apache Kid, a White Mountain Apache scout who had been convicted of mutiny and desertion in 1887. By 1893, the Apache Wars had been over for more than six years. However, the Arizona Territory was still a frontier, and its residents and legislators were eager to bring the Apache Kid's story to a definitive conclusion. While working toward statehood, Arizonans desired to do away with reminders of how bloody the road had been, and emphasize a bright future as one of the United States, complete with a territorial university, library, and museum. (The Apache Kid was never captured, and the date and circumstances of his death are variously reported.) The legal mandates of the Arizona State Museum have changed little over the years. The Arizona Antiquities Act of 1960 explicitly gave legal protection to archaeological sites, artifacts, vertebrate paleontological specimens (fossils), and human remains and funerary objects (Arizona Revised Statutes 41–841 to –844 and 41–865), with ASM being responsible for permits to excavate and collect these materials. The Arizona Board of Regents continues to oversee ASM's activities (*ABOR Policy Manual*, chapter 8). (Photograph by J. Weakly of page from copy of *Laws of Arizona* loaned by UA Special Collections.)

Two

The Museum's Homes

A visit to the University of Arizona campus leaves many with memories dominated by red bricks and red roof tiles. The main difference between the buildings that are quite old and merely old is that the older buildings have nicer, intricate brickwork (compare the images on the top and bottom of page 28). Of the seven buildings that ASM has occupied on the main campus (see pages 38 and 39), five are in the older, western portion of campus that is designated a 33-acre campus historic district in the National Register of Historic Places (NRHP). Both Old Main and ASM North (the old Main Library) have individual nominations to the NRHP as well.

ASM might not be at UA today except that, in 1893, the territorial library in Phoenix was too full to accommodate a housemate. Once at the university, the museum was ensconced in Old Main with all other departments. The university library outgrew its space, and, fearing the legislature would not approve funds for a library building alone, the proposal tacked on the museum. The Library and Museum Building was approved and constructed; 10 years later, the building that was supposed to house the library "for all time to come" had reached capacity. Curator Herbert Brown had died, and, with no one to object, the museum collection was put into storage in the new Agriculture Hall. With Byron Cummings's arrival in 1915, exhibits were set up, and ASM then enjoyed 15 years of stability before again being evicted because the landlord needed the space. In 1930, ASM moved into another newly built, semi-empty facility: the underside of the football stadium. In 1935, the Public Works Administration constructed 10 buildings on campus, including the first home built specifically to house ASM, which, of course, it outgrew. The Anthropology Building, built in 1962, housed some ASM offices. Anthropology grew, and was pleased when ASM inherited the old Main Library and moved out. Having filled ASM South and ASM North, the museum is now hoping for a newer, bigger hand-me-down. As for Old Main, ASM's first home—in 2013–2014, it received an extensive, well-deserved, and badly needed renovation (the first since 1979), as well as some excavation work by ASM archaeologists (see page 70). And, 110 years after moving out, ASM was asked to install new anthropology exhibits in Old Main.

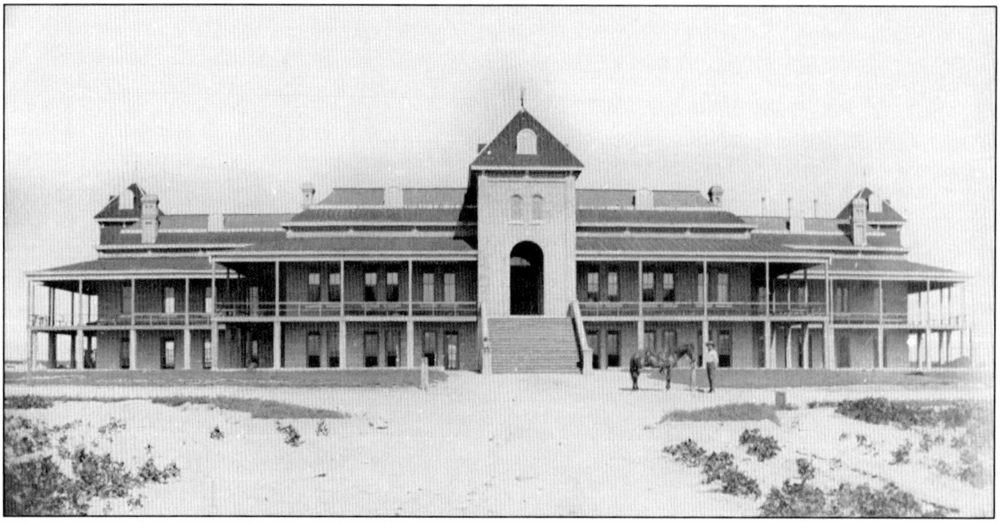

The view in this 1897 photograph is looking east at the front of Old Main, the first instructional building on the University of Arizona campus and the first home of the Arizona Territorial Museum (1893–1904). The foundation was set below grade, and the entire building was encircled by upper and lower roofed porches to shade windows and people. The museum was a second-floor room, probably the six windows to the right of the main entrance and above the man and horse. The original museum exhibits (below) were dominated by natural history specimens, including minerals donated by Thomas Sorin. The first curator of the museum, Herbert Brown, donated his collection of native bird skins, nests, and eggs, which can be seen in the center, upper left, and lower left of this photograph, taken around 1899. Note the newly built exhibit cases that would move with the museum to four future homes in as many decades. (Both, J.W. Toumey; above, UASC N-4681, below, N-10,947.)

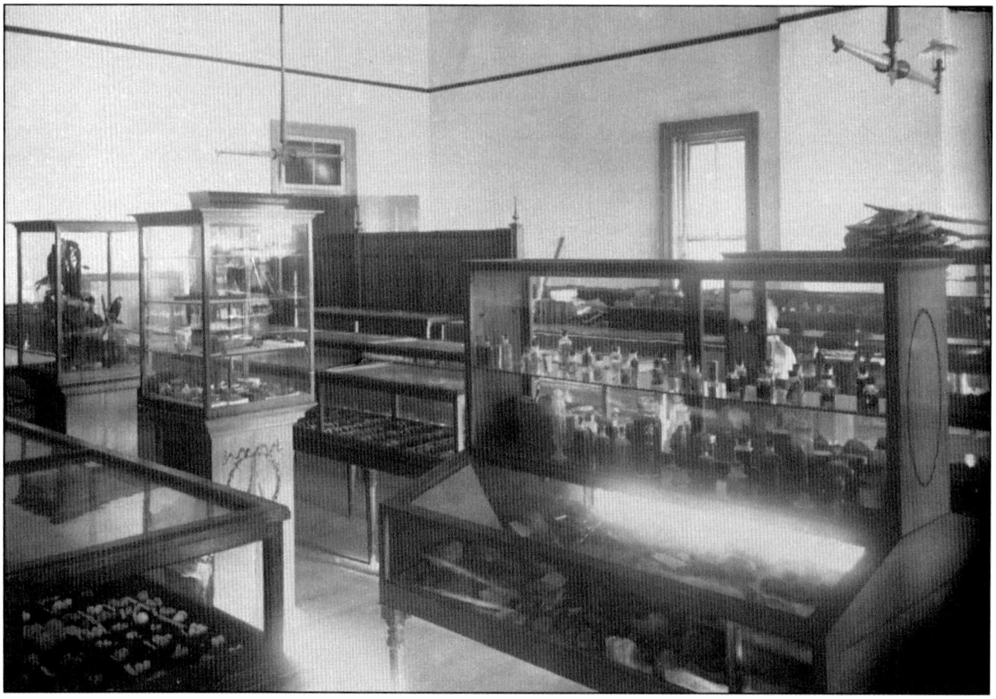

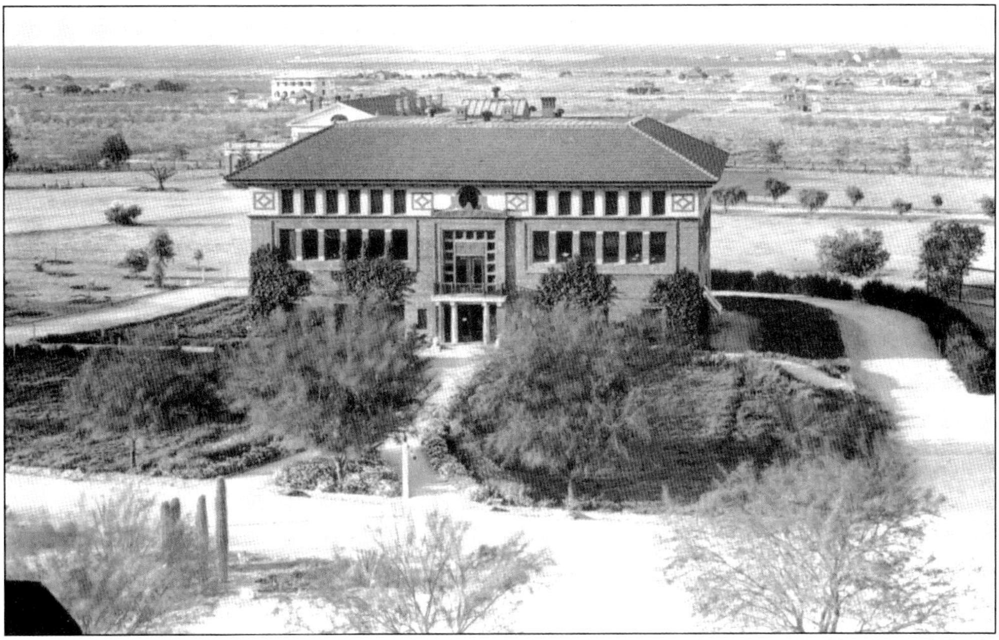

Completed in 1905, the Library and Museum Building (now the Douglass Building) took both departments out of Old Main. The museum occupied the northwest corner of the second floor (the two rows of windows at upper right). This 1911 view looks south. With statehood on Valentine's Day in 1912, the museum became the Arizona State Museum. Below is the only known photograph of museum exhibits in the Douglass Building, probably from 1905, in this view looking north-northeast. The displays closely resemble the previous ones in Old Main (see opposite page). Mostly in the same cabinets, and still dominated by rock specimens, at the back of the room (left center) can be seen cases holding Native American artifacts, bird skins, and 62 plaster figurines showing traditional Mexican costumes that had been donated in 1903. Curator Herbert Brown resigned in 1912 because of illness and died in 1913. Collections were boxed and moved in 1915 to the nearly completed Agriculture Hall. (Above, UASC N-2917; below, N-631.)

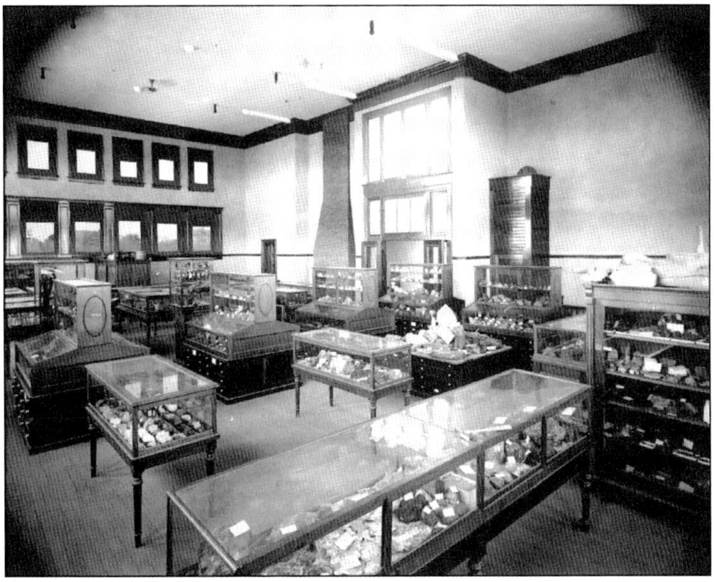

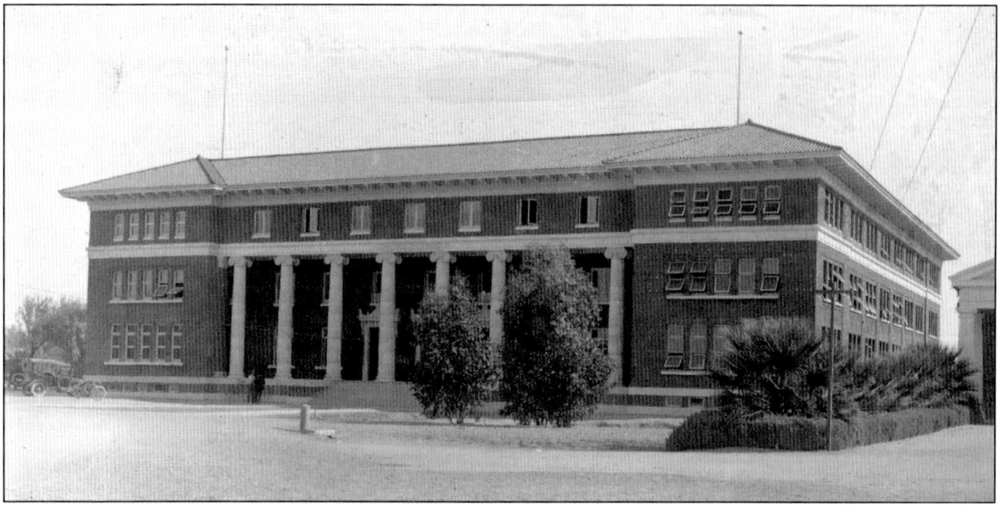

Agriculture Hall (now the Forbes Building), completed in July 1915, became the Arizona State Museum's third home (1915–1929). In September, Dean Byron Cummings was hired as the first director of ASM. The museum occupied the northwest corner of the third floor (five windows at left) and straddled the central hallway, lit by seven windows above the columns on the west face and three overlooking the courtyard on the east. There was also a basement workroom. Below is the only known photograph of the museum's collections in Agriculture Hall, in front of the two southern courtyard windows. The mammoth teeth at the far left could be those excavated by Cummings at Double Adobe in 1927 (see page 57). Prehistoric pots from northeastern Arizona, Chihuahua, and the Gila Bank Ruin, excavated by Cummings and students in 1928 and 1929, all sit on newspapers, presumably waiting to be packed for the museum's move in 1930 to the newly built West Stadium. (Above, UASC N-4679; below, R.B. Streets, UASC N-2065.)

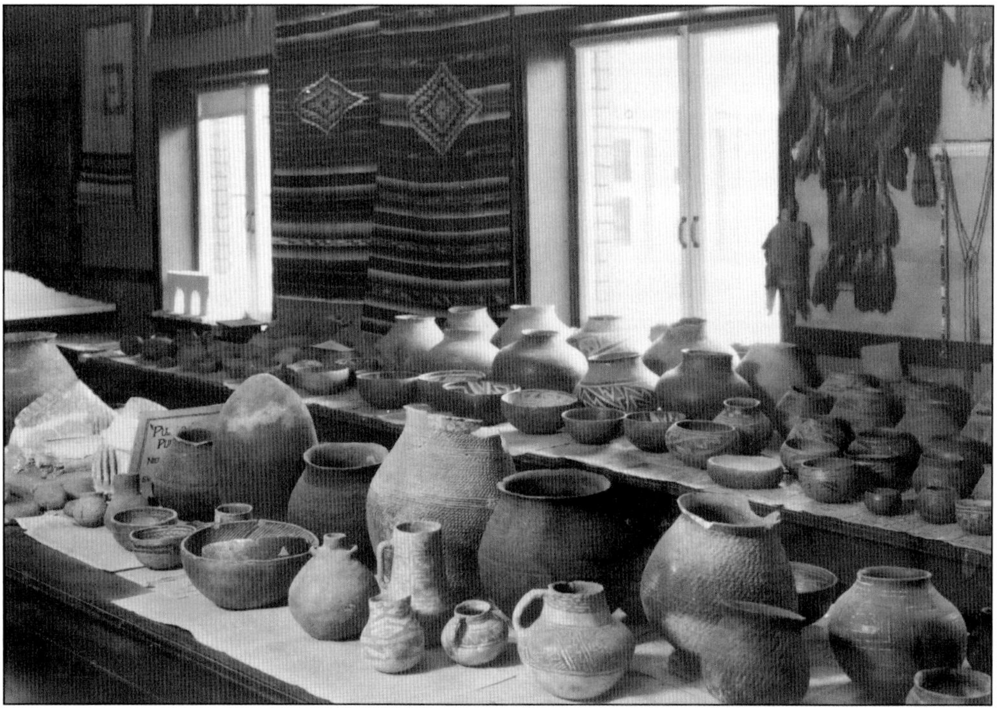

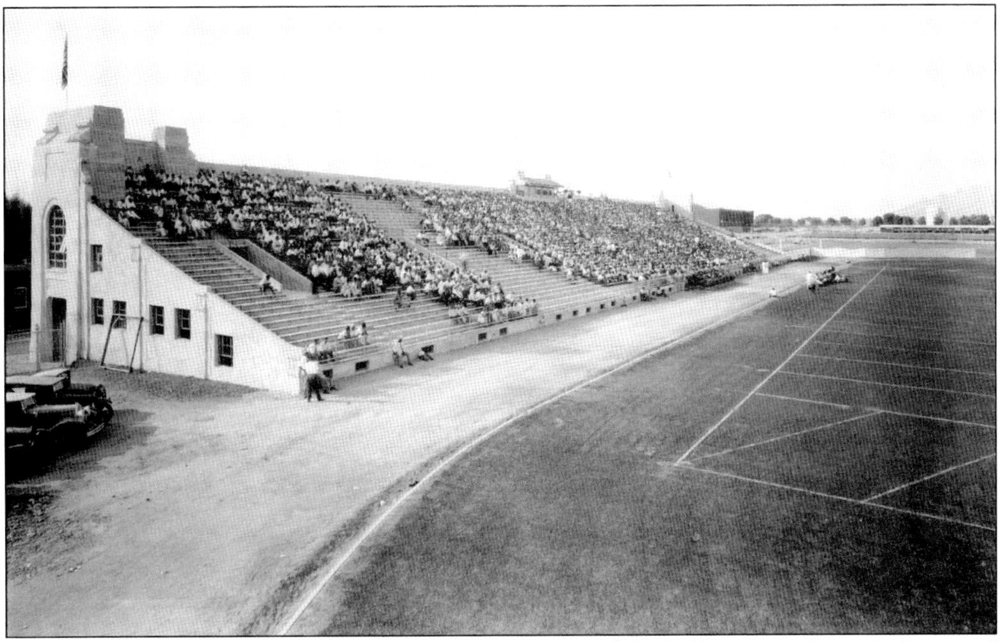

A growing College of Agriculture needed more space, and football came to the aid of arts and culture. Dedicated on October 12, 1929 (above), the West Stadium sheltered the Art Department, the Drama Division, ASM (1930–1935), and the Arizona Pioneers' Historical Society in the rooms built literally under the bleachers. Below is a 1934 view looking northeast through the museum exhibits. The support pillars, beams, and stepped ceiling are all the poured concrete of the stadium supports and seating. Cummings made ingenious use of this unusual space to display hundreds of historic Native American baskets, prehistoric pottery in the center of the room from his various excavations, prehistoric Mexican ceramics in the foreground, and, at right, small artifacts in legged display cases (survivors from Old Main), with bows and edged weapons on the walls and the lowest portions of the ceiling. (Above, UASC N-6339; below, R.B. Streets, AHST 72899.)

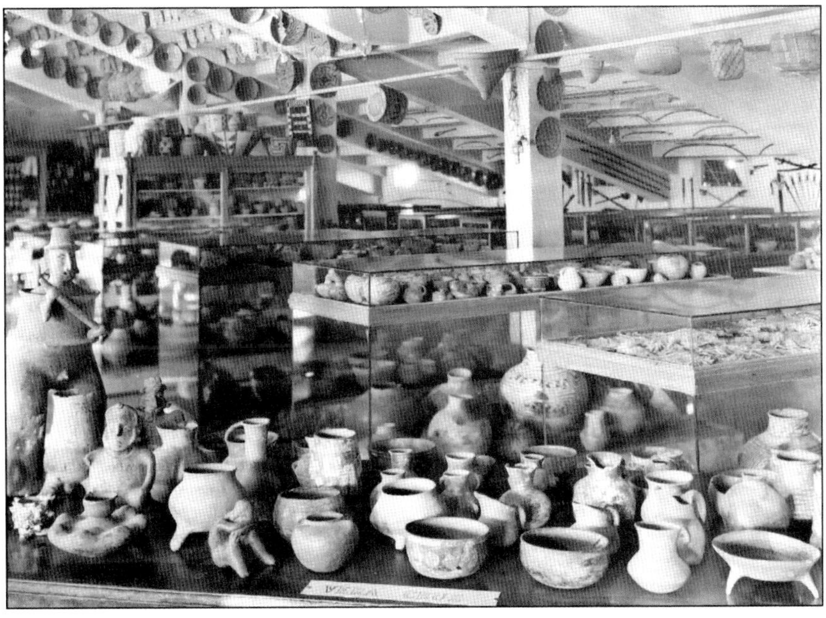

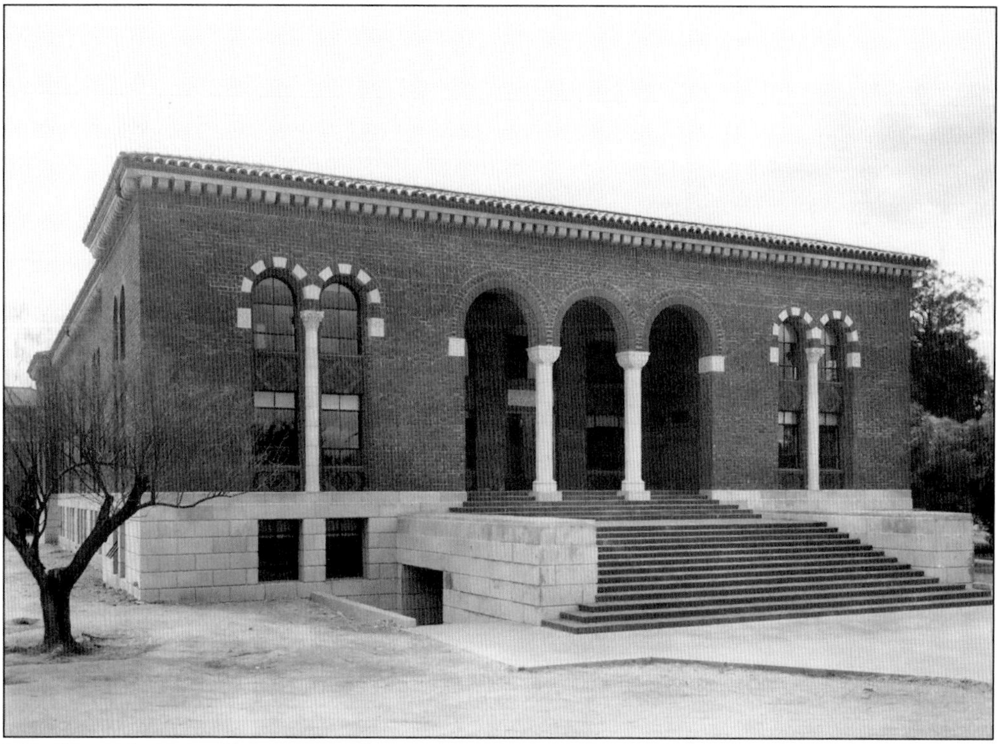

Thanks to the Great Depression, the Arizona State Museum was completed in December 1935 as one of ten buildings constructed at UA by the federal agency best known (from 1935 onward) as the Public Works Administration (PWA). In early 1936, the museum moved in. Above was a two-story exhibit hall, with mezzanines suspended by decorative ironwork. The semi-subterranean basement housed work and storage rooms, with offices and classrooms shared with the Department of Archaeology. When built, it was envisioned as the first wing of a larger museum. The view in this photograph looks south-southwest. (UASP N-629.)

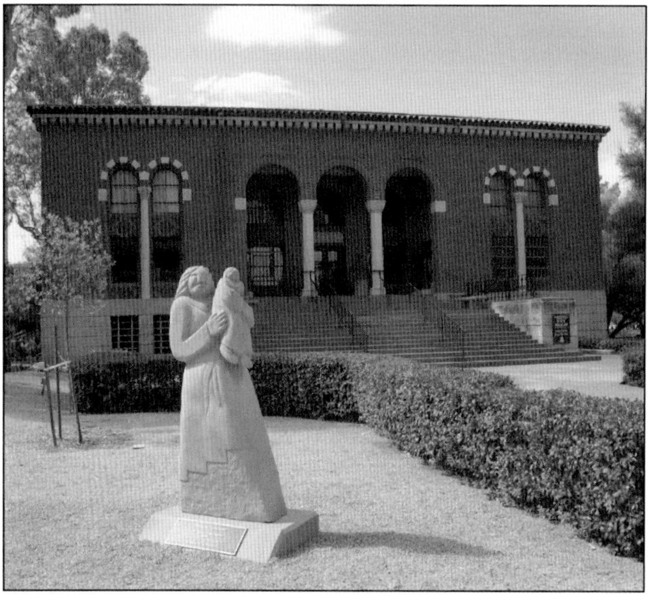

In 2013, at 77 years of age, the exterior of ASM is little changed. Iron railings and landscaping were early additions. Evaporative cooling was installed in 1954, making the interior especially inviting in Tucson's summer months, whether visitors were interested in anthropology or not. The limestone sculpture in the foreground, *Waiting for Grandfather*, by Taos Pueblo artist John Suazo, was dedicated on January 29, 2013. It was a generous gift from the Burt and Brenda Lazar family. (J. Weakly, ASM.)

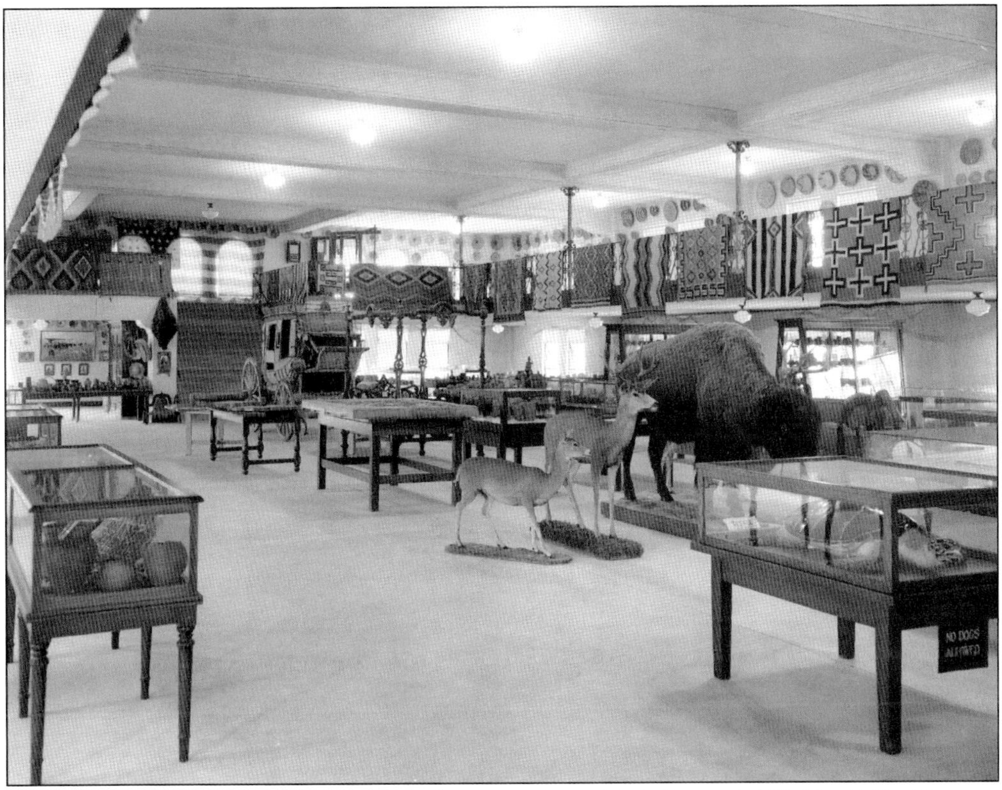

The view in this photograph looks southwest at the exhibit floor of ASM in 1936. Director Cummings believed in displaying everything. At the front left, in a case from Old Main, are Apache pots on loan from Grenville Goodwin (see page 47). At the top of the stairs hangs a flag that flew over Washington, DC, on Arizona statehood day (February 14, 1912), and at bottom is a bell that hung in Old Main to call early UA students to class, as well as a stagecoach. Mezzanine banisters are draped with Navajo textiles. The baskets near the ceiling and the bison had been displayed in the West Stadium. (R.B. Streets, AHST 73191.)

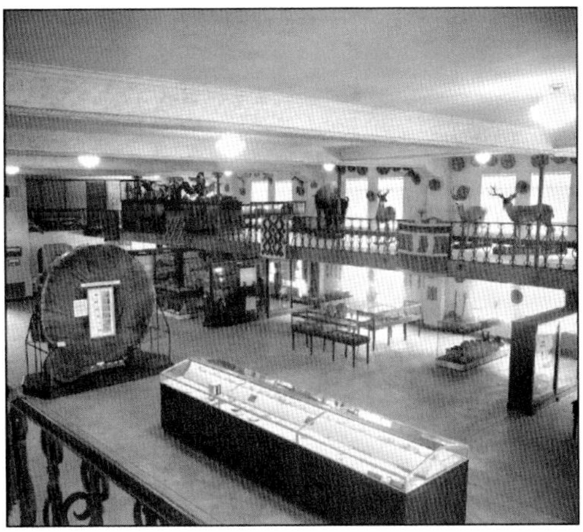

Looking northeast at the exhibit hall in 1941, this view shows the front door at the extreme left. The rugs on the mezzanine banister are fewer now, but exhibit cases from Old Main are still in use. In 1938, retiring director Byron Cummings authorized the installation of a 10-foot-diameter section of a redwood tree from Sequoia National Forest to highlight the science of dendrochronology (tree-ring dating), recently developed by UA astronomer A.E. Douglass (see page 102). In 1939, incoming director Emil Haury added a long exhibit case fully explaining the technique. They would remain on display until about 1995. (UASC N-136.)

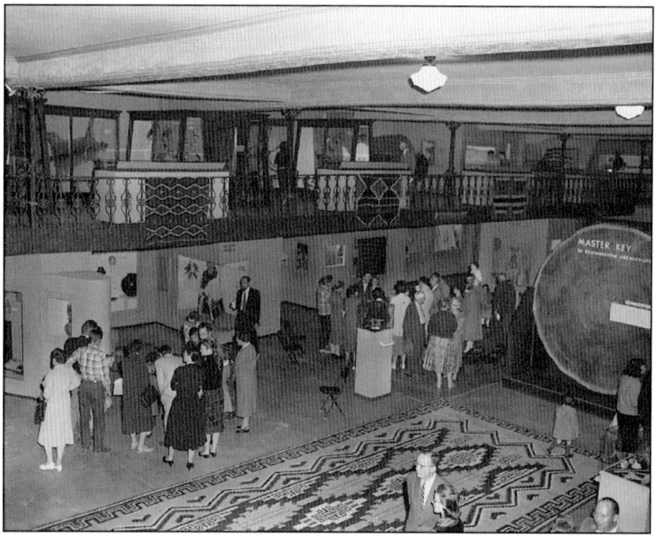

Between about 1946 and 1952, the museum slowly and permanently covered over all of the exhibit hall and mezzanine windows, both to reduce damaging light levels and to allow construction of more appropriate exhibit cases. The large Navajo rug, measuring about 11 feet by 25 feet, was on the floor from at least 1948 to 1968. This view shows exhibits along the east wall during an open house on January 31, 1958, attended by 302 visitors. (James Pollock, ASM 2010-556-1.)

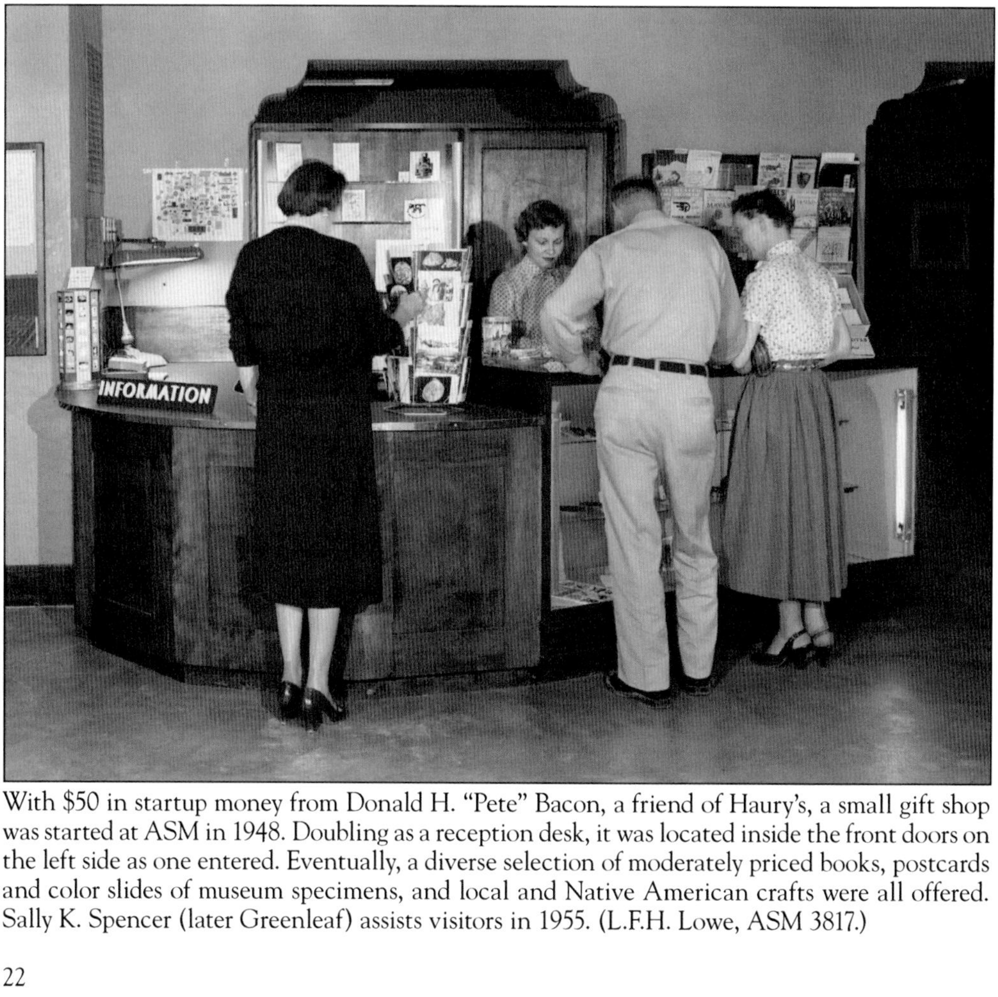

With $50 in startup money from Donald H. "Pete" Bacon, a friend of Haury's, a small gift shop was started at ASM in 1948. Doubling as a reception desk, it was located inside the front doors on the left side as one entered. Eventually, a diverse selection of moderately priced books, postcards and color slides of museum specimens, and local and Native American crafts were all offered. Sally K. Spencer (later Greenleaf) assists visitors in 1955. (L.F.H. Lowe, ASM 3817.)

By December 1966, all of the Navajo rugs had been removed from the mezzanine banister. Haury's vision of how to organize exhibits for educational purposes and reflect the topics outlined in the museum's founding legislation were now fully realized. The main floor was dedicated to Native Americans in the Southwest, with historic tribes featured on the east side and archaeological cultures on the west. The east half of the mezzanine held natural history displays, and the west half was used for temporary exhibits. (H. Teiwes, ASM 15875.)

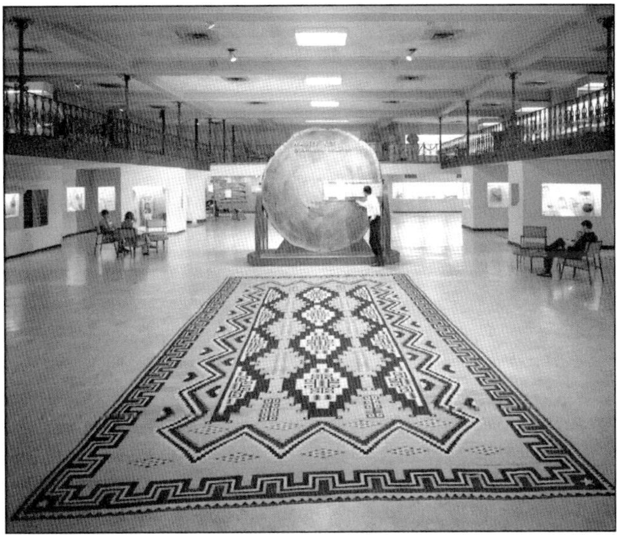

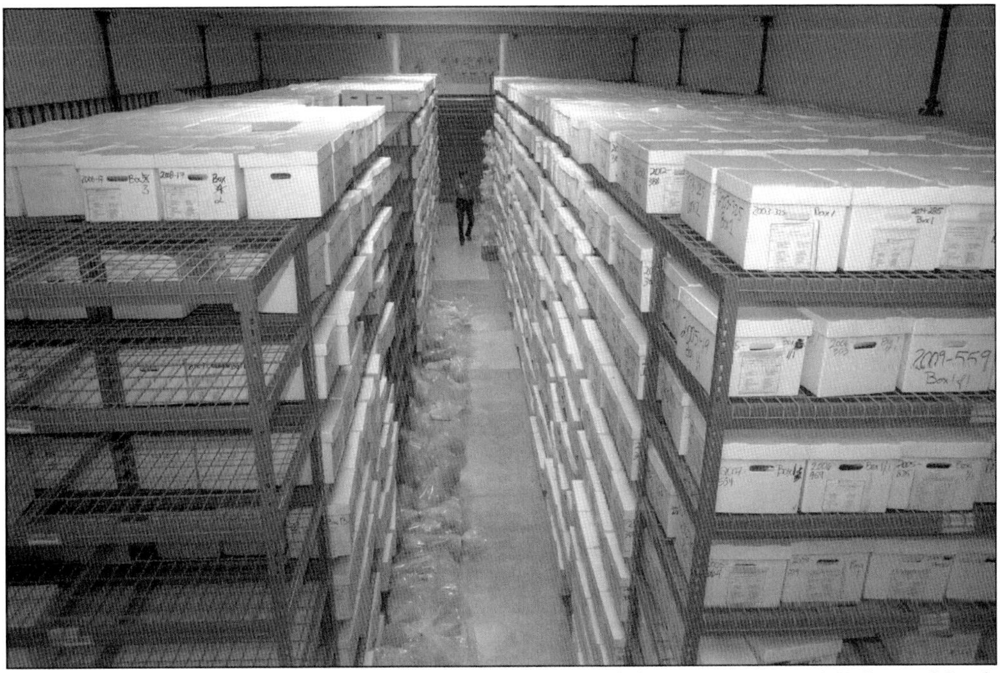

About 1995, the building was closed to visitors, with new exhibits now open in ASM's new North Building (see page 32). The mezzanines were enclosed to create laboratory space for archaeological field projects run jointly with the UA School of Anthropology. In 2010, an off-campus storage facility (see page 40) was closed, and its 12-foot-tall shelving moved to the old exhibit floor to store some 4,900 cartons of artifacts from contract archaeological projects from all over Arizona, including artifacts, animal bones, and soil samples. This is the same view as the 1966 photograph at the top of the page, but from the mezzanine. (J. Weakly, ASM.)

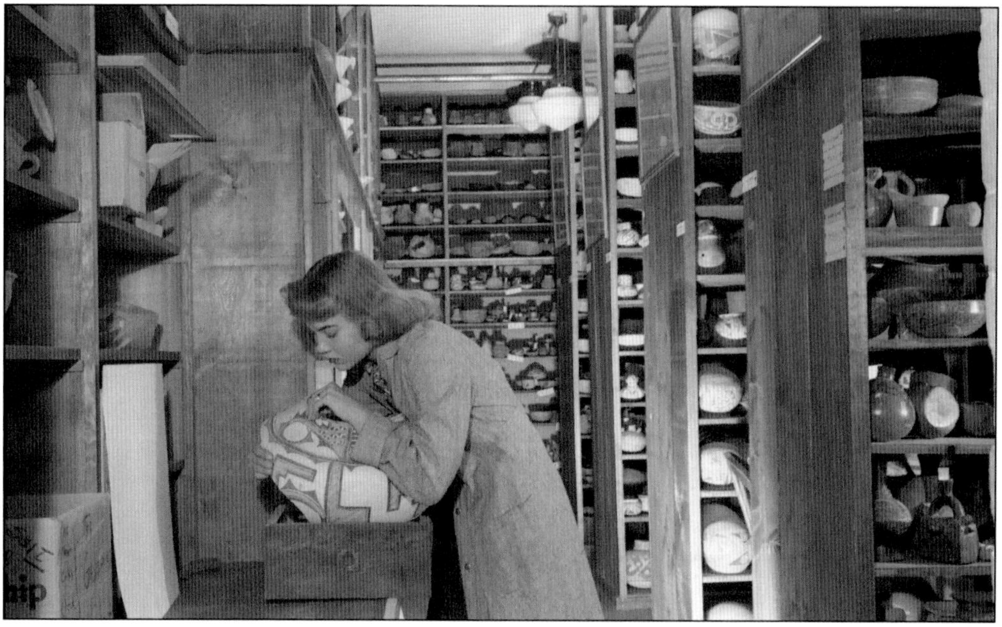

Room 112, in the ASM basement, is pictured here in the spring of 1958, when it was the pottery storage room. Undergraduate senior Inez Lindsey is shown mending a large historic Zuni polychrome jar. All of the other pots visible in this photograph are prehistoric, from the Hohokam, Ancestral Pueblo, Casas Grandes, central Mexican, and Peruvian areas. This room was later turned into a machinery room. The Southwestern pots were moved to Anthropology Room 125 (see page 29), and the Central and South American pots to Room 106/108. (ASM 4564.)

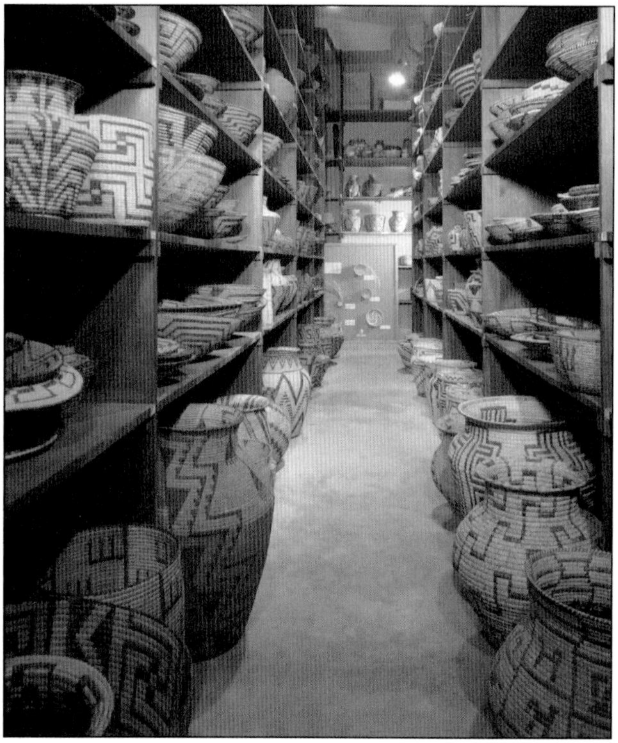

Room 109, also in the basement, the basketry storage room, is seen here in September 1968. The wooden shelves held about 4,000 baskets, most from the Southwest but with significant collections from Californian and other North American tribes, as well as comparative examples from around the world (see the cover). In 2013, these baskets were moved into new, climate-controlled, less-crowded storage in ASM North (see page 37). (H. Teiwes, ASM 18829.)

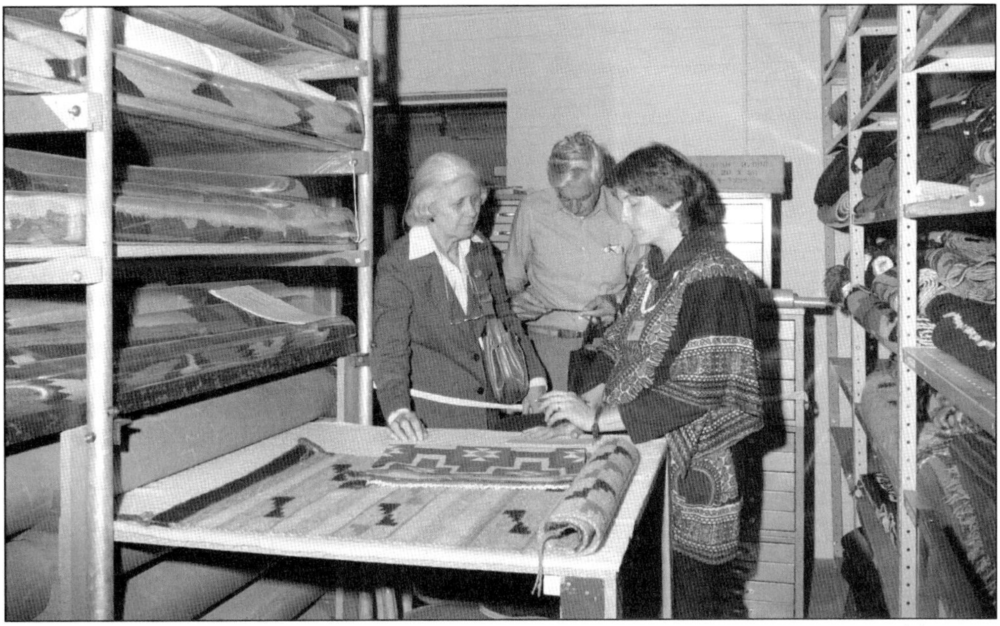

Another room in the ASM basement, Room 107, the textile storage room, is pictured here on March 12, 1985, during an ASM open house celebration of the University of Arizona's 100th anniversary. Ethnological Collections curator Diane Dittemore (right) is showing Navajo weavings to UA alumni Tad and Mary Jane Nichols. Tad was an internationally known photographer, and Mary Jane an ornithologist. (H. Teiwes, ASM 64994.)

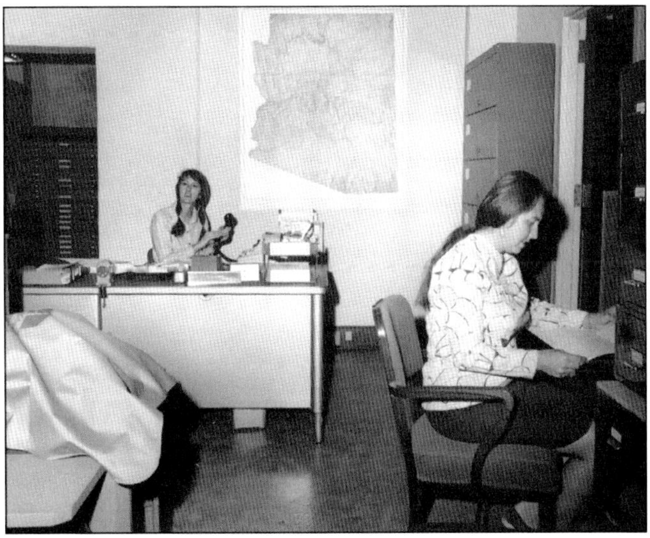

Basement Room 100B/100C, the museum administrative office, is seen here in November 1971, with museum secretary Shirley Pettengill (left) and archaeological assistant Sharon F. Urban. At this time, the museum's records of archaeological sites in Arizona consisted of five-by-seven-inch cards filled out with information (in the drawers to Urban's right), with site locations plotted mostly on USGS topographic sheets (in flat files in the room behind Pettengill). (H. Teiwes, ASM 29003.)

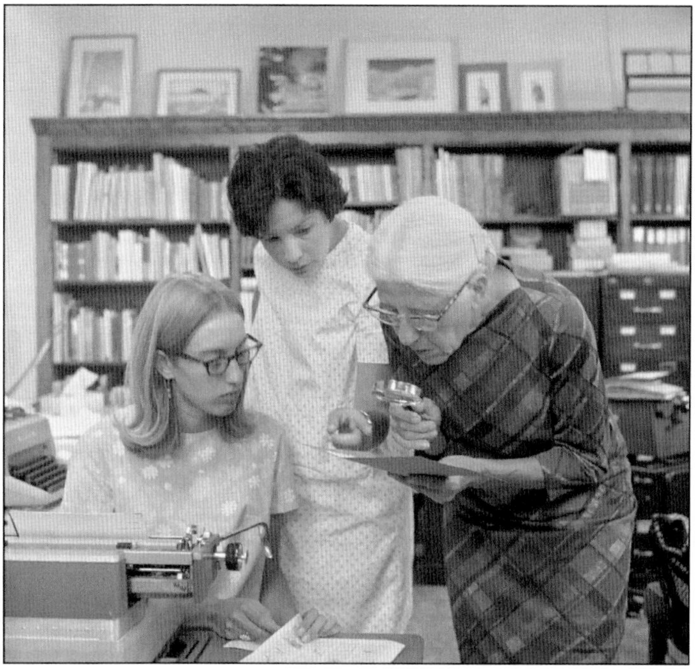

Room 101, in the ASM basement, was first a seminar room with built-in bookcases, visible here on the south wall. In 1957, director Emil Haury designated it the first ASM library in order to accept a bequest of Rev. Victor Stoner's library. After the library moved in 1962 (see page 29), the room housed the entire collections division staff. Seen here in 1969 are, from left to right, assistant curator Nancy L. Foster, curatorial assistant Carmen Prezelski, and curator of Collections Wilma Kaemlein. (H. Teiwes, ASM 22904.)

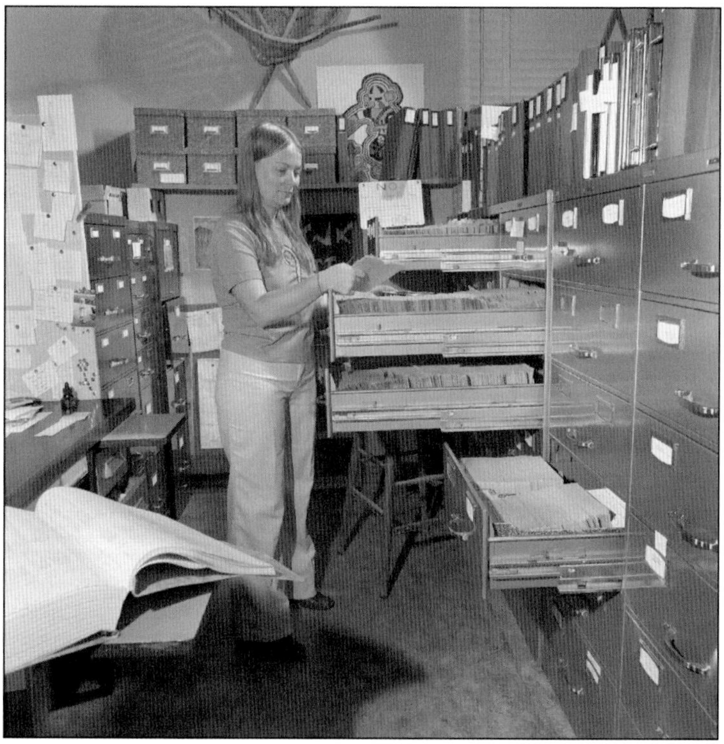

In 1974, the northwest corner of ASM Room 101, in the basement, was both an office for curator of photographic collections Alice Holmes and the entire storage area (behind and in front of her) for all negatives, slides, and prints. ASM photographic collections in 2013 number more than 500,000 images, including video, film, and digital holdings. (H. Teiwes, ASM 38598.)

A Tucson Transfer & Warehouse Co. crane, free of charge, lifts an enormous boulder with a prehistoric petroglyph on it into the east side of the ASM portico on February 5, 1963. The boulder was found about 40 miles northwest of Phoenix and donated by the estate of I.W. Lively. The design was pecked (hammered) through the darker surface of the basalt boulder with a hammerstone, exposing lighter-colored rock beneath and creating the glyph. Based on the design, it was probably made by a Hohokam artist sometime between about AD 1030 and 1230. (Jim Tallen, ASM 8813.)

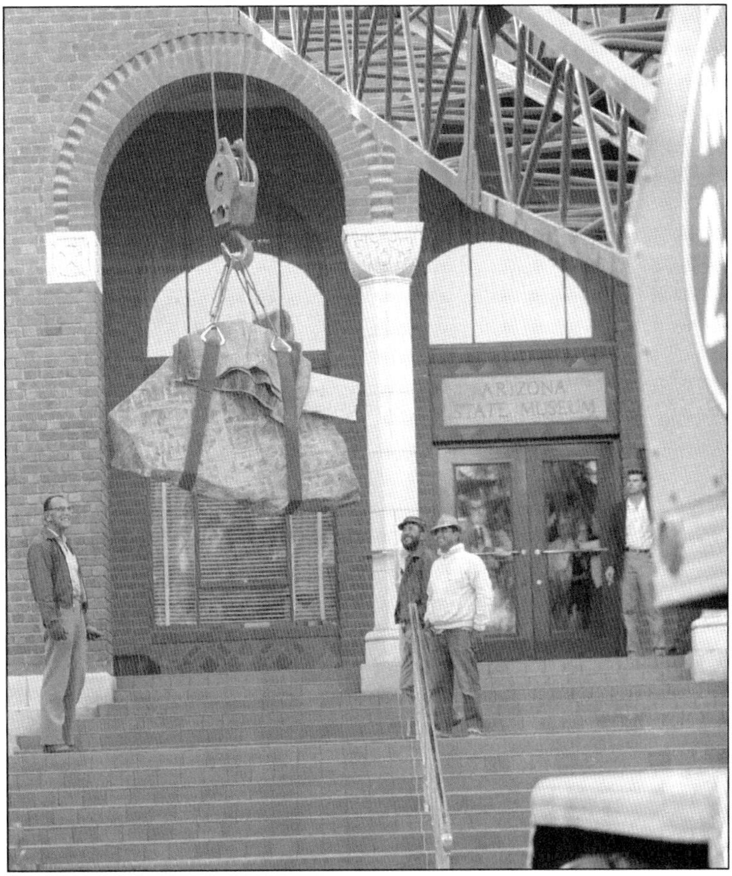

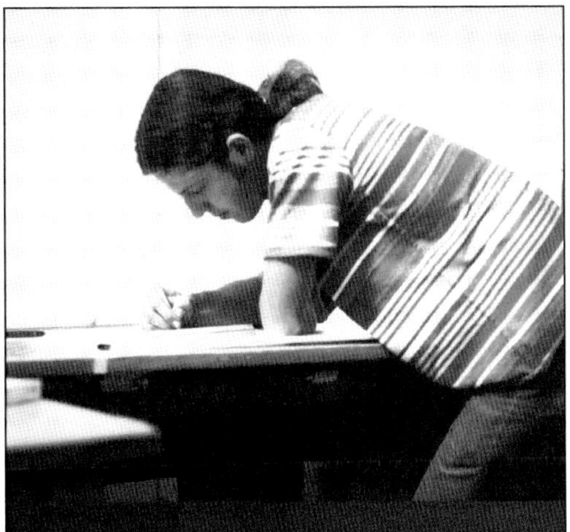

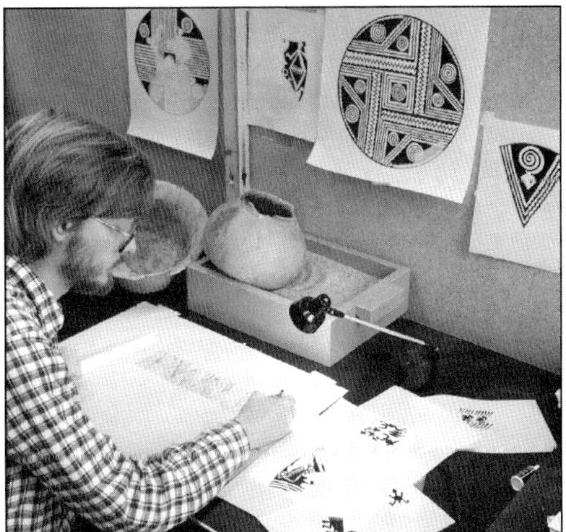

Charles Sternberg (left) works at the drafting table in ASM Room 100 in October 1971. Sternberg worked at ASM from 1969 to 1988 doing archaeology and drafting. He was famous for his skills with a plane table and alidade, and for his beautiful final maps. Ronald J. Beckwith (right) worked at ASM from 1978 to 1988 doing archaeology, photography, and drafting. Beckwith is well known for his excellent illustrations of pottery, as shown here, in the ASM North archaeology laboratory in April 1984. (Left, Pamela Haas, ASM 32404; right, H Teiwes, ASM 64042.)

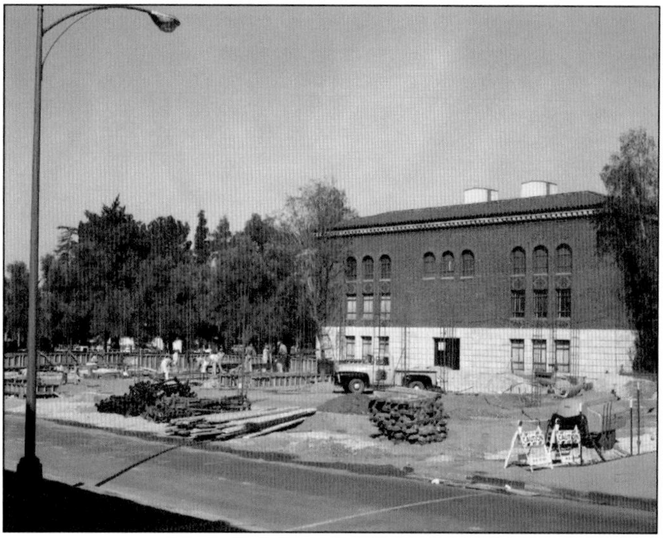

Since 1936, museum and anthropology staff had shared space in the basement of ASM. In February 1961, foundations for a new Anthropology Building were poured immediately south of ASM (pictured). Space between them housed a loading dock, and they were joined by hallways on the first and second floors. Both buildings were supplied with refrigerated air from UA's central power plant, replacing ASM's old evaporative coolers. (G. Bartell, ASM 6984.)

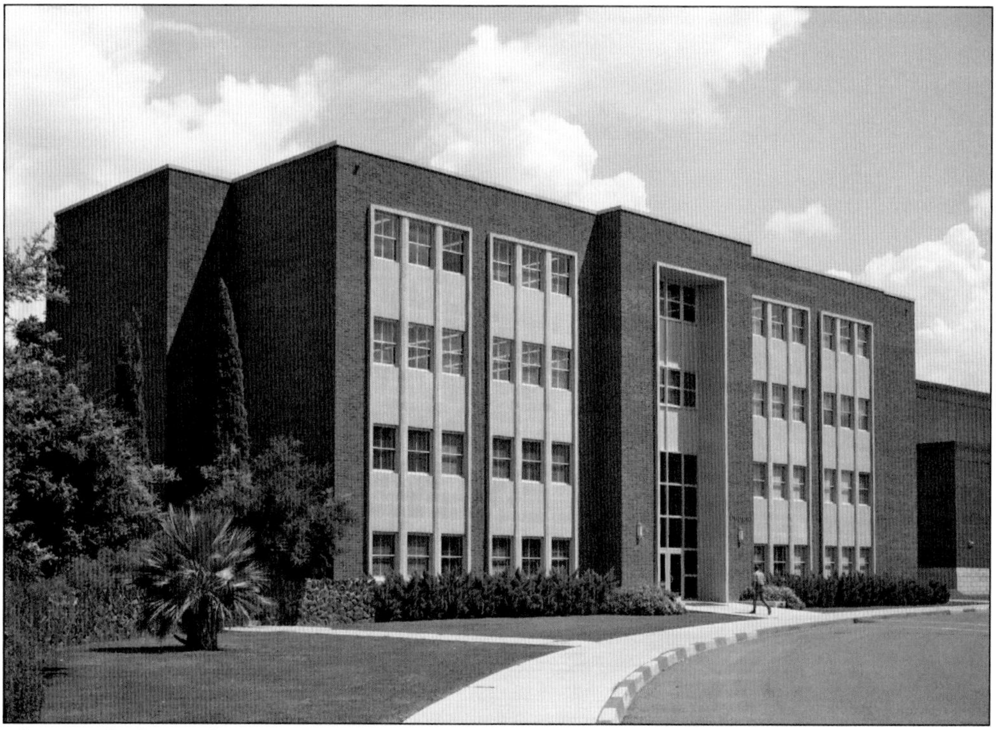

This view looks northeast at the front of the new Anthropology Building in October 1962. Three stories were completed in 1961, followed by a fourth, funded by the National Science Foundation, in 1962. All anthropology programs moved into this building, along with museum rooms for artifact storage, photography, contract archaeology programs, the library, a human osteology laboratory, and shared space for the archaeological field school collections. In 1991, the building was officially named the Emil W. Haury Anthropology Building. (H. Teiwes, ASM 13272.)

As part of modifications associated with construction of the Anthropology Building, ASM Room 112 (see page 24) was converted into a machinery room. The bulk of the museum's prehistoric Southwestern pottery was then moved into Anthropology Room 125, shown here, where it remained from 1962 to 1982. At right, in September 1968, curator of Collections Wilma Kaemlein is moving some of the larger jars. This view is looking toward the northeast corner of the room. (H. Teiwes, ASM 18832.)

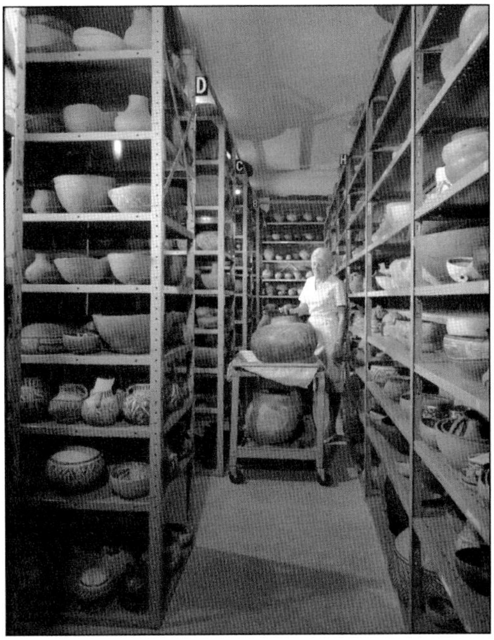

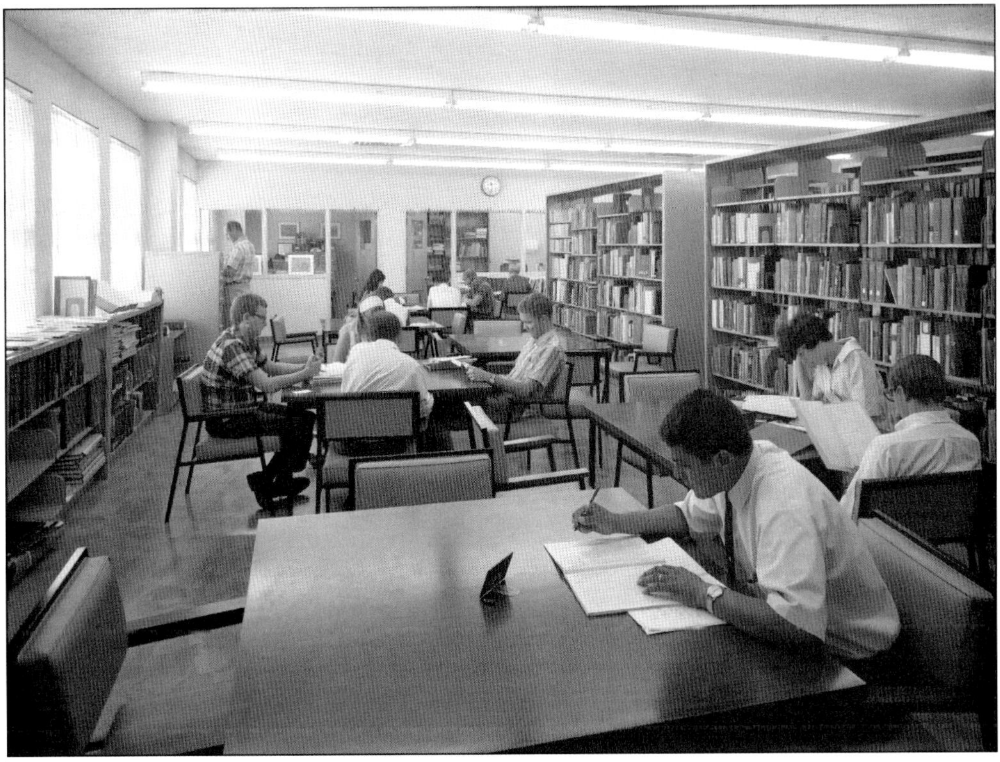

This view looks west across Anthropology Room 317, which received the museum library in 1962, where it finally had room for all of its books, periodicals, and a reading area. Five small interior rooms housed the librarian's office (back left), a workroom (back center), a storage room (back right, behind bookshelves), and, behind the camera, a microfilm room (317C) and Room 317B, which probably housed the ASM Archives, after its creation in 1964. (H. Teiwes, ASM 18849.)

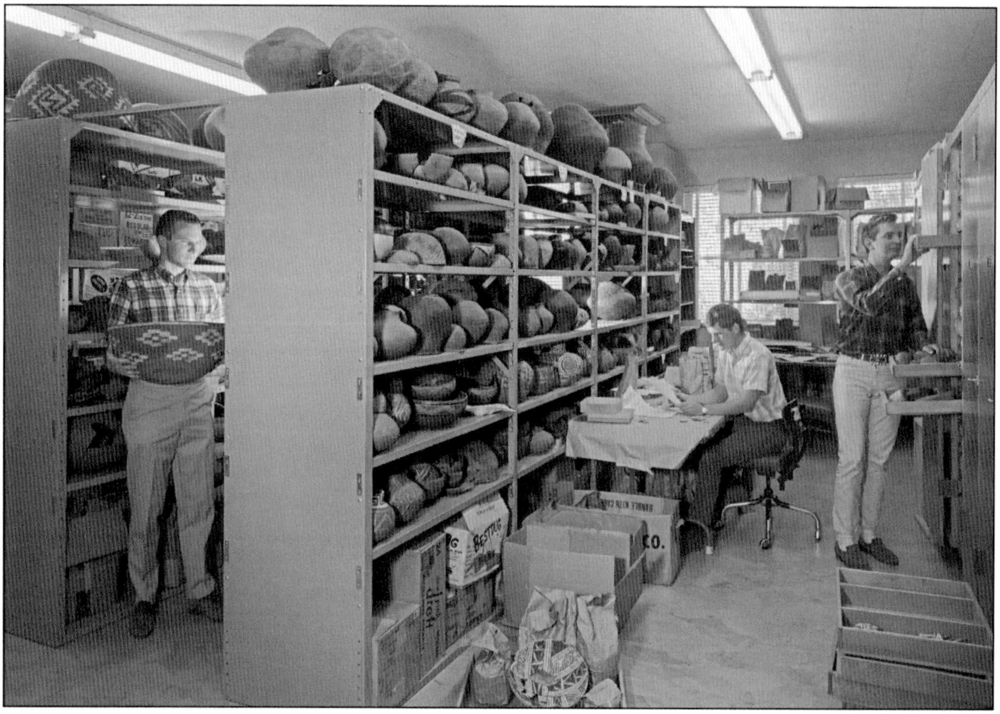

Anthropology Room 402 has always housed the Anthropology Department's archaeological field schools' collections. Seen here in a staged photograph are, from left to right, ASM assistant archaeologists James E. Ayres, R. Gwinn Vivian, and Laurens C. Hammack, looking at items from the Point of Pines Field School (see pages 76 and 77), which would make way for those from the Grasshopper Field School, and, in turn, the Silver Creek Archaeological Project. This view is looking at the northeast corner in November 1966. (H. Teiwes, ASM 13283.)

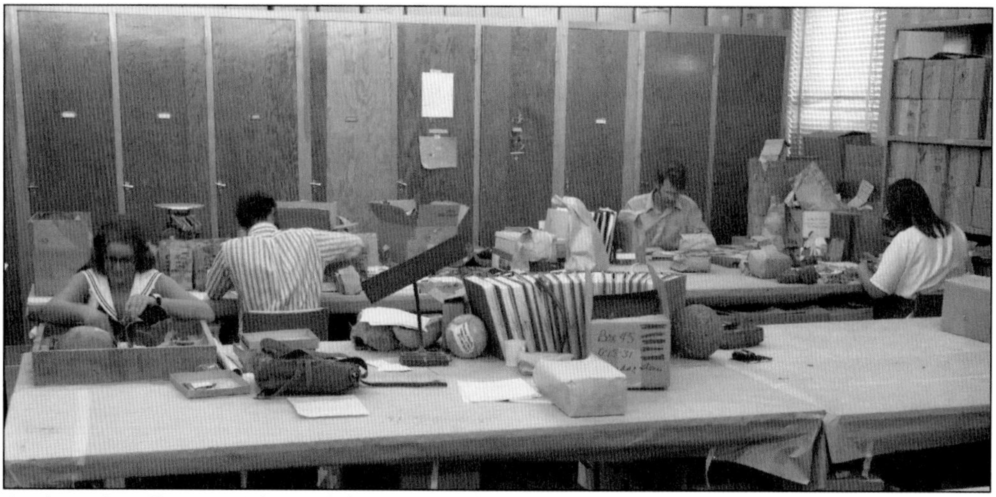

Anthropology Room 408 housed the ASM Highway Salvage laboratory and the Cultural Resource Management Section contract archaeology offices. Here, from left to right, Donna K. La Rocca mends a pot, while Bruce B. Huckell, Jonathan Haas, and Carol S. Weed analyze artifacts—all of them UA anthropology students employed by Highway Salvage. This view is looking southeast in October 1971. (Pamela Haas, ASM 32409.)

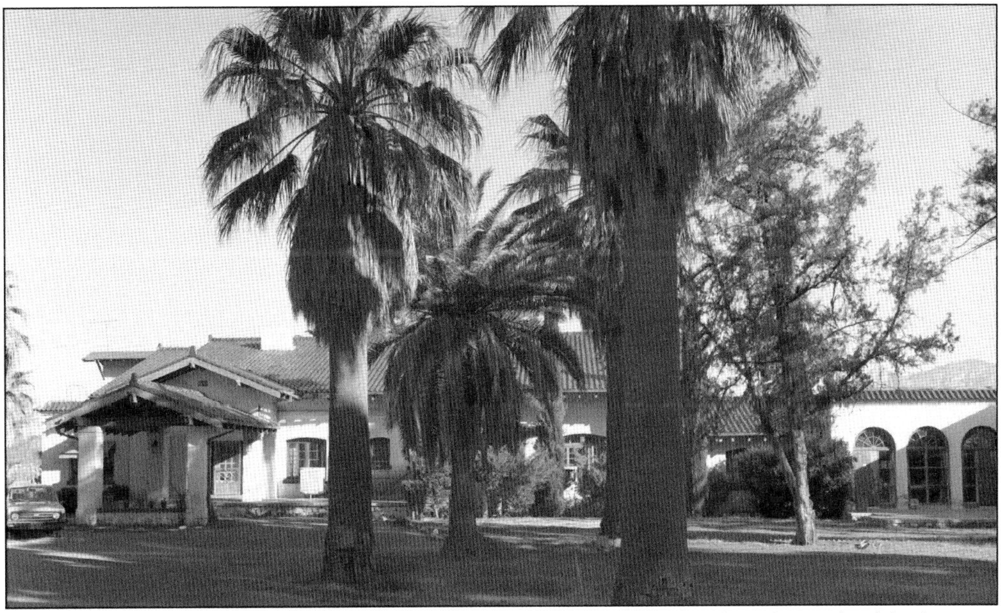

This photograph shows Casa Elizabeth Seton, located on Potter Place, directly north of the historic Arizona Inn, northeast of the UA campus. Built around 1910 as a private home, it was run as a postulant home and kindergarten by the Sisters of Charity of Seton Hill from 1953 to 1971. It was rented to ASM from about 1974 to 1976. An anthropology student served as a live-in caretaker, and the museum had offices (see page 123) and space for its archaeological survey collections and comparative animal bone collections (see next image). (H. Teiwes, ASM 43294.)

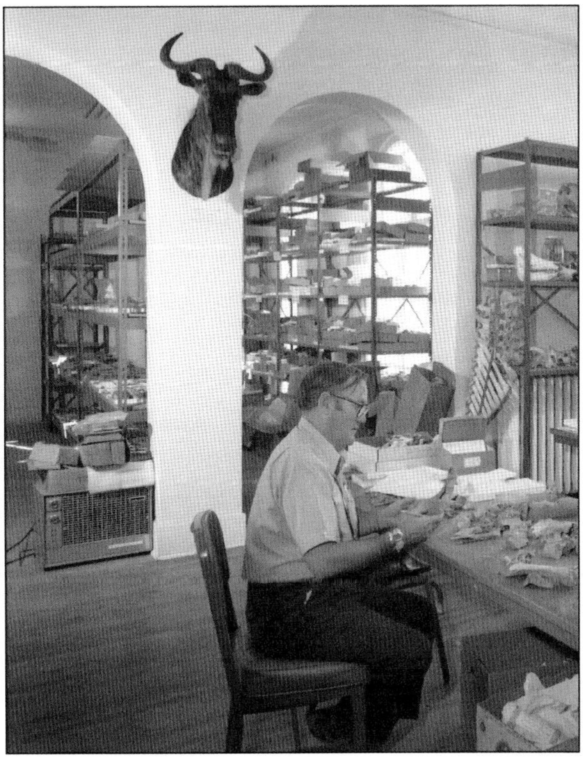

Stanley J. Olsen was ASM's first curator of zooarchaeology (1973–1997). His collections, combined with those lent by the National Park Service (NPS), formed a valuable reference "library" used by Olsen and his students to identify animal bones recovered from archaeological sites. Olsen is shown here in 1976 in Casa Seton in his laboratory, which was moved in 1977 to the third floor of ASM North. In 2002, it was joined by Charmion R. McKusick's animal bone collection, and, in 2004, it was named the Stanley J. Olsen Laboratory of Zooarchaeology, housing more than 4,000 catalogued skeletons. (H. Teiwes, ASM 43311.)

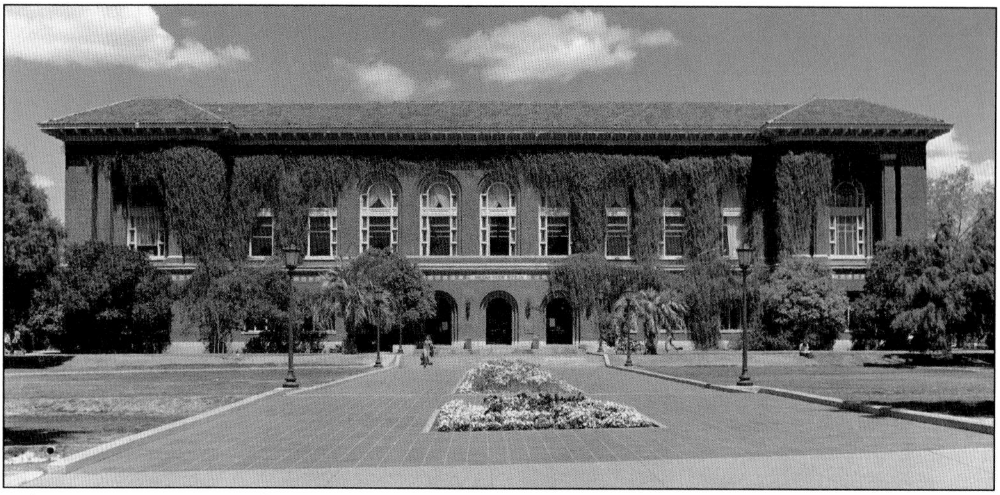

When a new UA Main Library was built, ASM inherited the 1925 library. Here, in a view looking north in April 1977, soon after ASM moved in, there is a new name over the entrance, but its exterior is otherwise unchanged. From 1977 to the present, the original ASM building is now known as ASM South, and the old Main Library is now ASM North. The luxuriant draperies of yellow trumpet vines (*Macfadyena unguis-cati*) had come and gone at least once before, but when those on the east side of the entrance blew down in a 1994–1995 winter storm, the rest were removed for the sake of the building's brick face, and to eliminate habitat for troublesome insects and squirrels. (H. Teiwes, ASM 44759.)

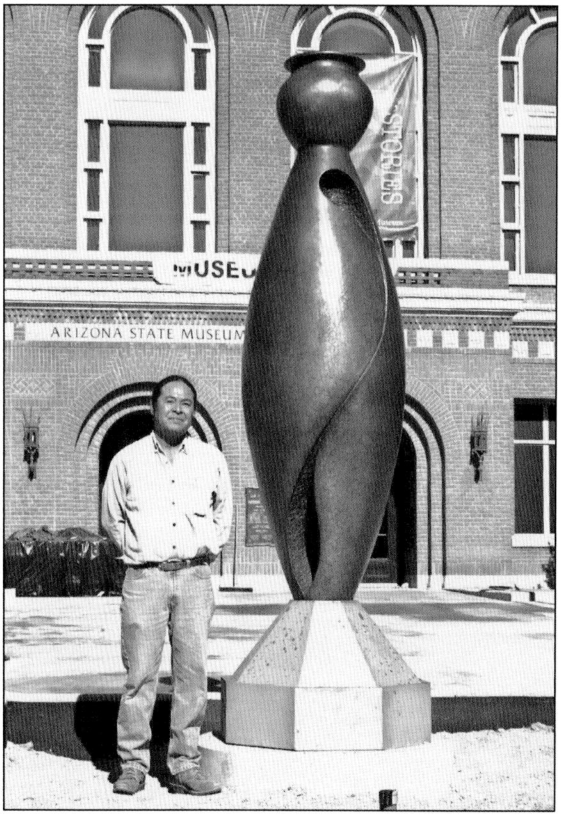

The ASM North entrance got a physical and aesthetic makeover. *Water Carrier*, an eight-foot-tall bronze, shown here with its sculptor, San Carlos Apache artist Craig Dan Goseyun, was installed on December 8, 2006 (a gift of Arnold and Doris Roland). The entire walkway between the museum doors and the street was replaced with a continuous, more fully accessible ramp that looks like its predecessor but eliminated its steps. It was completed in February 2007. (J. Weakly, ASM.)

The two-story-high reading room of the "old"/second UA Library is seen here in a 1930 view looking southwest. Considered one of the more beautiful spaces on campus, then and now, it featured a faux-beam ceiling (actually sculpted plaster on steel mesh) painted with elaborate floral decorations, intricate chandeliers, paneling, and built-in bookshelves of dark-stained "Mexican amapa" hardwood, and 29 oak tables 12 feet in length with matching chairs. (R.B. Streets, UASC N-1990.)

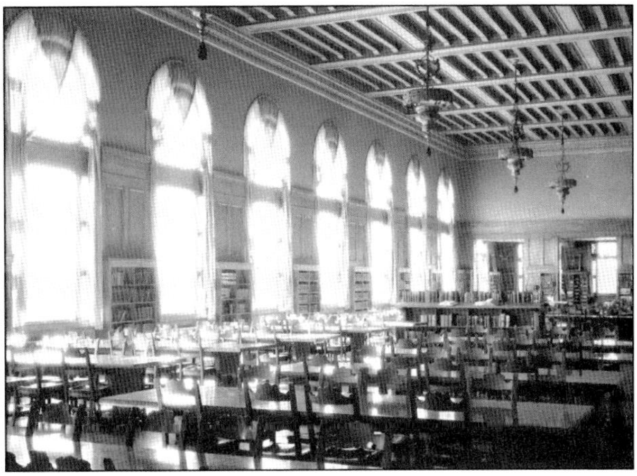

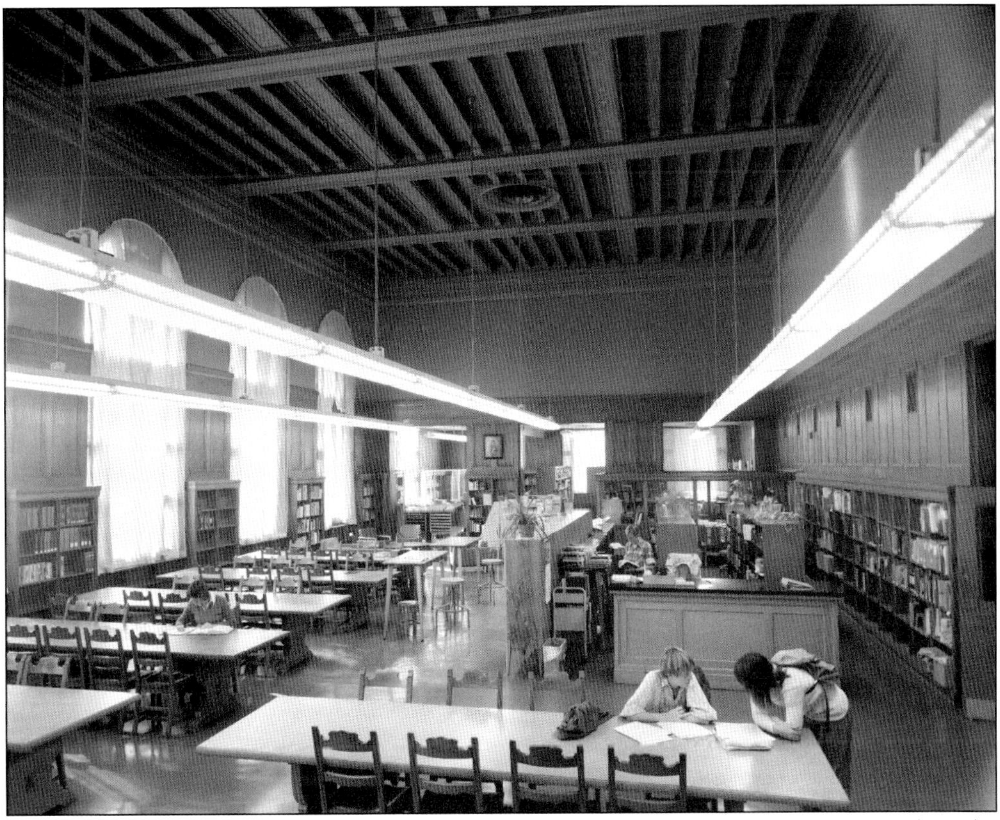

In late 1977, the ASM Library was moved from Anthropology Room 317 (see page 29) to the ASM North reading room. In this view looking west-southwest in February 1978, one sees many of the original tables and chairs retrieved from around campus. The black-topped circulation desk (right foreground) started life in the first UA Library (Library and Museum Building) in 1904, was resurrected in 1959 for Special Collections in the 1925 library, and continues in use to the present. The glassed-in office beyond was built in 1963. Fluorescent lights replaced chandeliers in 1950. Shade-cloth screens replaced the cloth drapes in 1996. (H. Teiwes, ASM 45918.)

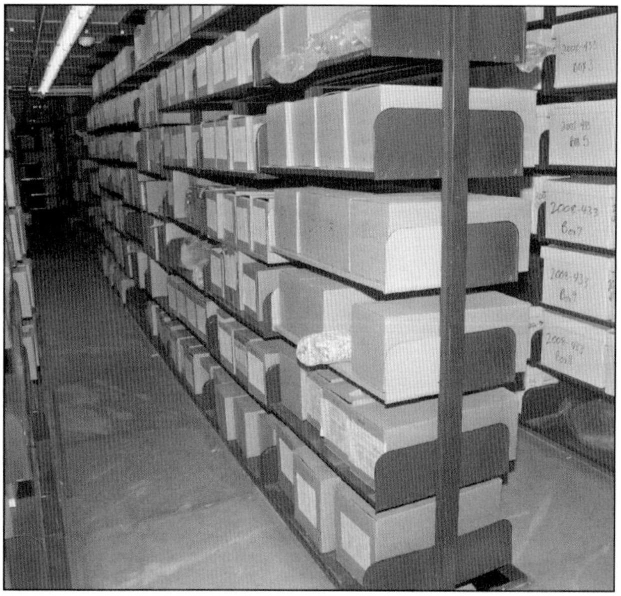

Everyone who used this building when it was the UA Library remembers "the Stacks": five tiers of metal shelving with marble floors and low ceilings holding untold thousands of books, with secluded study carrels decorated with names, dates, promises, and chewing gum. ASM now uses the same shelves to store about 23,000 boxes of artifacts. Earlier collections are in corrugated cardboard boxes (left aisle), which are being superseded by white polyethylene cartons (right), which will last longer and shed water should the fire sprinkler system ever go off. It is seen here in November 2012. (J. Weakly, ASM.)

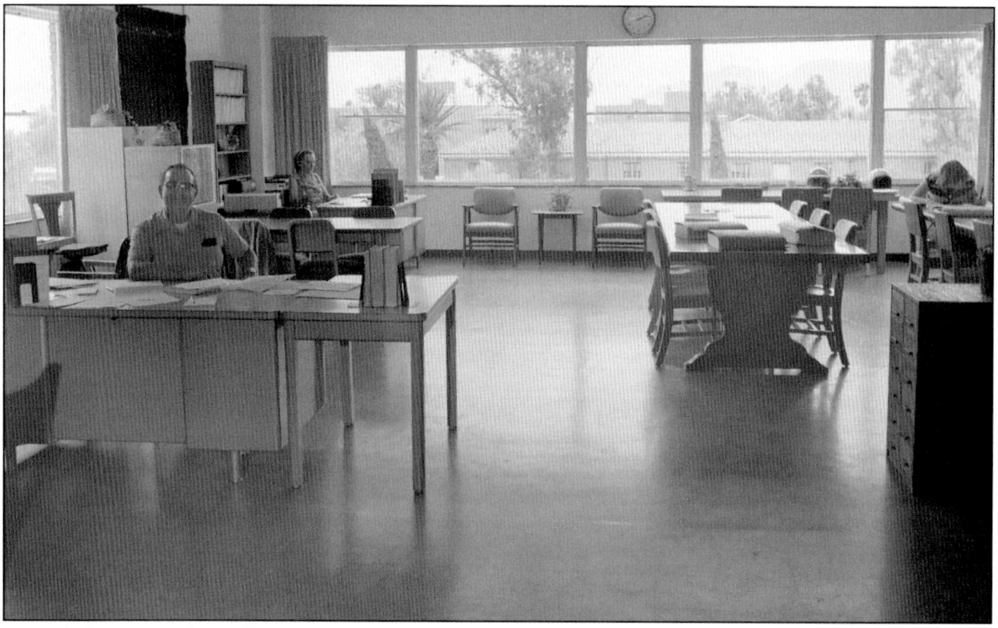

Founded in 1975, the Office of Ethnohistorical Research (OER) conducts research on the Spanish and Mexican periods in the American Southwest and Northern Mexico, drawing on records of all kinds, including over 1,300 reels of microfilmed documents. Here, in March 1977, are, from left to right, head of OER Rev. Charles W. Polzer, assistant ethnohistorian Madeleine T. Rodack, and an unidentified student, newly moved into the northwest corner of ASM North Room 320, the former Main Library Special Collections reading room. (H. Teiwes, ASM 44756.)

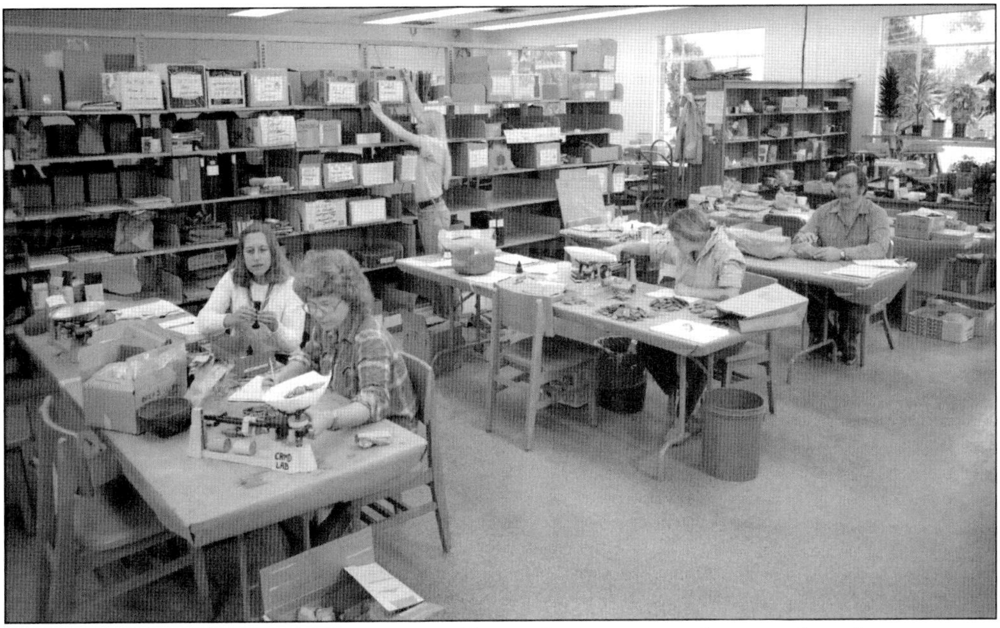

In 1963, the library building had one-story additions built on its northwest and northeast corners. When the museum moved in, all of the northwest addition became the processing area and writing cubicles for the contract archaeology division. Here, in April 1984, from left to right, Jennifer Strand, Kim Beckwith, Deni Seymour, and Nancy Kress analyze potsherds and chipped stone under the supervision of Arthur W. Vokes. The view looks toward the north windows. (H. Teiwes, ASM 64033-x.)

This photograph looks north along the east wall of the first tier of Room 328 in the early 1980s, at what had been the dedicated storage area for Special Collections when the building was the UA Library. ASM adapted the bookshelves to hold ethnographic Tarahumara, Mayo, Tepehuan, Warijio, and Pima Bajo Indian textiles from Northwest Mexico, rolled on old commercial carpet tubes covered in acid-free paper, and protected, yet visible, through a wrap of clear Mylar sheeting. (ASM.)

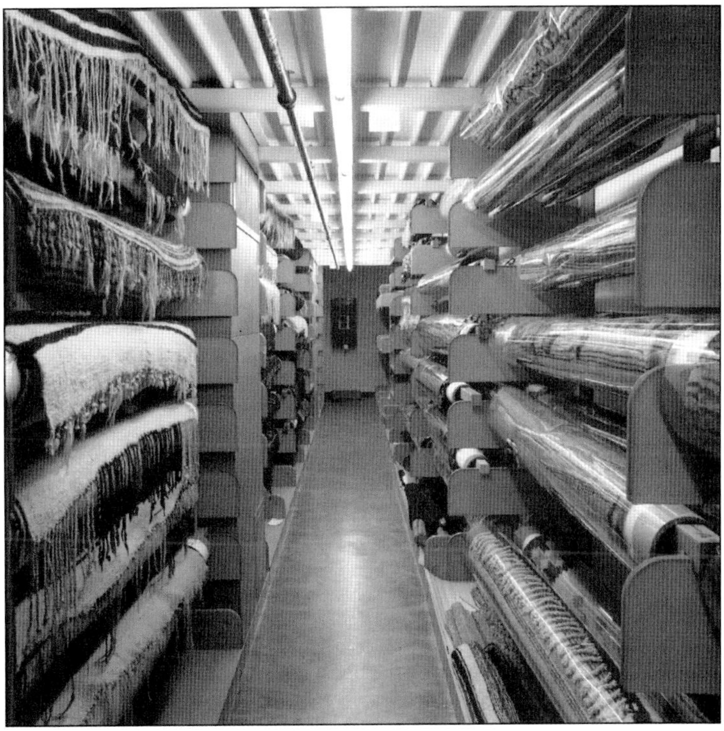

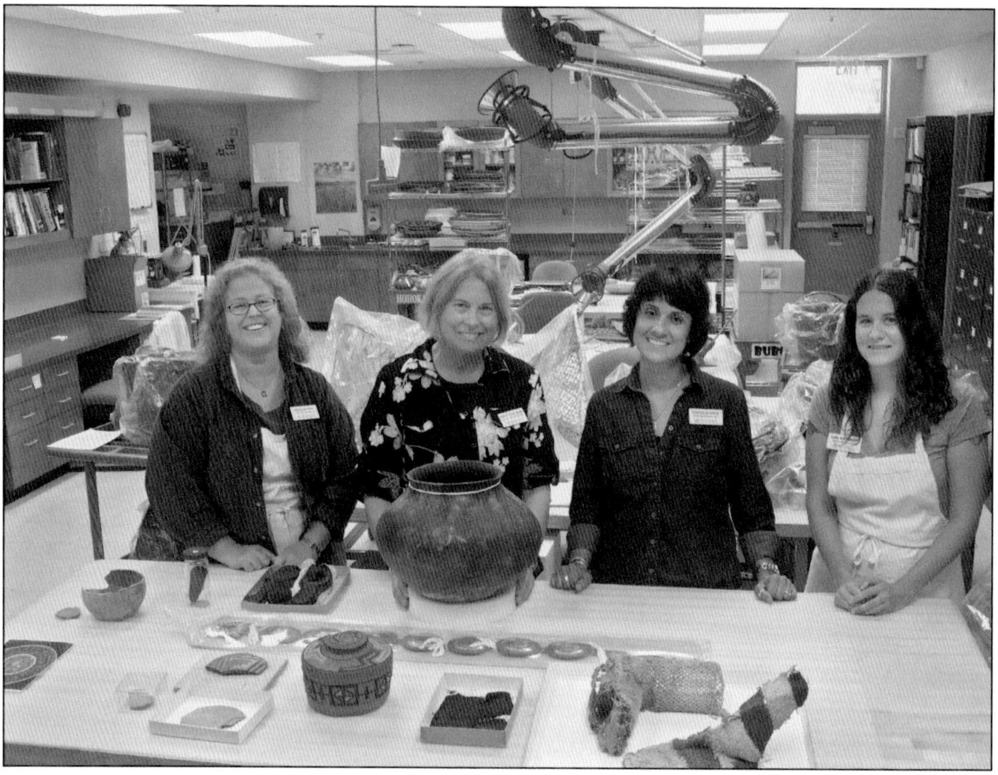

In 2008, construction of a conservation laboratory and the Agnese and Emil Haury Southwest Native Nations Pottery Vault in ASM North was completed inside, respectively, the gutted 1951 and 1963 one-story additions to the northeast corner of the Main Library building. Both were funded with a grant from the Save America's Treasures program (a Clinton White House preservation initiative), a National Endowment for the Humanities Challenge Grant, donations from Agnese N. Haury and the Ak-Chin, Gila River, the Salt River Pima–Maricopa Indian communities, and a host of other contributors. Both areas are temperature- and humidity-controlled. Seen above in the lab are, from left to right, objects conservator Marilen Pool, head of Preservation Nancy Odegaard, associate conservator Teresa Moreno, and conservation assistant Gina Watkinson. Below, in the vault with its 20,000 prehistoric and historic Southwestern pots, is Archaeological Collections curator Mike Jacobs in August 2013. (Both, J. Weakly, ASM.)

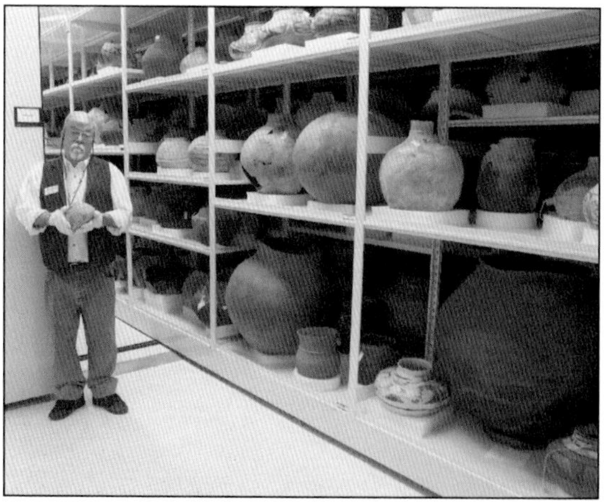

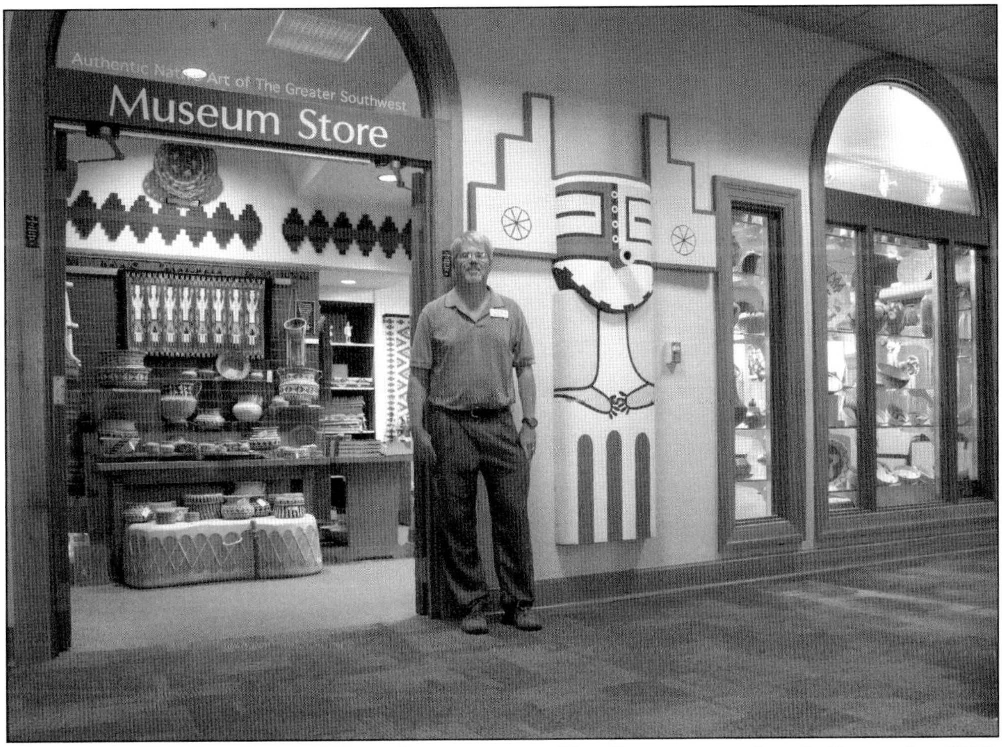

The museum store, in ASM North, and store manager Tim Price are seen here in September 2013. The store supports ASM's mission by selling Native American arts, crafts, and music recordings, along with books, posters, and related educational materials. Profits go into museum programs. The seven-foot-tall replica of a Hopi kachina doll was originally made by exhibits assistant Eura Rhodney "Rhod" Lauffer as part of the entryway for the 1989 exhibit *Hopi Spirits: Contemporary Kachina Doll Carving*. (J. Weakly, ASM.)

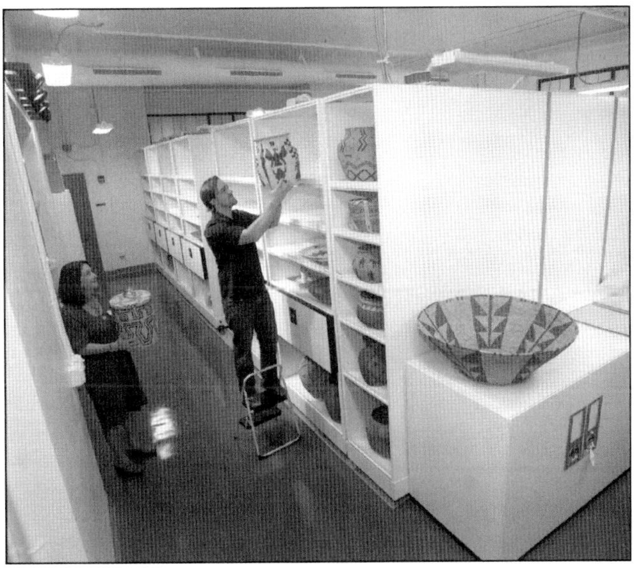

With one of the last Save America's Treasures program grants as seed money, a new climate-controlled vault for the museum's collections of 25,000 historic and prehistoric Southwestern baskets and vegetal artifacts was built in the southwest corner of the first floor of ASM North. Here, in September 2013, Ethnological Collections curator Diane Dittemore and assistant curator Andrew Higgins begin bringing in baskets, including a large Tohono O'odham bowl displayed 80 years earlier under the West Stadium (see page 19). (J. Weakly, ASM.)

The view in this aerial photograph of the University of Arizona, taken in late 1937, looks due east from the western edge of campus, showing the locations of all seven homes (as of 2014) of the museum: (1) the Arizona Territorial Museum in Old Main (1893–1904); (2) the Arizona Territorial Museum, changing to Arizona State Museum in 1912, in the Library and Museum Building (now Douglass Building) (1905–1914); the Arizona State Museum in (3) Agriculture Hall (now Forbes Building) (1915–1929), then (4) the West Stadium (1930–1935), then (5) the Arizona State Museum (now ASM South) (1936–present), then (6) the Anthropology Building (now Haury Building) (1962–mid-1990s) (building not yet constructed in this photograph), then (7) the second University Library (now ASM North) (1977–present). (Ben D. Gross Photography, UASC N-3692.)

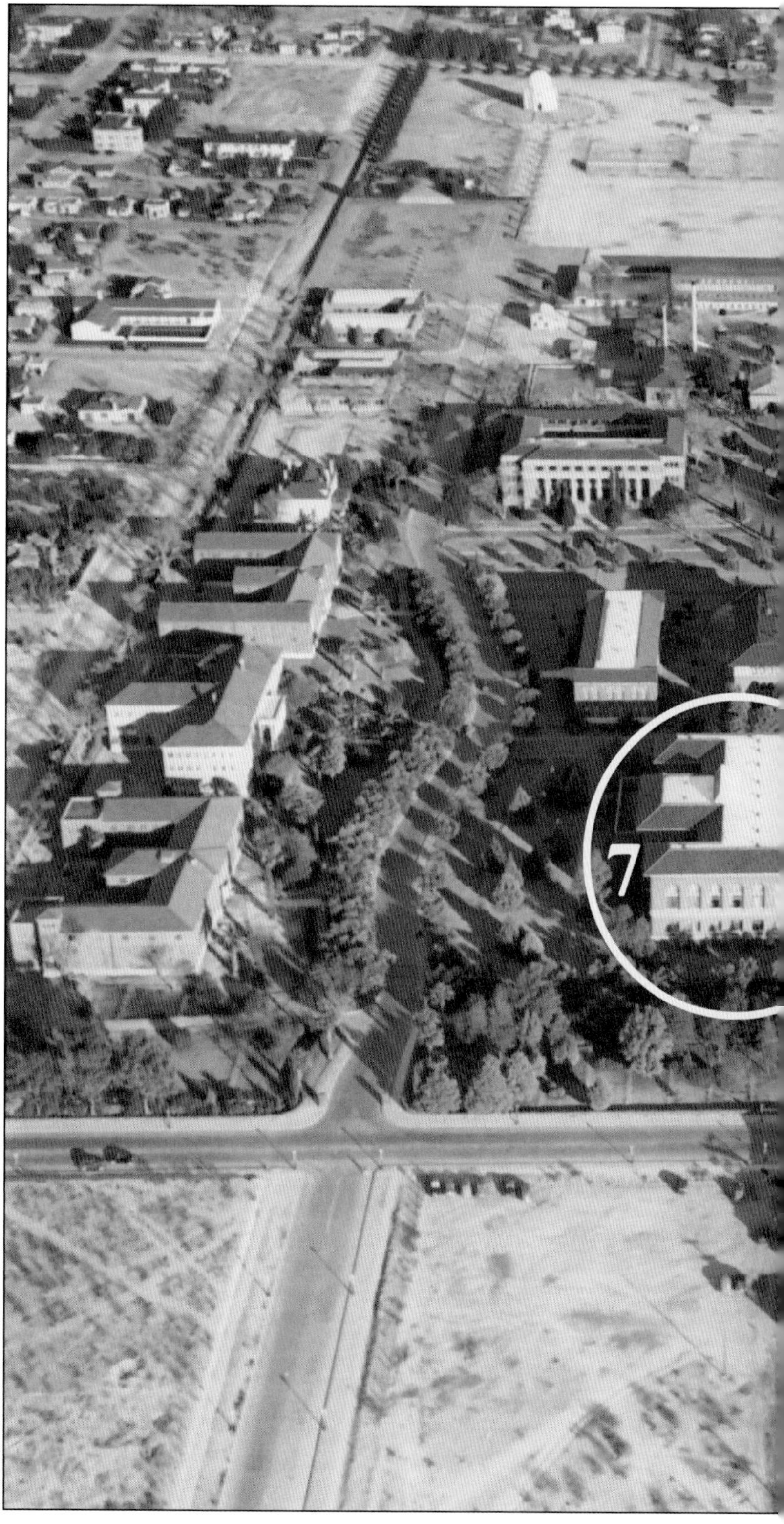

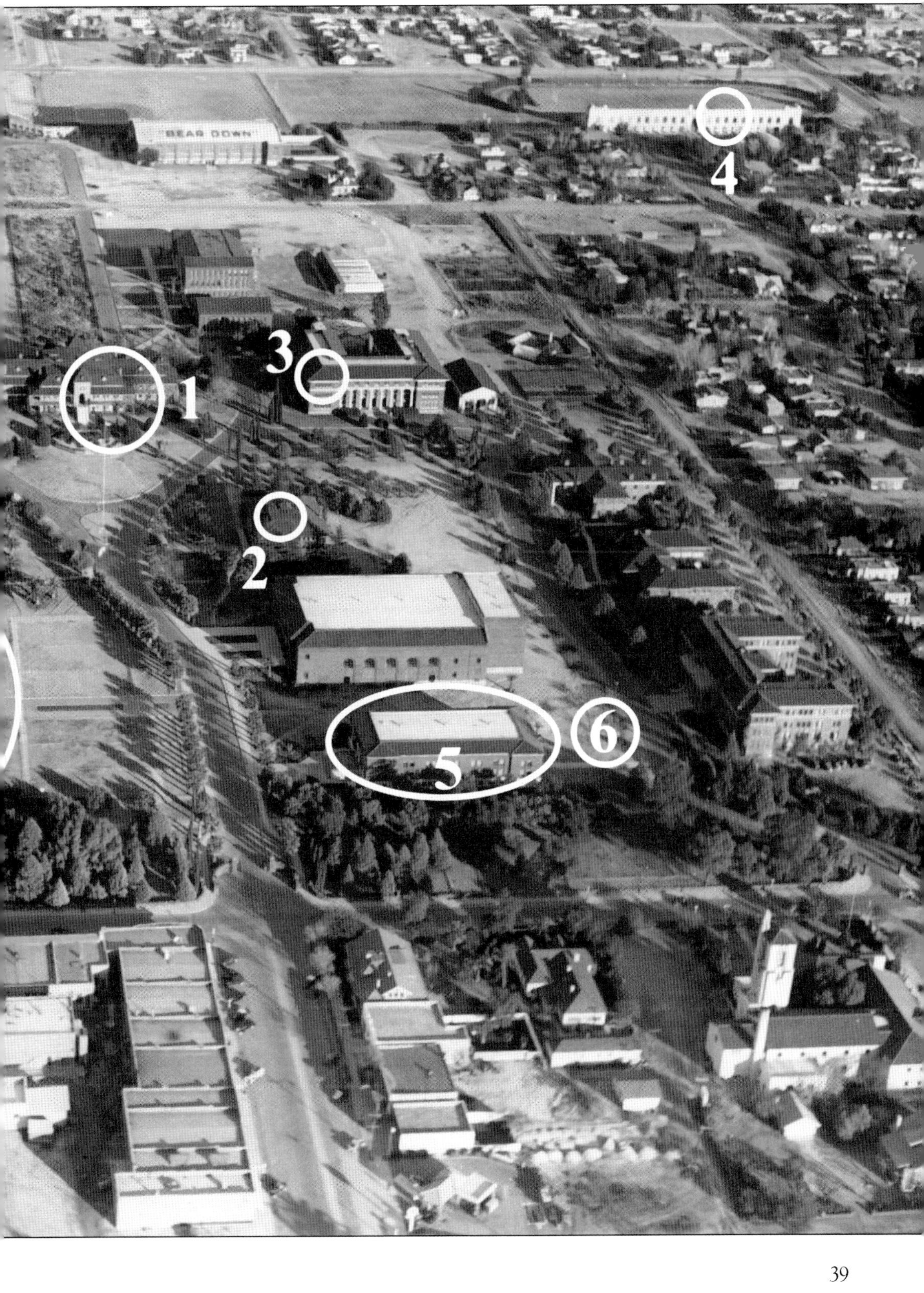
BEAR DOWN
1
2
3
4
5
6

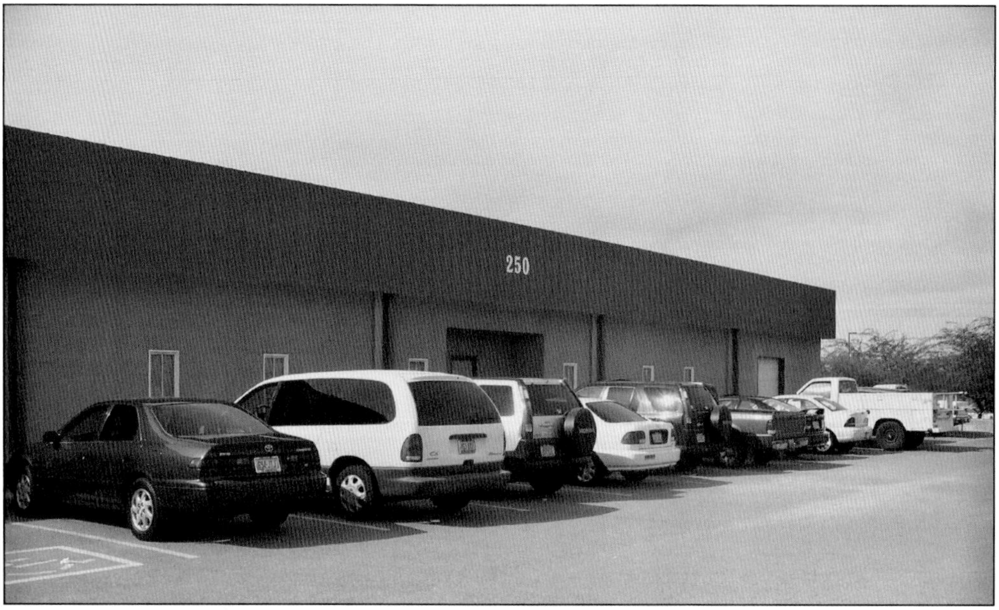

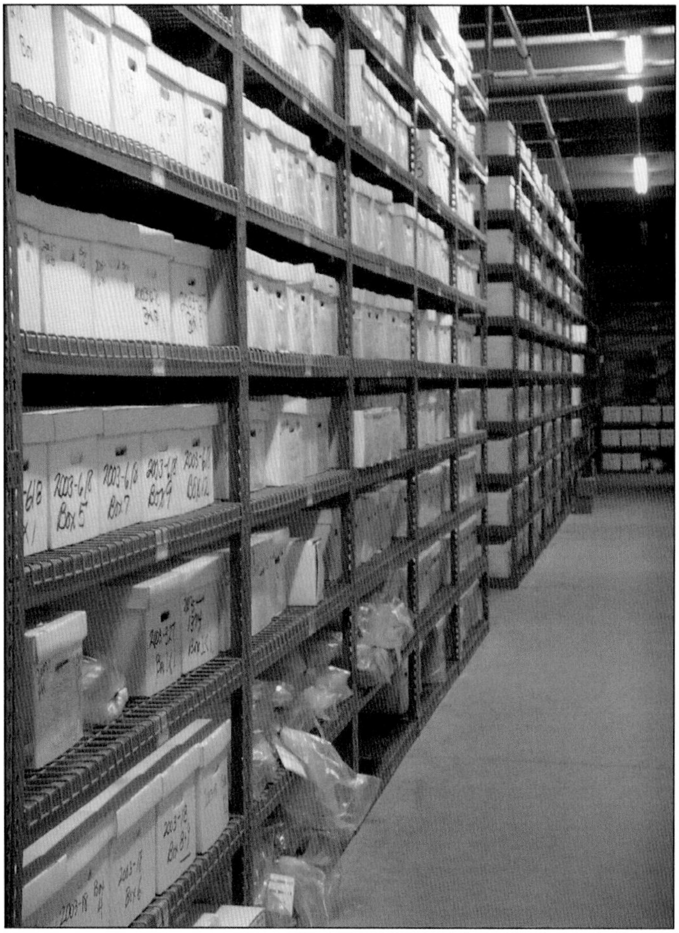

In November 2004, ASM leased part of a warehouse at 250 South Toole Avenue (above), southwest of campus, to store boxes of artifacts from contract archaeology projects throughout Arizona, for which the museum has perpetual curation responsibilities. Twelve-foot-tall shelving capable of holding 12,000 boxes was assembled (at left). However, less than six years later, finances necessitated moving the shelving and 7,000 boxes of potsherds, chipped stone, ground stone, animal bones, and soil samples back to campus, to be housed on the former main exhibit floor of ASM South (see page 23). The last day at Toole for Archaeological Repository Collections curator Arthur Vokes and his staff was August 6, 2010. (Both, Arthur W. Vokes, ASM.)

Three

Ethnological Projects and Collections

The Arizona State Museum holds very large collections of both old and new examples of the arts and crafts made by historic Native Americans in the Southwest and northwestern Mexico, including pottery, basketry, textiles, jewelry, clothing, tools, masks, dolls, games, musical instruments, carvings, and paintings. The photographs in this chapter touch on many of the most significant collections and collectors. Some additional collections not pictured are worth noting.

ASM received more than 120 items (mostly Plains Indian material) collected during the 1870s by John A. Logan, a Civil War general who went on to be a US senator, and a few objects from the Southwest, probably collected by his daughter Dollie Tucker in the 1880s. The collection was donated by Logan's grandson John A. Logan III. In 1948, Nancy Margaret Pinkley Whiting donated 100 Pima baskets collected by her father, Frank Pinkley, presumably during his employ at Casa Grande National Monument, from 1901 to 1915 and 1918 to 1940.

Photographic collections containing important ethnographic components include those of Forman Hanna, Julian Hayden, Daniel Boone Linderman, Tad Nichols, and E.B. Sayles. ASM holds archival materials from Muriel Thayer Painter, Agnese N. Lindley Foundation documents related to court interpreters, and Edward Spicer's files about the War Relocation Authority.

Ethnographic research by ASM staff has been on a variety of topics. Photographer Helga Teiwes generally took pictures for other people, but she also wrote and published about her visits during the 1980s to document the work of Tohono O'odham potter Rupert Angea, trips from 1986 to 1989 to the Hopi mesas to photograph kachina doll carvers, and from 1991 to 1994 to record Hopi basket weavers. Jan Bell, the head of Collections, conducted field projects focused on pottery making among Yaquis and Mayos (1970s), Navajos (1980s), and the Mexican community of Mata Ortiz in Chihuahua, Mexico (1990s), as well as a study of wire baskets (1980s). Documentation and objects from all of these studies are curated at ASM. Ethnological Collections curator Diane Dittemore continues her long-term research on Southwestern Native American basketry and the major collections assembled by early Arizonans.

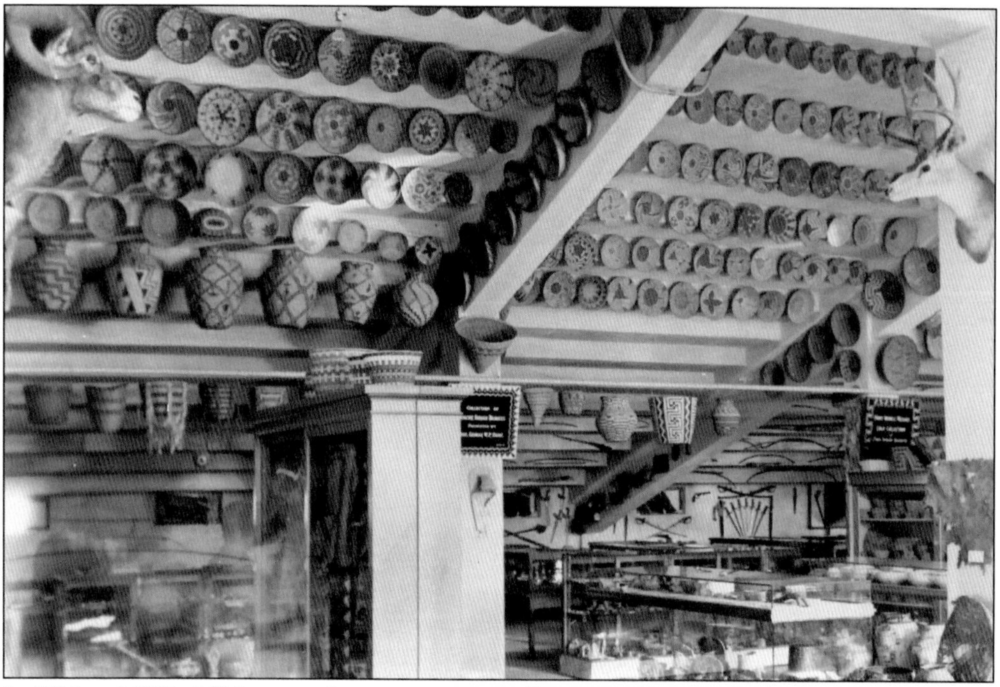

In 1916 and 1917, ASM received two important collections of historic baskets. While ASM was under the West Stadium (1930–1935), the baskets were displayed on the ceiling (see page 19). The view above is looking southeast. The sign on the left reads "Collection of Apache Indian Baskets Presented by Hon. George W.P. Hunt" and refers to the baskets at upper left. Hunt's baskets probably came from his wife, Helen Duett Ellison (below left), whose family traded with Apaches at the Ellisons' Q Ranch, east of Young and just west of the Fort Apache Indian Reservation. The sign on the right says, "Perry Merrell Williams Loan Collection of Pima Indian Baskets," and refers to the baskets at upper right. Williams (below right) and his brother operated a hotel and saloon in Maricopa, just south of Phoenix, and sold Indian crafts through the mail. His loan of 300 Pima baskets was converted to a donation in 1968 by his son Perry Merrell Williams Jr. (Above, R.B. Streets, UASC F1F10A; below left, ASL 97-6617; below right, Maricopa Historical Society, Maricopa.)

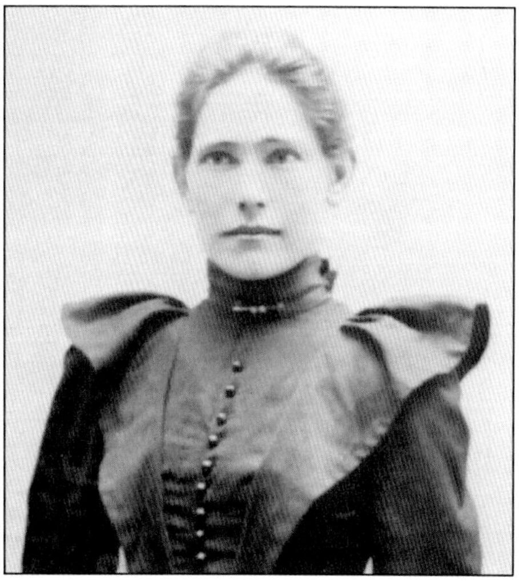

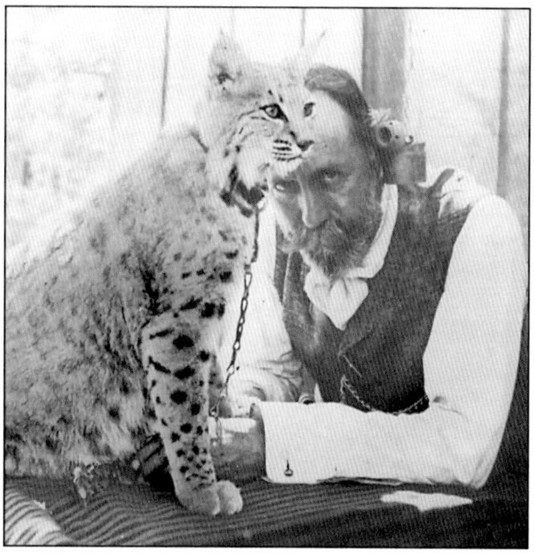

The Miller Collection consists of over 2,000 archaeological and ethnographic objects. It is perhaps best known for the more than 275 examples of ancestral and historic Hopi Indian pottery. This photograph appears in the January 1897 issue of *Land of Sunshine* magazine, showing a selection of late Sikyatki Polychrome bowls from the Hopi area and polychrome jars from both Zuni and the Hopi pueblos, most of which came to ASM. (ASM.)

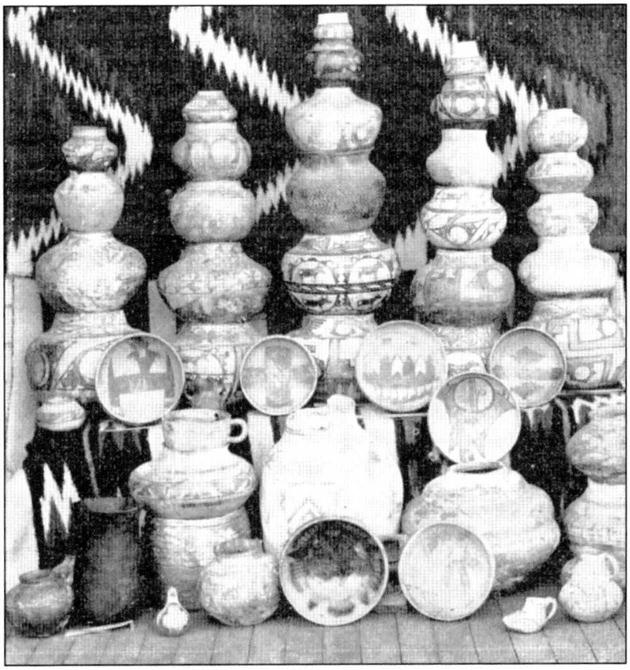

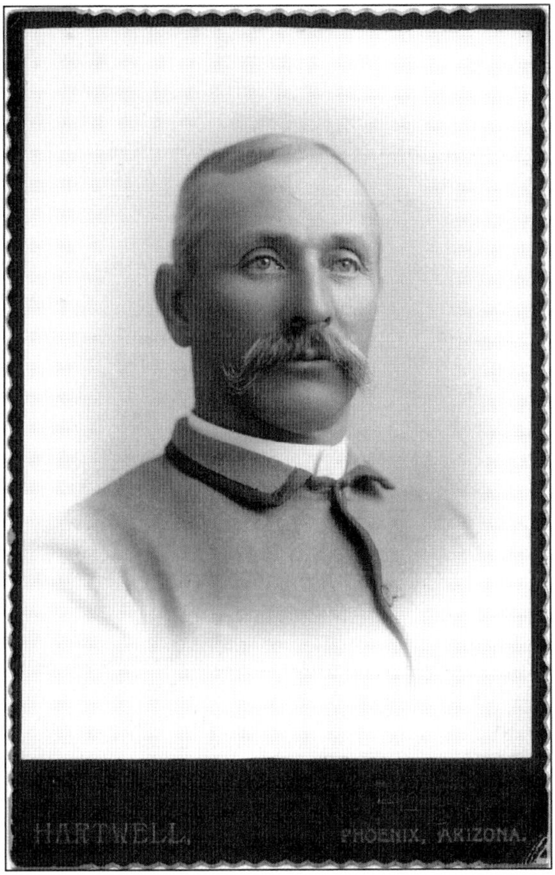

Joshua Miller, shown here about 1910, a physician in Prescott, was twice appointed superintendent of the insane asylum in Phoenix by Gov. Nathan Murphy (see page 12). In 1895, Miller helped found the Arizona Antiquarian Association, which, in 1897, proposed a new museum be built at the normal school (now Arizona State University) in Tempe, in part to house Miller's collection. Territorial museum curator Herbert Brown squelched that plan, but it was 20 years later (1917) before serendipitous events culminated in Miller's collection being purchased from his widow for the Arizona State Museum by the newly formed Arizona Archaeological and Historical Society in Tucson. (Courtesy of Sharlot Hall Museum, Prescott, PO-0104P.)

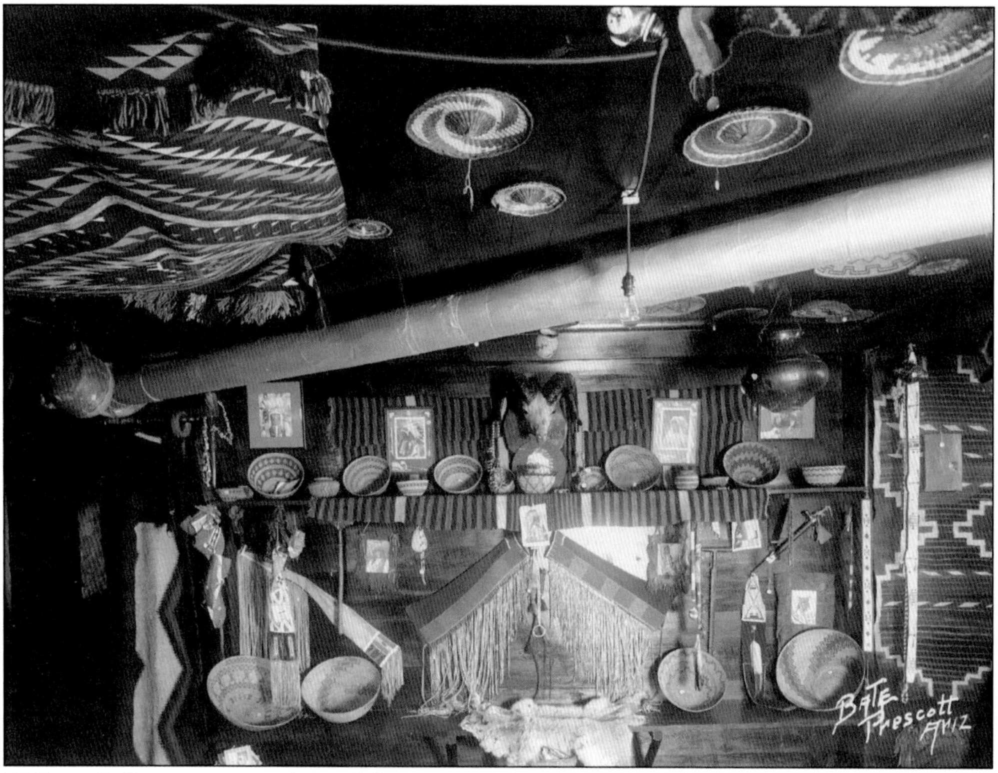

William F. Dermont, president of the Saginaw & Manistee Lumber Co., and his wife, Nelle, moved from Michigan to Williams, Arizona, in 1901. Enthusiastic collectors, they filled their home with Native American objects, as seen here. Prescott photographer Thomas Bate took at least a dozen images of the home, including one with a 1914 calendar visible. William died in May 1915. Whether these photographs were taken before his death, or soon after, as a record of the Dermonts' possessions, is unknown. (Thomas Bate, ASM.)

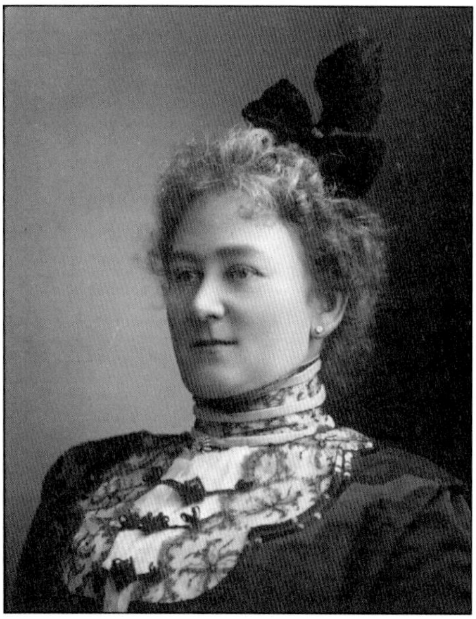

After her husband's death, Nelle A. Dermont, shown here in an undated photograph from the Root Studio in Chicago, loaned her collection to the Southwest Museum in Los Angeles. However, in 1920, she sold 235 baskets (mostly from Arizona and California), 90 pieces of Southwestern pottery, 65 Navajo and Hopi textiles, 131 "Indian curios," and a group of 41 antlers, furs, animal heads, and stuffed birds to UA, for ASM, in order to keep them in Arizona. (Courtesy of Arizona Historical Society Flagstaff Collections, Cline Library, Northern Arizona University, Flagstaff.)

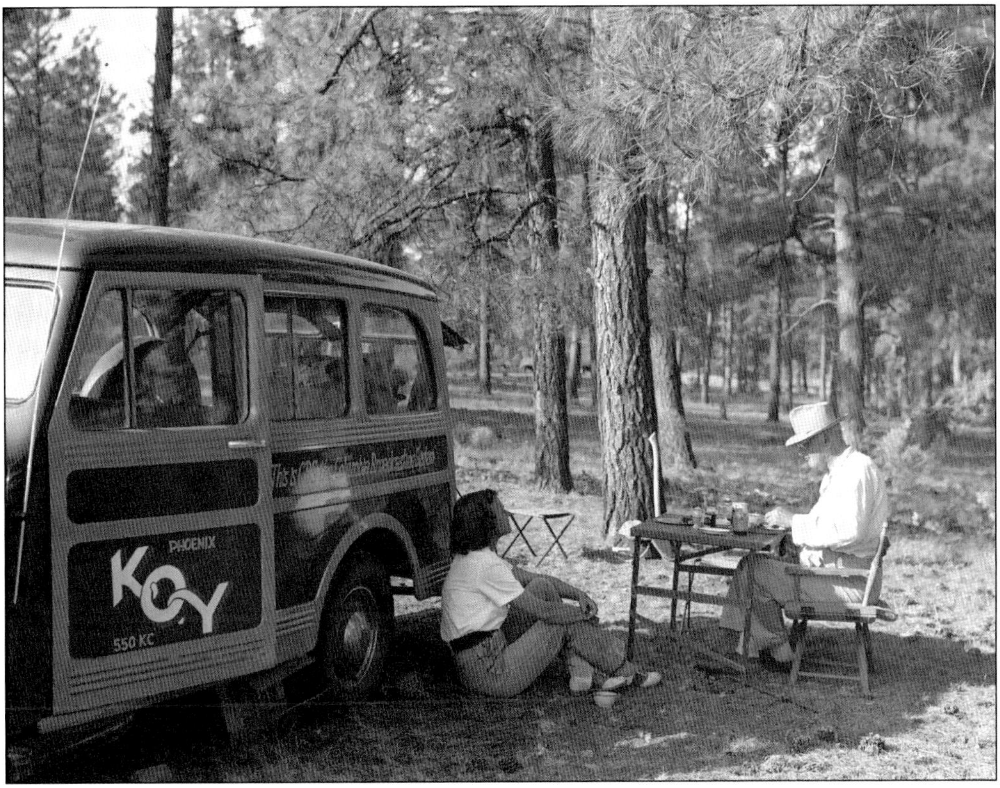

Hard times during the Depression forced Caroline Smurthwaite to sell a collection of 350 Maricopa Indian pots collected by her mother and herself between 1898 and 1907. She offered the collection to ASM director Emil Haury, who convinced Chicago businessman Burridge D. Butler to buy the pots in 1938, dividing them between ASM and the Pueblo Grande Museum, in Phoenix, where he owned the KOY radio station. Later, Butler also made donations to the Point of Pines Field School. Here, during a 1947 visit, he sits (right) with laboratory assistant Gladys Sayles. (E.B. Sayles?, ASM 3208b.)

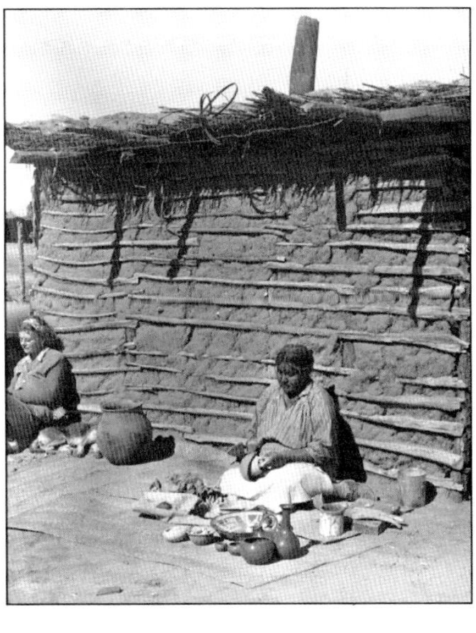

In 1940, ASM curator E.B. Sayles took 108 photographs of accomplished Maricopa potter Ida Redbird making pottery. Here, Ida (right) sits surrounded by her tools and some unfinished pots. Ida is using a paddle to thin the wall of a bowl, while Gladys Sayles takes notes. Some of Redbird's tools, and pots in various stages of manufacture, were collected and placed in ASM. A summary of this documentation appears in the January 1948 issue of *Arizona Highways* magazine. (E.B. Sayles, ASM 21138.)

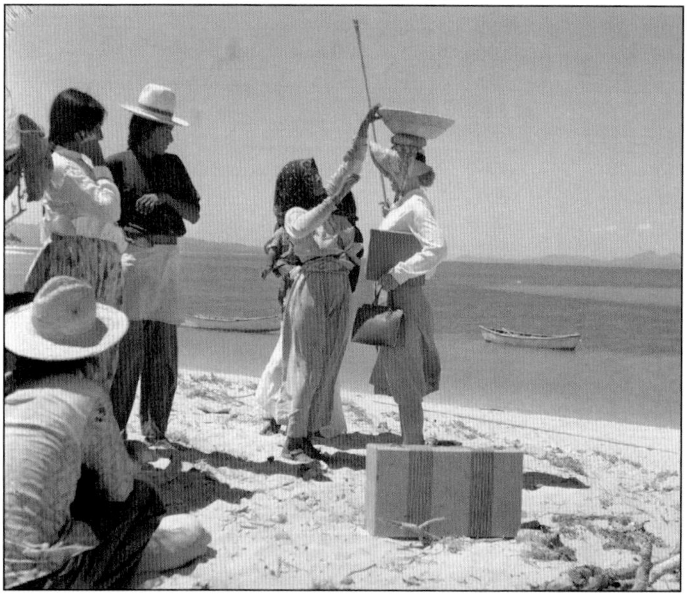

Gwyneth (Browne) Harrington (later Xavier, later Wulsin) held anthropology-related jobs with such diverse employers as the Soil Conservation Service, the Indian Arts and Crafts Board, and the Amerind Foundation. She made five visits to the Seri Indians in Sonora from 1937 to 1944, and donated her notes, photographs, and over 200 artifacts to ASM. Here, on Tiburón Island in June 1941, a Seri woman helps her adjust a head ring and carrying basket. (Julian Hayden, ASM 21038.)

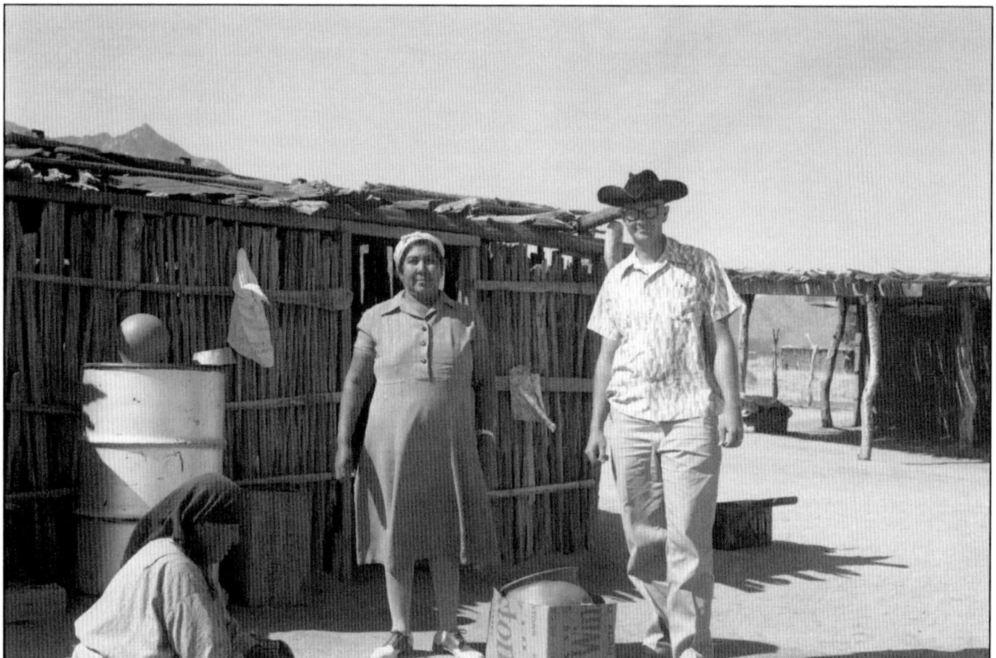

In 1958 and 1959, four UA anthropology students, Bernard L. Fontana, William J. Robinson, Charles W. Cormack, and Ernest E. Leavitt Jr., studied archaeological collections and interviewed Tohono O'odham potters on the reservation southwest of Tucson. The result was a seminal book, *Papago Indian Pottery*, with photographs, notes, and pottery deposited at ASM. Here, interpreter Isabel Miles (center) stands with Fontana (right) and a jar (in box) made by Listiana Francisco (left) at Pan Tak (Coyote Village) in April 1959. (ASM 9324.)

Frederick Rhodes Pleasants studied languages at the Sorbonne and anthropology at Harvard, where he worked at the Peabody Museum. During World War II, he served in the Office of Strategic Services (OSS) and the Red Cross, and, afterward, he was at the Central Art Collecting Point in Munich, one of the "Monuments Men" repatriating stolen artworks. After retiring as curator of Primitive Art at the Brooklyn Museum, he moved to Tucson in 1958, where he taught at both ASM and the UA Anthropology Department (at the time of this 1967 photograph) until he retired again in 1973. He donated only 32 objects to ASM, but each was a major piece of African or Latin American art. (H. Teiwes, ASM 14913.)

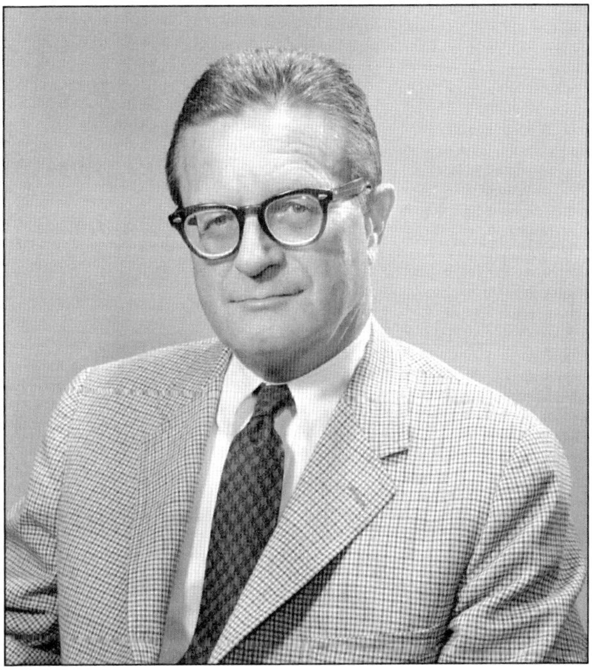

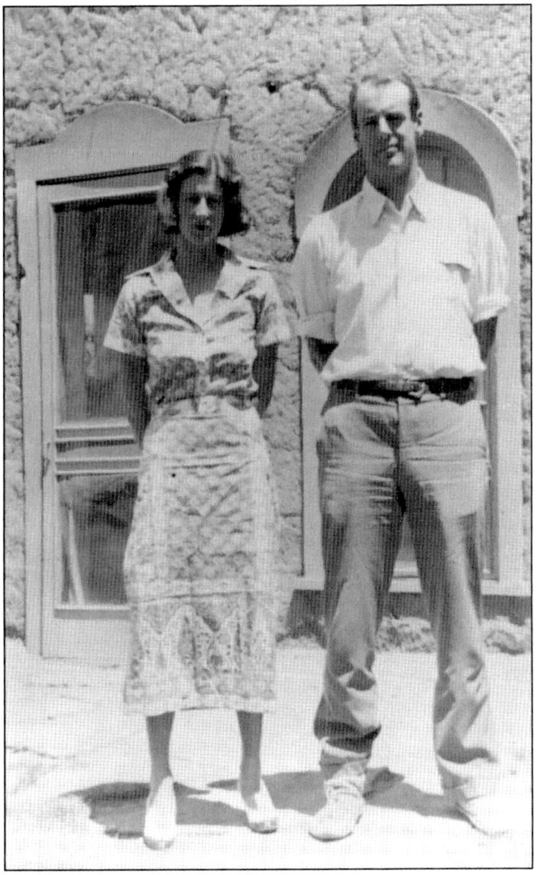

Self-taught anthropologist Grenville Goodwin was introduced to the Southwest when he attended the Mesa Ranch School in Mesa and met Byron Cummings. Intrigued by Apaches and possessed of an aptitude for languages and a friendly demeanor, he spent 1930–1936 living on the San Carlos Indian Reservation, interviewing elders, taking photographs, and collecting some 300 artifacts. Married in 1936, Grenville and his wife, Janice, are shown here in 1937. Grenville died in 1940 at age 32. In 1968, Janice and their son Neil donated to ASM all of Goodwin's research materials, including over 2,000 pages of notes. Goodwin's materials continue to serve as one of the most thorough records of Western Apache culture of the late 1800s and early 1900s. (Courtesy of Neil Goodwin.)

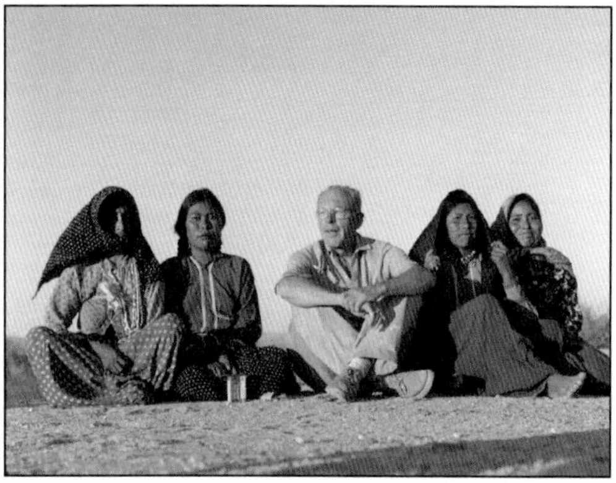

James "Jimmy" W. Manson served in World War I and then ranched in the Yaqui Valley, in Sonora. As early as 1922, he began collecting miscellaneous items. In 1928, he opened the Pacific Brokerage Company in Nogales, Arizona, and, until his death in 1968, he spent many weekends in Seri Indian villages fishing or taking photographs. His more than 500 ethnographic, archaeological, and natural history specimens and over 600 photographs (mostly of Seris) were donated to ASM by his wife in 1969. Here, he sits with four Seri women. (ASM 24902.)

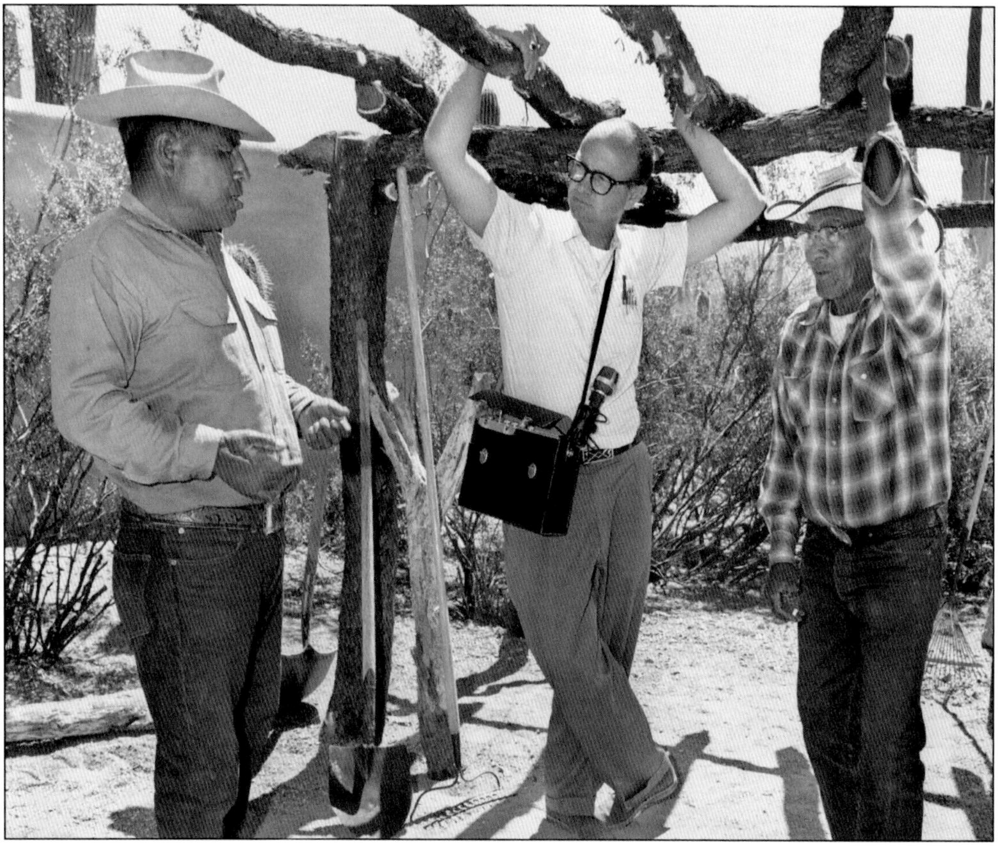

From 1967 to 1972, Bernard L. Fontana directed the Doris Duke American Indian Oral History Program at UA, which was funded there, and at seven other universities, by tobacco heiress Doris Duke. Tallies show that 48 anthropology students and staff interviewed 506 individuals from 32 cultural or ethnic groups (primarily Native American), in 16 languages, resulting in 615 sound recordings (787 hours), for which the transcription of a small fraction resulted in over 7,000 typed pages. All materials reside in the ASM Archives. Here, Fontana (center), with his faithful Uher-brand reel-to-reel tape recorder, interviews Tohono O'odham Lorentino Noceo (left) and Frank Lopez in May 1968. (H. Teiwes, ASM 18290.)

Pál and Elisabeth Kelemen (left) visit a prehistoric site at Malinalco, Mexico, with anthropologist Robert Weitlaner in 1940. The Kelemens spent 40 years traveling in Latin America, researching pre-Columbian and Spanish Colonial art and publishing extensively on both. Between 1974 and 1978, they donated to ASM 42 linear feet of archives, about 1,100 books and journals, and 19,000 negatives by William Harold Eagle, which will be a treasure trove for future researchers. (Courtesy of Diane Halász.)

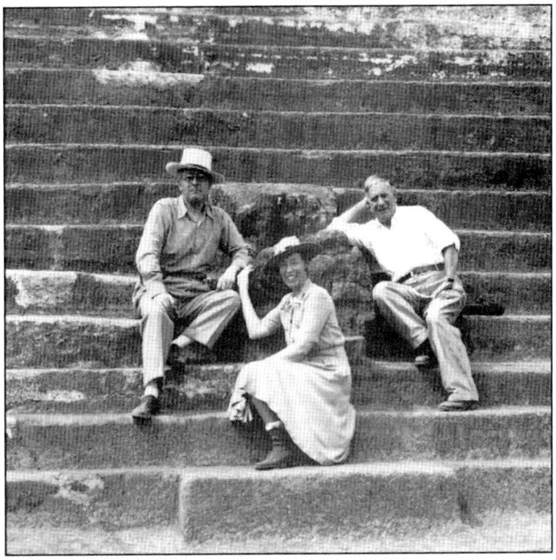

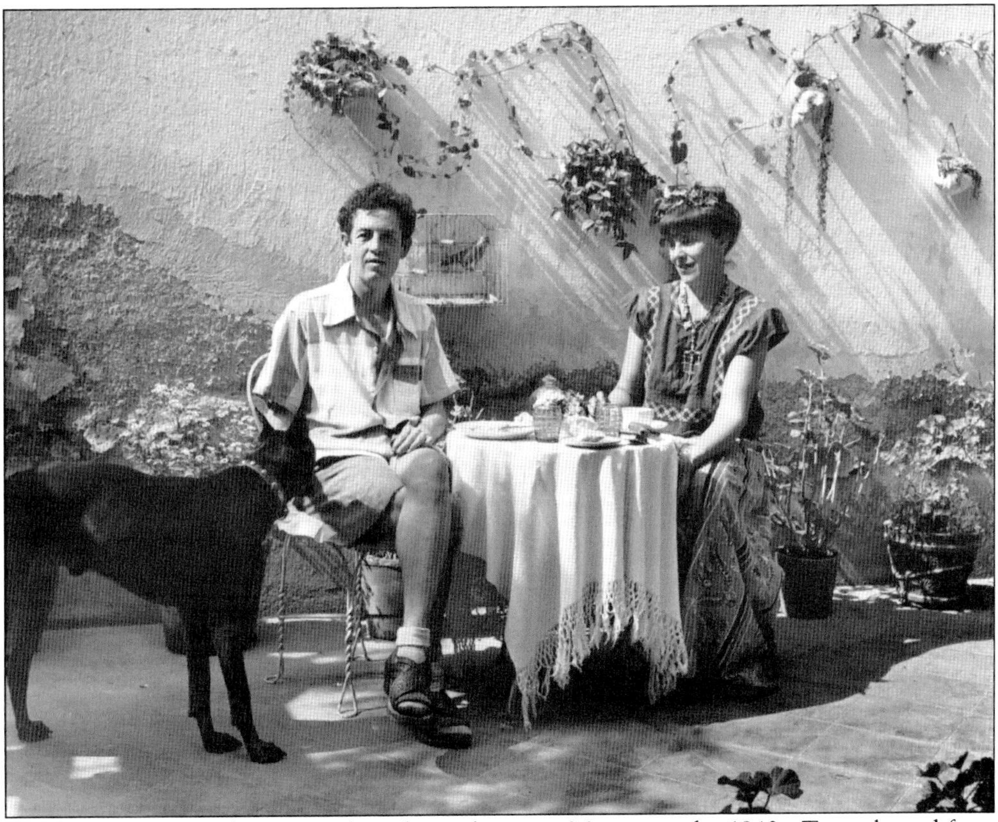

Donald B. and Dorothy M. Cordry relax at home in Mexico in the 1940s. Transplanted from Minneapolis, Minnesota, these two artists, entrepreneurs, folk art connoisseurs, and authors fell in love with Mexico. Their extensive collections were sold and donated to numerous institutions. In 1979, UA president John P. Schaefer and the UA Foundation purchased for ASM some 350 Mexican costumes and 550 masks collected between 1931 and 1978, as well as over 340 Cuna Indian textiles and artifacts from the Cordrys' 1969 trip to Panama. (Courtesy of Science Museum of Minnesota.)

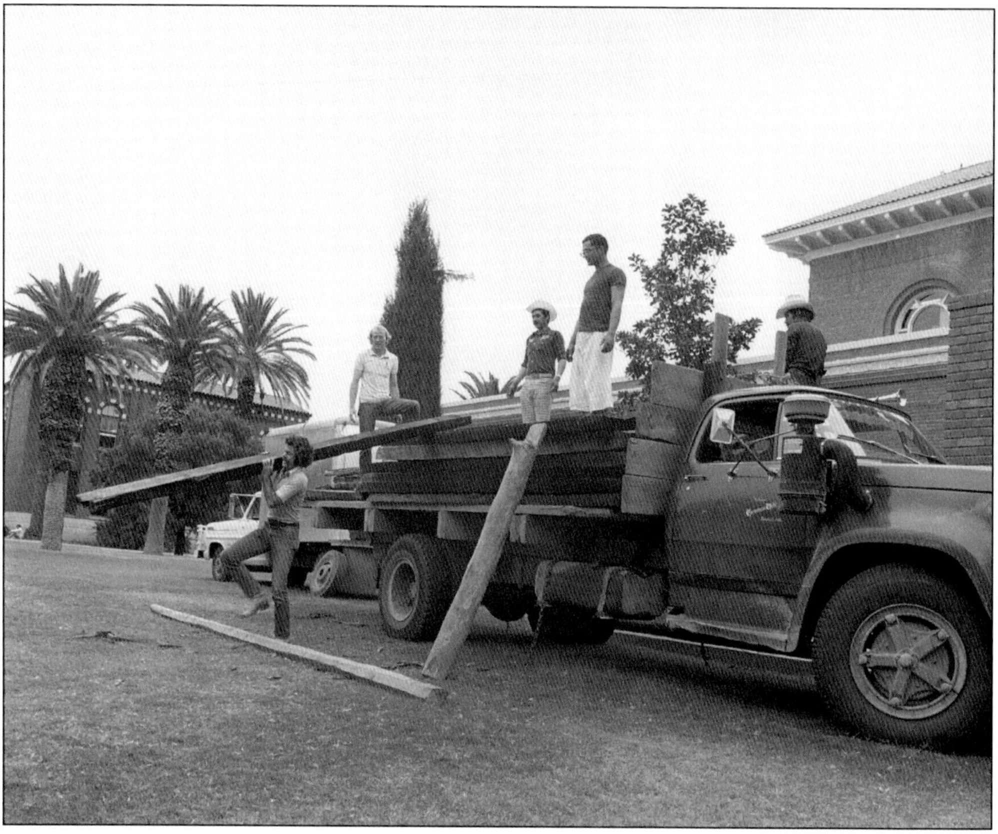

In 1977 and 1978, UA president John P. Schaefer, working with the UA Foundation, sponsored an ethnographic project: trader Edmond Faubert collected over 650 contemporary objects from Tarahumara Indians in Chihuahua, Mexico, and all were donated to ASM. Additionally, a log house, granary, chicken coop, and corral were purchased for use in a major ASM exhibit. Here, in September 1978, Faubert (in white pants), assisted by ASM registrar Steve Rogers (tail of truck) and three helpers, unloads logs on the north lawn of ASM North. (H. Teiwes, ASM 47741.)

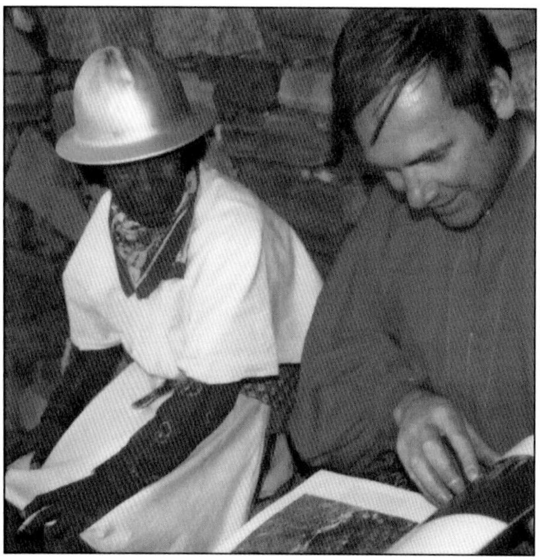

John Schaefer is seen at right with a Tarahumara man, looking at the May 1979 issue of *Arizona Highways* magazine, which features an article on the Tarahumara by Bernard L. Fontana, illustrated with Schaefer's photographs, which were extracted from their book *Tarahumara: Where Night Is the Day of the Moon*. Schaefer donated his extensive Tarahumara photographic archives to ASM. (Bryant Bannister, ASM.)

Edward P. Dozier, seen here in June 1966, was born at Santa Clara Pueblo, New Mexico. He became the second Native American to obtain a doctorate in anthropology, and the first to pursue a teaching career in the field. He did fieldwork in his own community, at Hopi, and, in 1959–1960, among the Kalinga of the northern Philippines, who would later be the focus of study by another UA anthropologist (see page 54). Dozier taught at UA from 1960 to 1971, and 27 linear feet of his personal and professional papers were later donated by his family to the ASM Archives. (Douglas Lindsay, ASM 11805.)

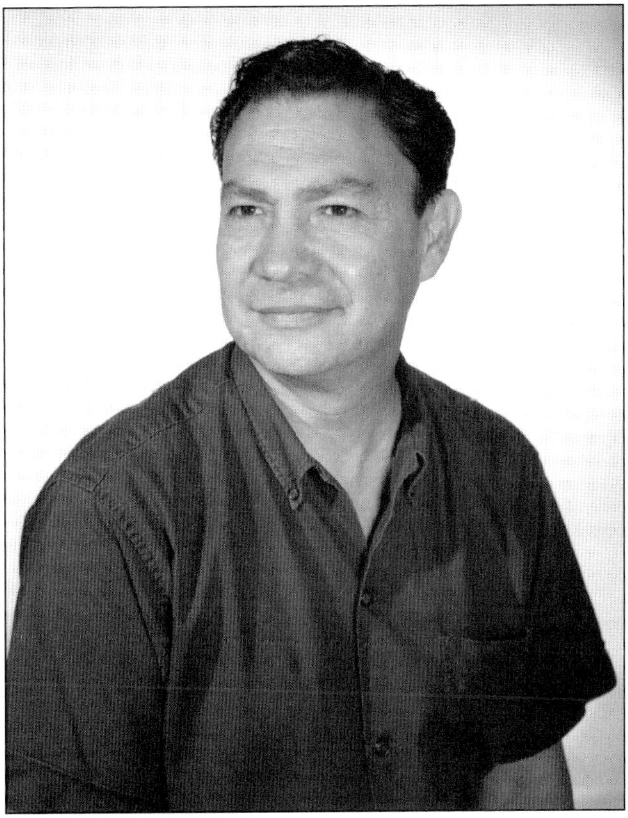

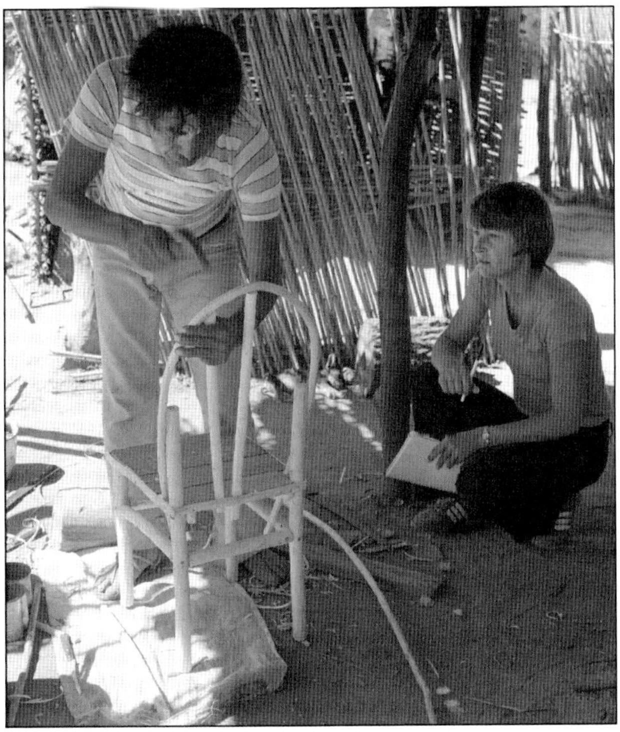

ASM curator Jan Bell studied the making of pottery and other crafts in Native American Yaqui and Mayo communities in Sonora and Sinaloa, Mexico, in 1979 and 1980. Here, Bell documents Placido Yolimea, a Mayo living in the Yaqui village of Bataconsica, Sonora, making Mayo-style wooden chairs in February 1980. Bell's photographs, field notes, and object collections are part of ASM's extensive ethnographic collections from northwestern Mexico. (H. Teiwes, ASM.)

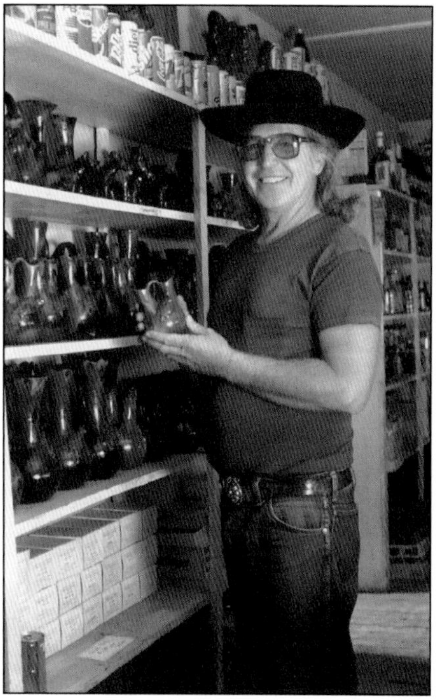

William T. "Bill" Beaver Jr. displays Navajo pottery for sale at his Sacred Mountain Trading Post, north of Flagstaff, in September 1986. In 1981, UA president John Schaefer arranged for the UA Foundation to purchase, for ASM, Beaver's collection of some 250 Navajo pots made between about 1950 and 1980. Beaver actively promoted Navajo potters in his years as a trader (1951–2009) and participated in over 13 hours of oral history interviews with Jan Bell to further document the evolution of the craft. (Jan Bell, ASM.)

Rev. Edgar Guenther and his wife, Minnie, pose at East Fork, Fort Apache Indian Reservation, soon after their arrival from Wisconsin in early 1911. The couple spent the rest of their lives as Lutheran missionaries and friends to the White Mountain Apache tribe. In her will, Minnie bequeathed to ASM 275 Apache artifacts that had been purchased or received as gifts up to 1981, expanding the time period covered by ASM's earlier donations of Apache materials (see page 47). (Photograph by E.E. Guenther, courtesy of the author.)

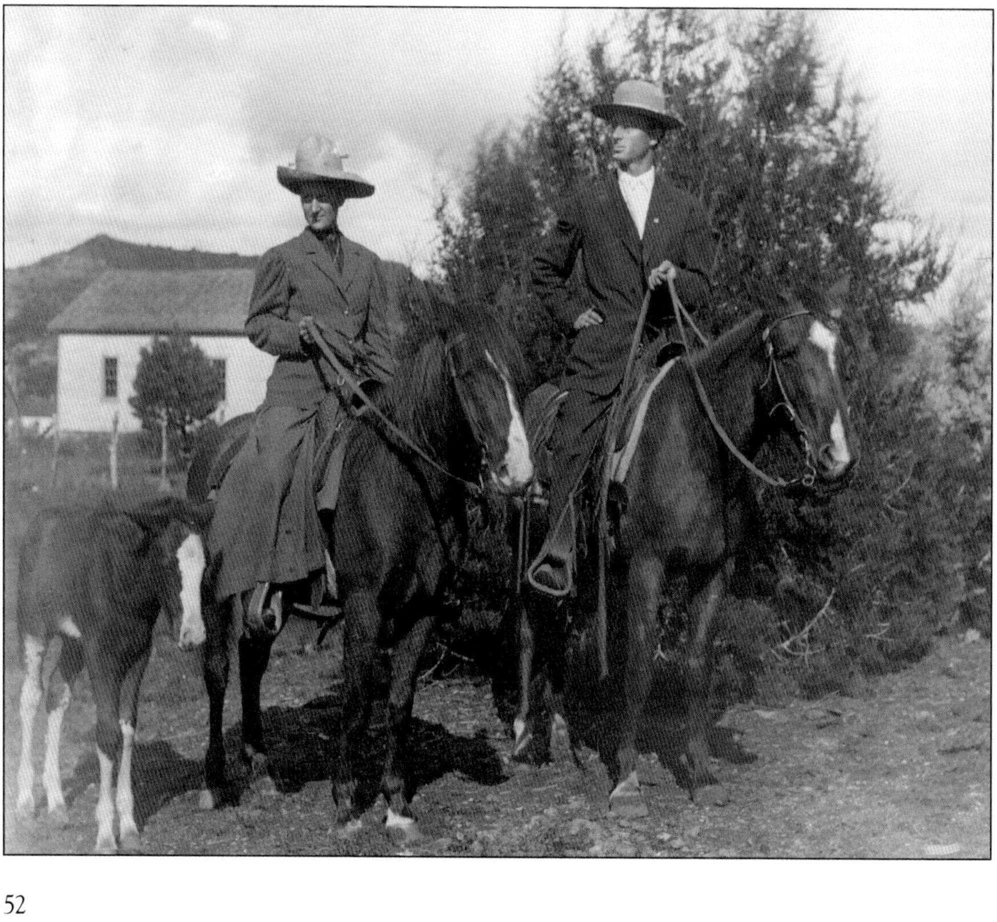

Between 1991 and 1994, ASM photographer Helga Teiwes traveled repeatedly to the Hopi mesas in northeastern Arizona to photograph the work of several dozen basket weavers, resulting in her book *Hopi Basket Weaving: Artistry in Natural Fibers*. In October 1991, Pearl Nuvangyaoma of Shipaulovi, Second Mesa, allowed Teiwes to photograph the complete process of weaving a *piiki* tray (*piiki* is a thin bread made from blue corn). Here, Nuvangyaoma holds the finished product, now in ASM. (H. Teiwes, ASM 86180.)

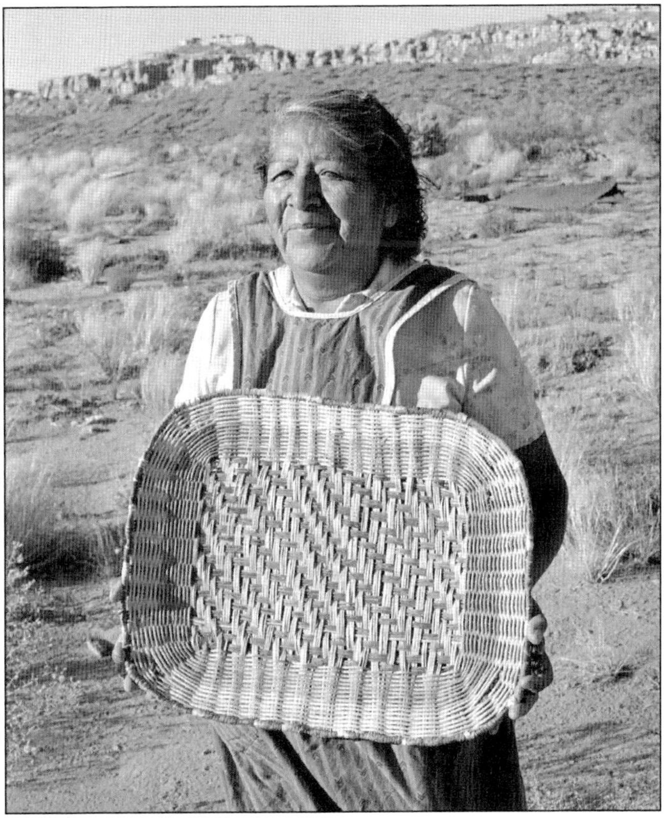

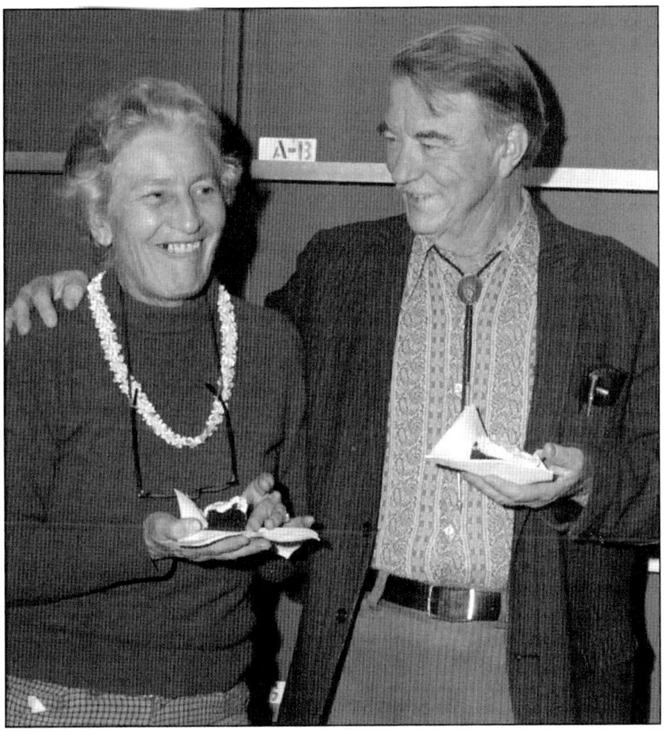

Rosamond B. "Roz" and Edward H. "Ned" Spicer share some cake at a 70th birthday party held for Ned in the UA Anthropology Department in November 1976. Ned was a prolific, world-renowned cultural anthropologist best known for his work on Yaqui culture and other "persistent peoples." Roz, a Yaqui scholar in her own right, completed several of Ned's projects after his death in 1983. She also organized some 120 linear feet of their archival materials (the largest collection in ASM Archives) and 1,500 of her own ethnographic photographs. (H. Teiwes, ASM 42389.)

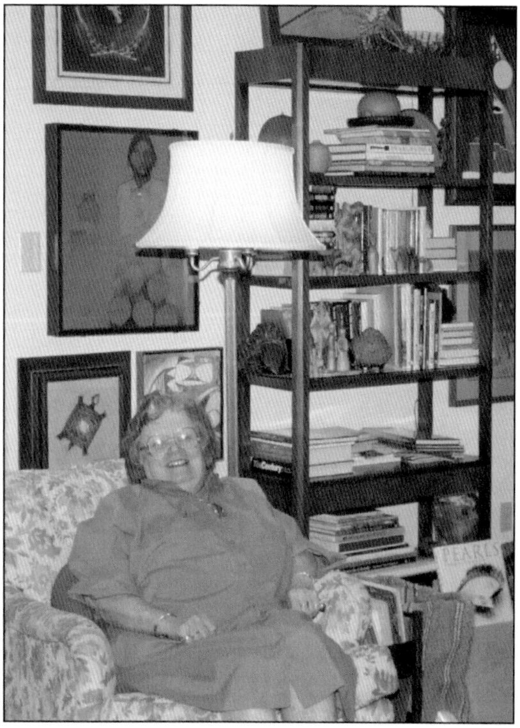

Marjorie Pierce Avery was born in Phoenix and studied art at UA. She led a family-supported adventure from 1960 to 2000, assembling an encyclopedic collection of 354 Native American paintings created between 1930 and 1991. Avery is shown above in her home, in 2001, the year she donated her collection to ASM. In 2002, the paintings were featured in an exhibit and catalog, both assembled by curator Diane Dittemore and both aptly titled *Connections Across Generations*. (Diane Dittemore, ASM.)

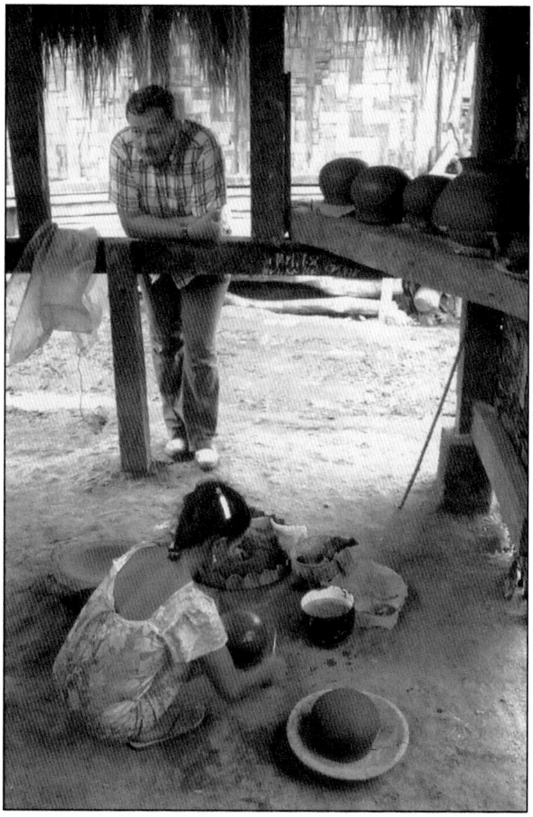

William A. Longacre watches a Kalinga woman make pottery in the village of Dalupa in the northern Philippines in 1988. Longacre began his career at the UA Anthropology Department doing archaeology in Arizona. In 1973, he launched the ongoing Kalinga Ethnoarchaeological Project to study a traditional culture that still made and used pottery. The resulting research collections of over 850 Kalinga objects (primarily pots and baskets), field notes, and over 1,500 photographs are all curated at ASM. (Photograph by and courtesy of James M. Skibo.)

Four

Archaeological Projects and Collections

Archaeological projects in the late 1800s and early 1900s were conducted primarily by museums, as their budgets allowed, and by private individuals or institutions, which limited the amount of such work. The federal Antiquities Act of 1906 provides protection to archaeological materials and sites located on federal lands. The Arizona Antiquities Act of 1960 explicitly gives legal protection to archaeological sites, artifacts, vertebrate fossils, and human remains and funerary objects located on state, county, city, and other municipal properties within Arizona.

In practical terms, this meant that the volume of prehistoric artifacts coming in to ASM in its early years was relatively small. In 1955, the Arizona Highway Department (renamed the Arizona Department of Transportation [ADOT] in 1974) agreed to fund surveys and excavations by ASM in advance of its projects; this work was overseen by ASM archaeologist William W. Wasley. The Highway Salvage Program at ASM was formally created in 1964, with the Highway Salvage archaeologist position occupied by R. Gwinn Vivian (1964–1967, 1968–1970), Laurens C. Hammack (1967–1968, 1970–1979), David A. Gregory (1979–1980), Alan Ferg (1980), and Alan P. Sullivan III (1980–1981), after which the position was incorporated into ADOT's offices in Phoenix.

Highway salvage work, combined with the 1960 Arizona Antiquities Act, created a boom in what became known as "contract archaeology," conducted by universities and museums as well as private companies. All of them employed the bumper crop of archaeologists who had been trained on the GI Bill following World War II, including many from the UA who had attended the UA Point of Pines Archaeological Field School (see page 71). The opportunity to be gainfully employed doing archaeology encouraged additional students to enter the field in the 1970s and 1980s. ASM had its own contract group, starting about 1970, known from 1972 to 1980 as the Cultural Resource Management Section (CRMS) and from 1981 to 1990 as the Cultural Resource Management Division (CRMD). The first head was Mark A. Grady (1972–1975). Starting in 1975, Lynn S. Teague directed and, ultimately, closed down the division.

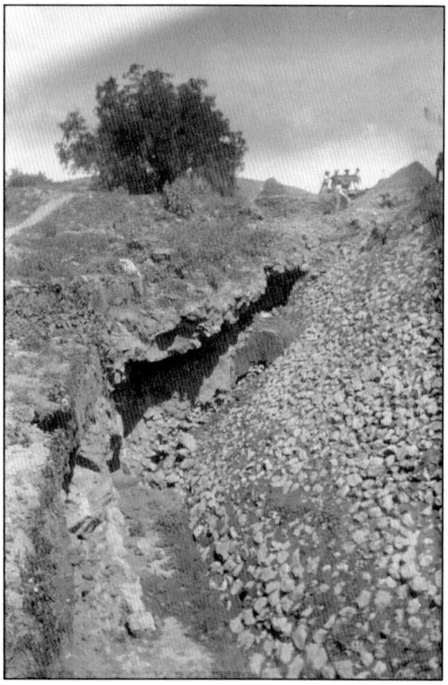

Invited by Mexican archaeologist Manuel Gamio, ASM director Byron Cummings excavated at the site of Cuicuilco, 12 miles south of Mexico City. Lava from Xitli volcano had flowed over the site and partially surrounded a hill, probably a few hundred years BC. Digging in 1922 showed the hill to be a man-made platform mound 50 feet high and 400 feet in diameter—the earliest known ceremonial structure of this type. At Cummings's invitation, Emil W. Haury, who had just completed his sophomore year at Bethel College in Newton, Kansas, joined the 1924–1925 season. At left, laborers work where the lava flow, under the tree, came near to the rock-faced mound at right. A layer of soil that accumulated after the site was abandoned shielded the mound. With that dug out (the dark shadow at center), the unsupported lava was removed by pick and hammer, as well as the judicious use of dynamite by assistant E.J. Hands. (E.W. Haury, ASM 7725.)

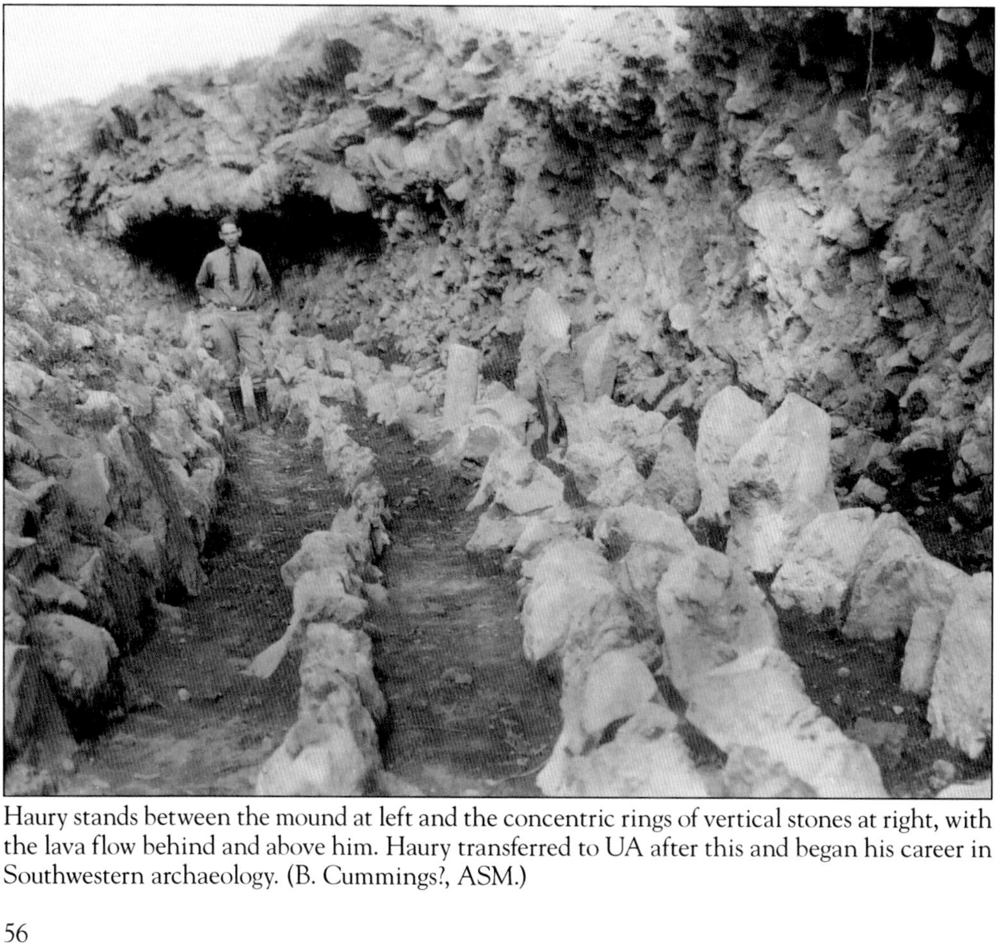

Haury stands between the mound at left and the concentric rings of vertical stones at right, with the lava flow behind and above him. Haury transferred to UA after this and began his career in Southwestern archaeology. (B. Cummings?, ASM.)

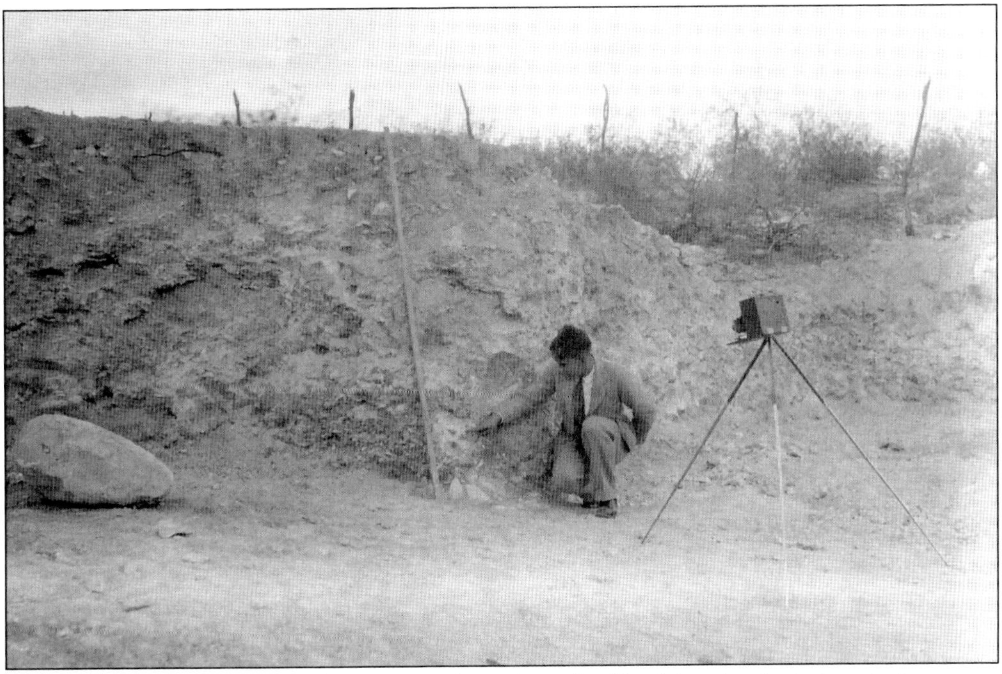

In 1924 and 1925, crosses, swords, spears, and wands made of lead, bearing Latin inscriptions, were excavated northwest of Tucson. Known as the Tucson Artifacts, the Silverbell Road Artifacts, or the Lead Crosses, their discoverer argued they were evidence of a lost colony of Romans dating from AD 775 to 900. Ultimately, their garbled Latin, the depiction of a dinosaur, and firsthand examination by Haury proved them to have been a hoax. Here, one artifact is photographed where it was found, below six feet of caliche. (A.E. Douglass, ASM 16233.)

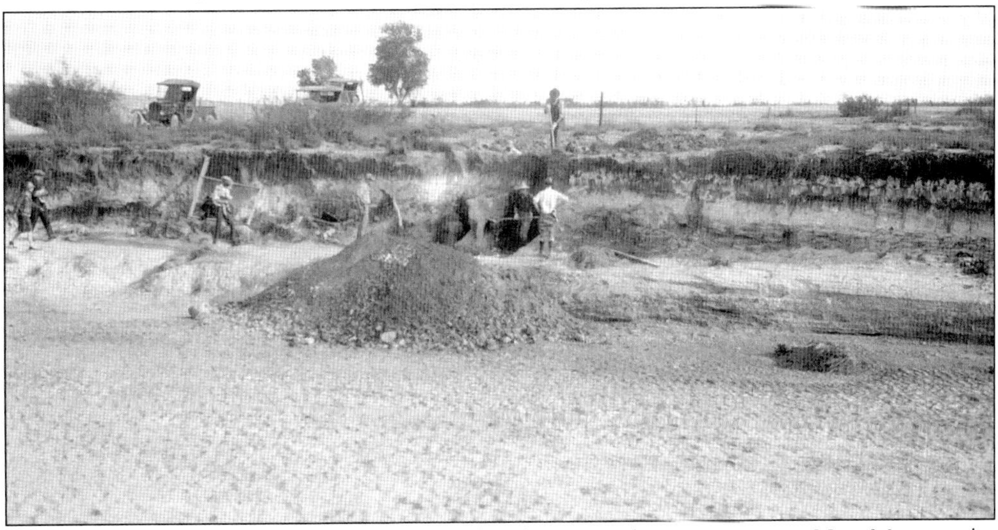

In 1926, Folsom spear points were discovered with ancient bison remains in New Mexico, the first association of humans and extinct animals in the New World. Here, also in 1926, Byron Cummings points his shovel blade at a mammoth skull discovered eroding from the bank of Whitewater Draw in southern Arizona, which he thought was associated with grinding stones. Later work at this Double Adobe Mammoth Site concluded that the association was the result of erosional events, not human coexistence with mammoths. (ASM 71.)

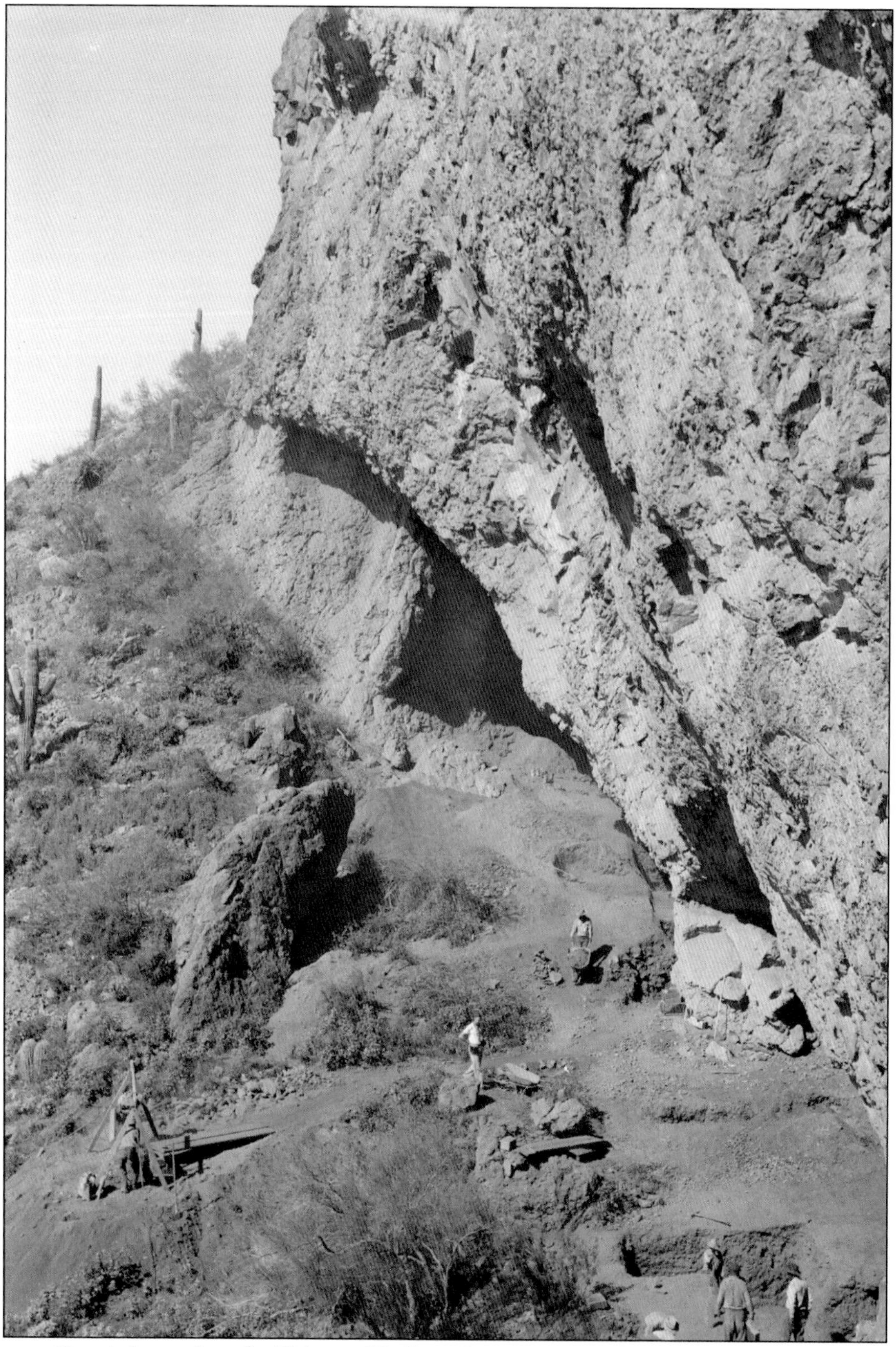

Ventana Cave is located on the Tohono O'odham Reservation and is actually a large rock shelter. The site's name refers to a nearby natural stone arch, La Ventana ("the Window" in Spanish). Excavations in 1941 and 1942 by Emil Haury, Wilfrid C. Bailey, and Julian D. Hayden found stratified cultural deposits spanning the entire known range of human occupation in the Sonoran Desert, from Paleoindian materials to historic Tohono O'odham artifacts. Here, the site is seen under excavation, at right, and with workers screening for artifacts, at left. (E.W. Haury, ASM 281.)

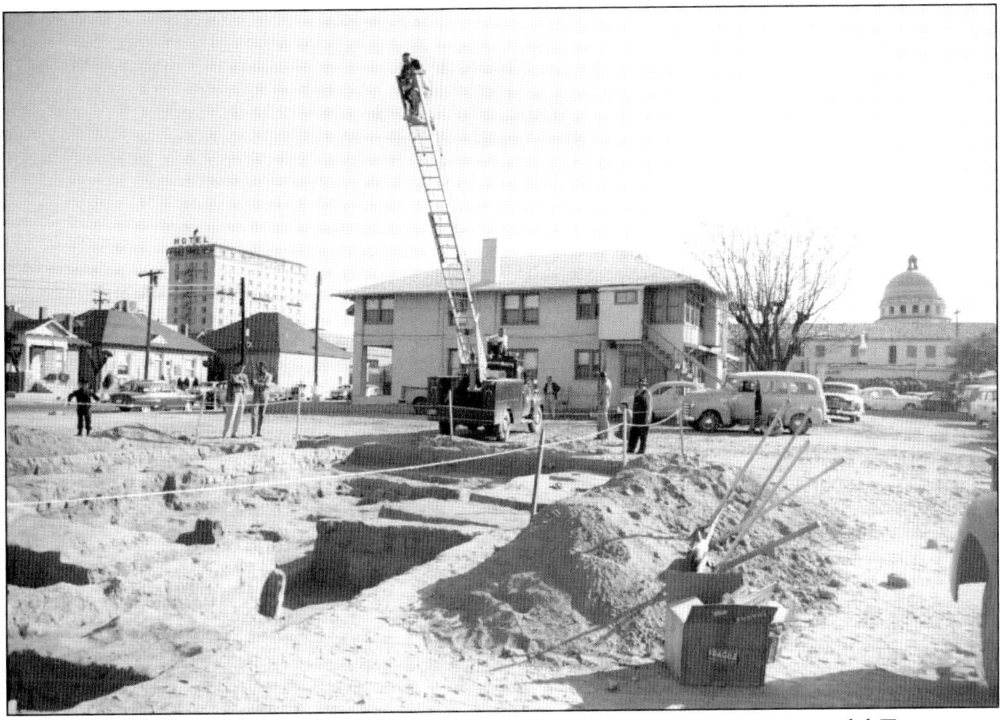

Tucson marks its founding as August 20, 1775, when the Presidio San Agustín del Tucsón was established. Its last piece of wall came down in 1918. In December 1954, a brief opportunity allowed Emil Haury, Alan P. Olson, and volunteers to excavate the northeast bastion. Here, Haury photographs the dig from a truck lent by Tucson Gas, Electric Light & Power Co. At back right is the Pima County Courthouse dome. The property was acquired by the city, and the bastion was rebuilt, opening in 2007 as a historic park. (George W. Chambers, ASM.)

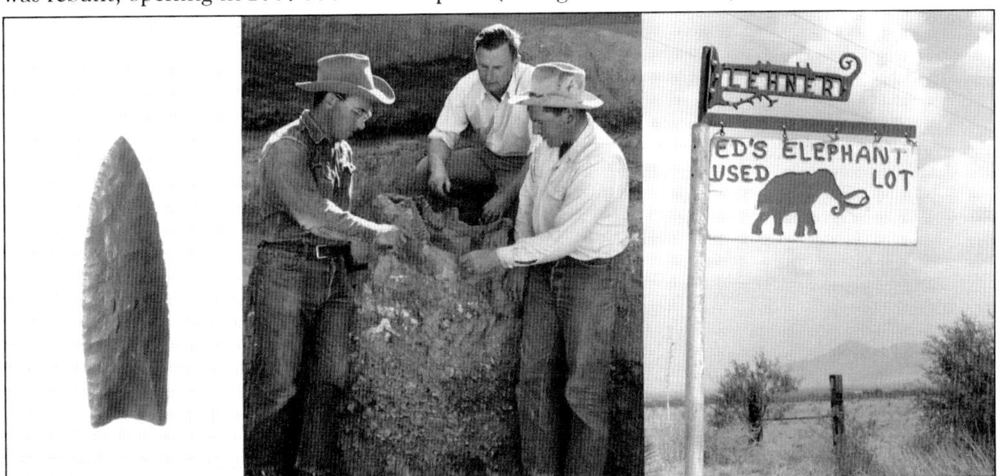

At the Naco Site in 1952, Haury, who had dug at Double Adobe in 1926, documented the first definite association in the Southwest of Clovis spear points with mammoths. In 1955–1956, he repeated the feat at the nearby Lehner Site, and radiocarbon-dated two fire pits to around 9,000 BC. Pictured are, from left to right, a Clovis point from Lehner Site; ASM archaeologist William W. Wasley (left) and Ed Lehner (right) examine a mammoth mandible; and the sign to Lehner Ranch in 1974–1975, while Vance Haynes conducted additional work at the site. (ASM.)

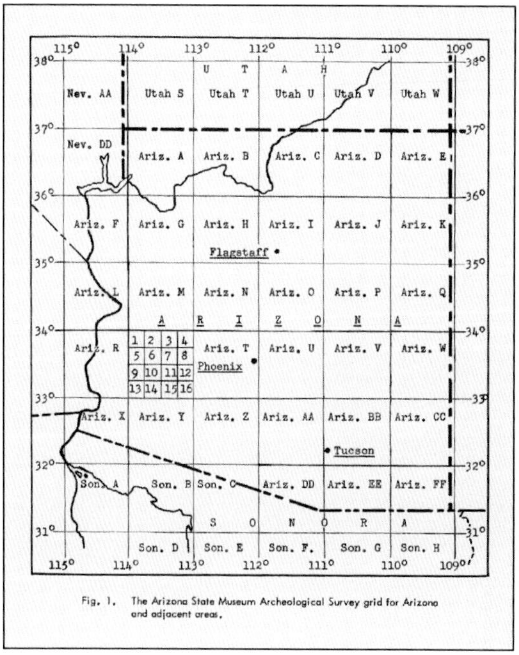

The ASM system of recording the location of archaeological sites throughout the state was adapted by Emil Haury from that created by the Gila Pueblo Archaeological Foundation in 1928. This 1957 map shows how the state was divided into lettered "quadrangles" one degree of latitude and longitude in size, which were internally divided into 16 rectangles, each 15 minutes on a side. The first site card (AZ FF:4:1) was filled out by Haury and E.J. Hands on May 13, 1937, while Haury was "between jobs" at Gila Pueblo and UA. The site is an early pit house village on Hands's ranch in the northern Chiricahua Mountains. (Photograph by J. Weakly of Figure 1 in W.W. Wasley's 1957 *The Archaeological Survey of the Arizona State Museum.*)

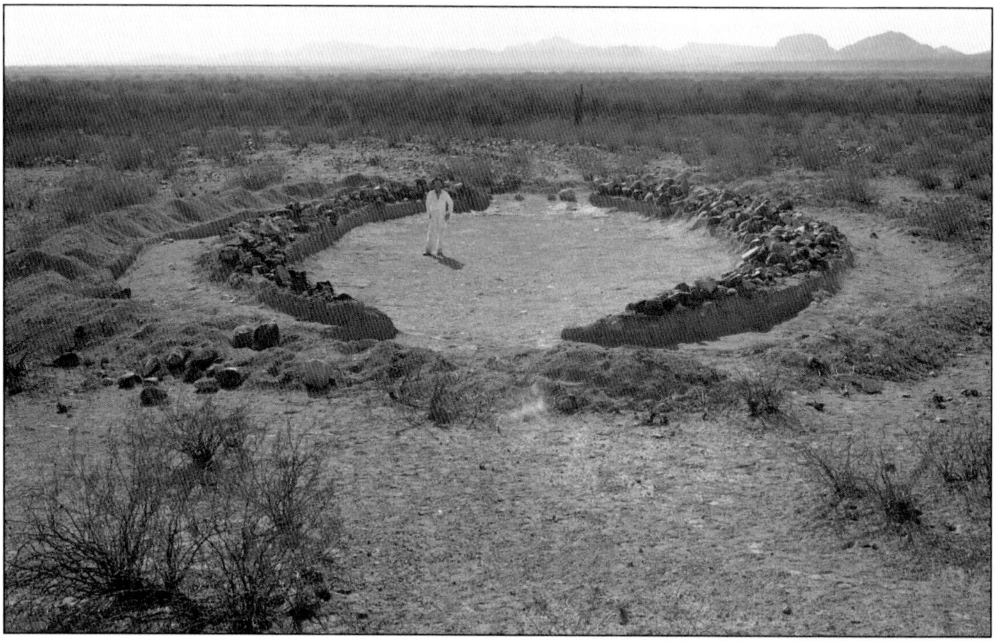

Over 50 Hohokam sites situated along the Gila River, west of Gila Bend, are within the possible flood pool of Painted Rocks Reservoir. Between 1958 and 1961, many were tested by ASM archaeologists W.W. Wasley and Alfred E. Johnson, funded by the National Park Service. This photograph shows the excavated namesake of the Rock Ball Court Site, with its stone embankments outlining an oval area where Hohokam Indians probably played a ceremonial game with a rubber ball derived from cultures in Mexico. (A. Johnson, ASM 6926.)

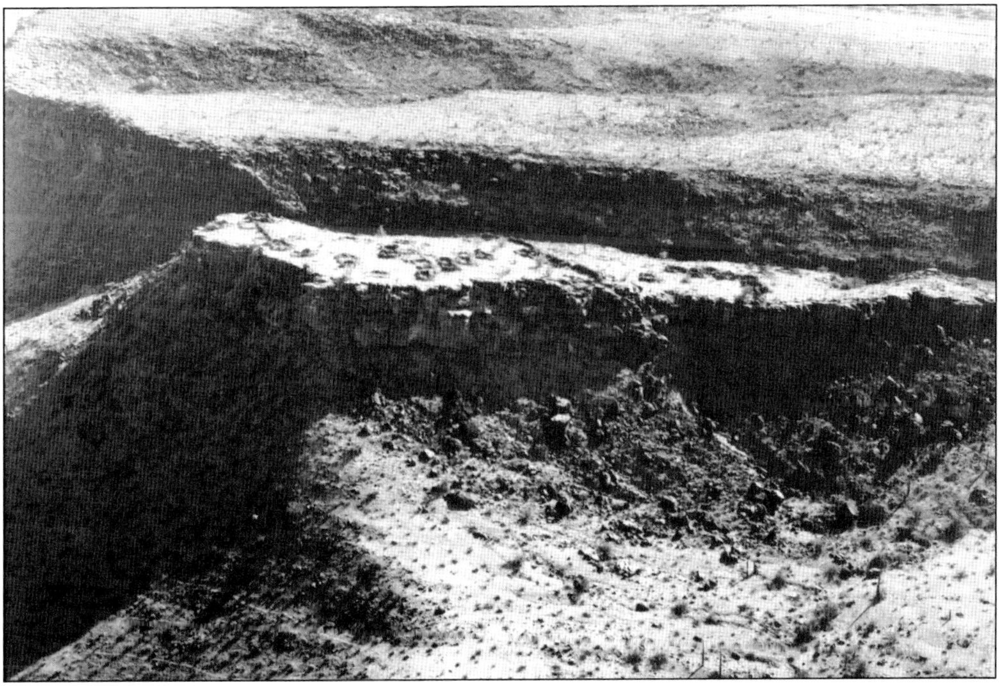

The Fortified Hill Site, or Fortaleza ("Fortress" in Spanish), in the San Lucy District of the Tohono O'odham Reservation, was excavated and reconstructed by J. Cameron Greenleaf and a Tohono O'odham crew in 1964. Built on an isolated hilltop, its dry-laid masonry rooms, walls built across the path up the hill, and the artifacts found within it all suggest the site was built around AD 1200–1275 by an immigrant Hohokam group with ties to the Tucson Basin. (D.D. Cassidy, Blanton and Cole Aerial Photography, ASM 9201.)

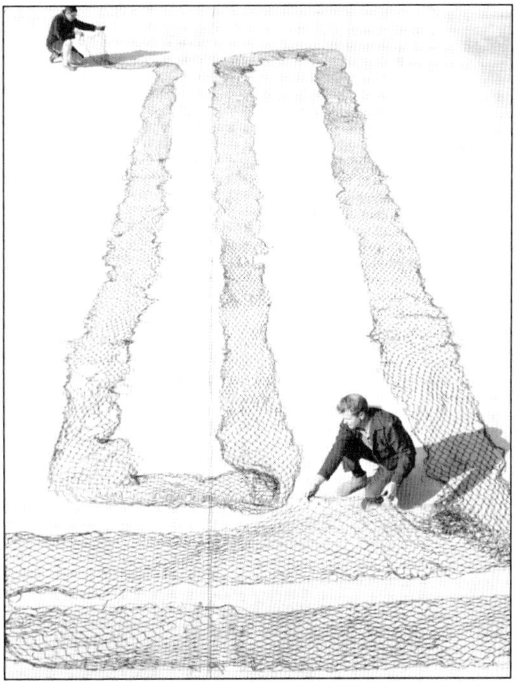

Historically, Southwestern rabbit drives involved flushing them toward a long, low net and then clubbing the rabbits that became entangled. Several prehistoric rabbit nets have been found, including this one, in 1962, which was dug illegally from a cave in the Altar Valley, southwest of Tucson. Laid out by curator of exhibits Ernie Leavitt (foreground), the net measures 43 inches wide and 165 feet long, was woven out of twine spun from human hair, and, based on associated pottery, was made between about AD 1250 and 1450. (H. Teiwes, ASM 15920.)

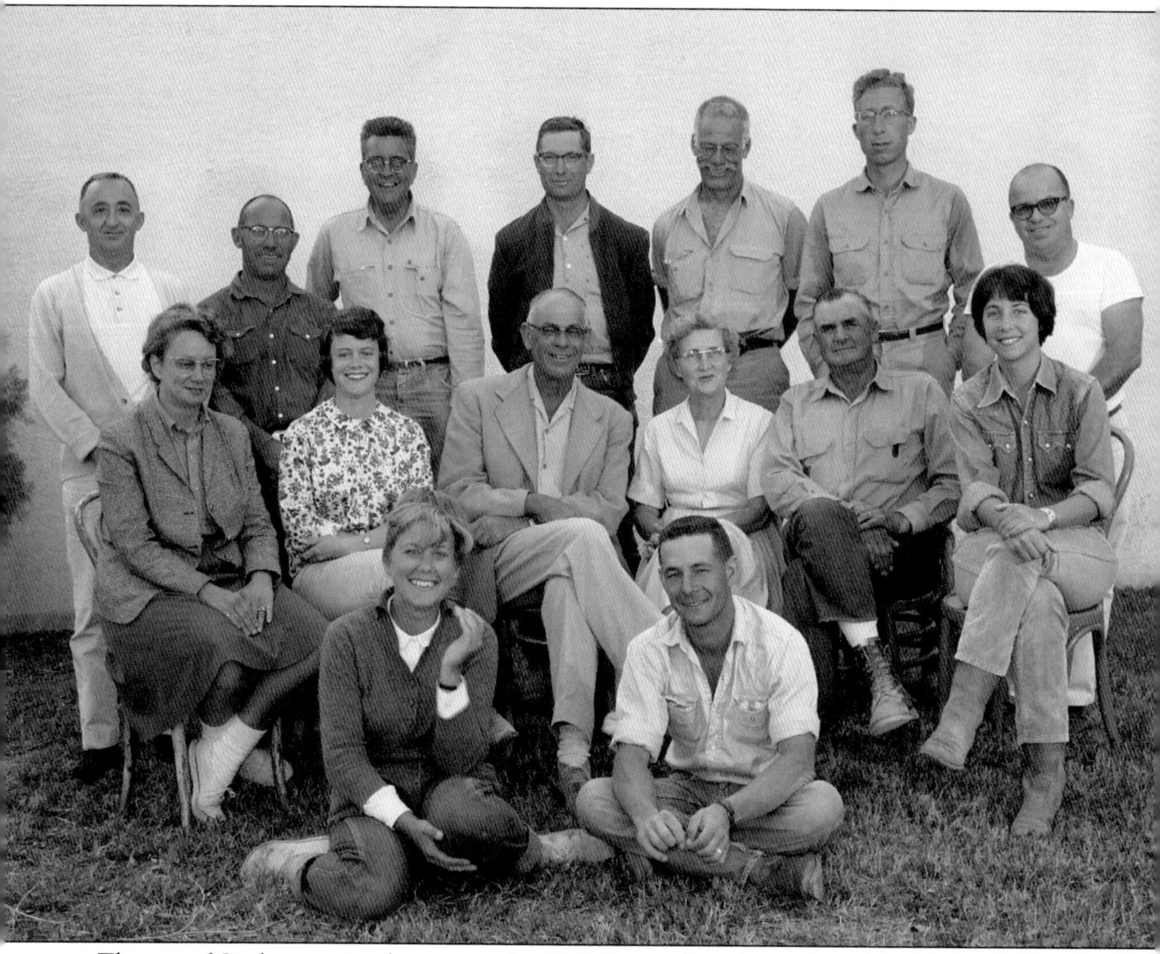

The site of Snaketown is a large, complex Hohokam village located on the Gila River (Pima) Indian Reservation, south of Phoenix. The Gila Pueblo Archaeological Foundation excavated part of the site in 1934 and 1935, with the results being the basis for the understanding of prehistoric Hohokam culture for decades to come. Emil Haury worked on that excavation and, in 1964 and 1965, as director emeritus of ASM, returned to Snaketown to learn more. Photographs of the excavations can be found in numerous publications. Haury himself published a photograph of his Pima crew members. Here, however, are faces to go with the names of the Snaketown II crew, photographed at the conclusion of the project, sunburned and happy. From left to right are (front) Helga Teiwes (photographer) and James V. Sciscenti (archaeologist); (seated) Agnese Lockwood (volunteer laboratory assistant), Mary Anne Stein (laboratory assistant), Emil W. Haury (field director), Hulda Haury (field director wrangler), James A. "Al" Lancaster (archaeologist), and Susan T. Adams (laboratory director); (standing) Theodore C. "Ted" Contes (business manager), William W. "Bill" Wasley (assistant field director), Manice "Chip" Lockwood (volunteer field assistant), Alfred E. "Al" Johnson (archaeologist), Julian D. Hayden (sage counsel/backhoe nurse), Jonathan Gell (cartographer), and Torance "Tut" Mock (cook). Of the four exposures Teiwes took of this group, running back to her seat each time after setting the camera timer, only in this one is everyone smiling. This is possibly because, for this one, Hayden had put a rock where Teiwes had to alight. (H. Teiwes, ASM 80394.)

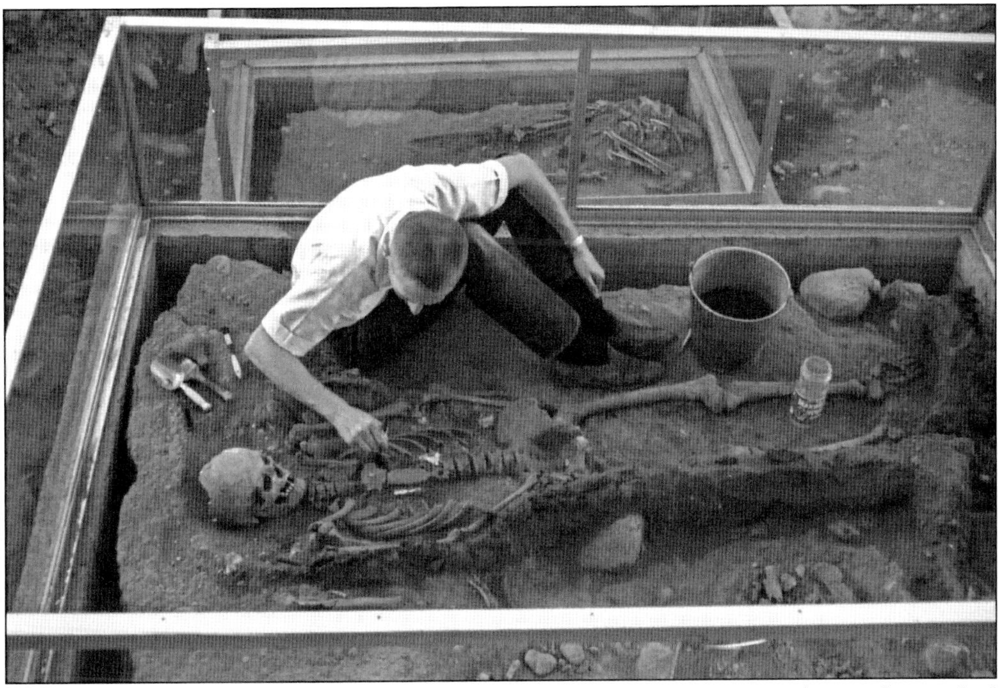

Father Eusebio Francisco Kino, arguably the most important Jesuit priest in the Southwest, died in Magdalena, Sonora, in 1711 and was buried, but the exact location of his grave was forgotten. In 1965 and 1966, Mexican archaeologist Jorge Olvera directed a successful search for the grave, with help from W.W. Wasley. Here, ASM forensic anthropologist Walter H. Birkby, who confirmed the identification of the skeleton, does final cleaning and stabilization of Kino's skeleton before the glass sarcophagus around the grave was closed. (W.W. Wasley, ASM 2013-508-58.)

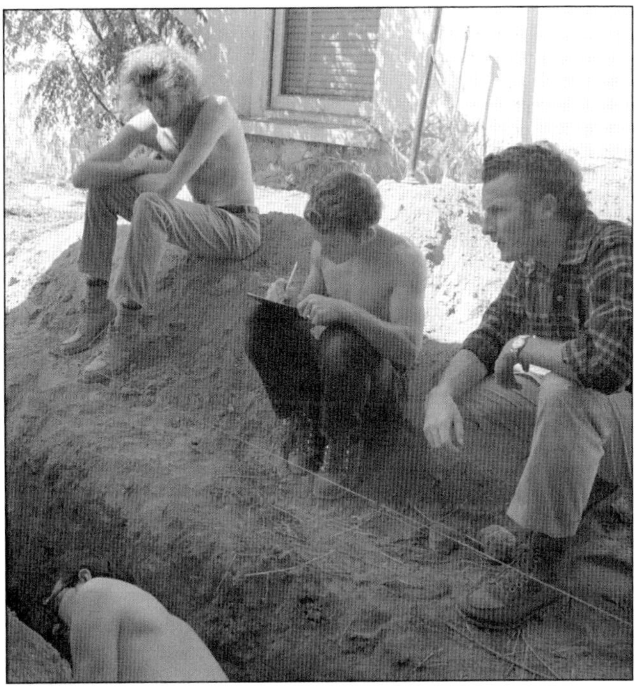

Funded by the Department of Housing and Urban Development, the City of Tucson demolished some of its oldest neighborhoods to build, among other things, a community center. From 1967 to 1972, ASM archaeologist James E. Ayres directed the Tucson Urban Renewal (TUR) Project to recover historical and archaeological information from the area. Starting a new trench in 1971 are, clockwise from right, Ayres and volunteer UA anthropology students Mark R. Barnes, Robert Powers, and James I. Mead. (Peter Urban, ASM 20587.)

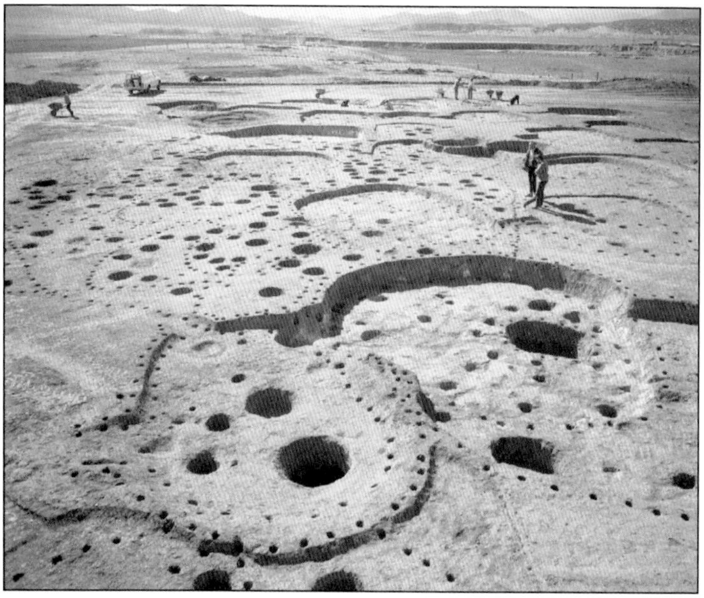

Highway construction near Dewey necessitated testing the Henderson Site in the winter of 1969–1970. About one-third of this Hohokam village, dating to around AD 700–900, was exposed, revealing a maze of superimposed pit houses and storage pits. The project was funded by ADOT, through ASM, and directed by Albert E. Ward of Prescott College, seen here discussing the site with Sharon F. Urban of ASM (right center). (H. Teiwes, ASM 26060.)

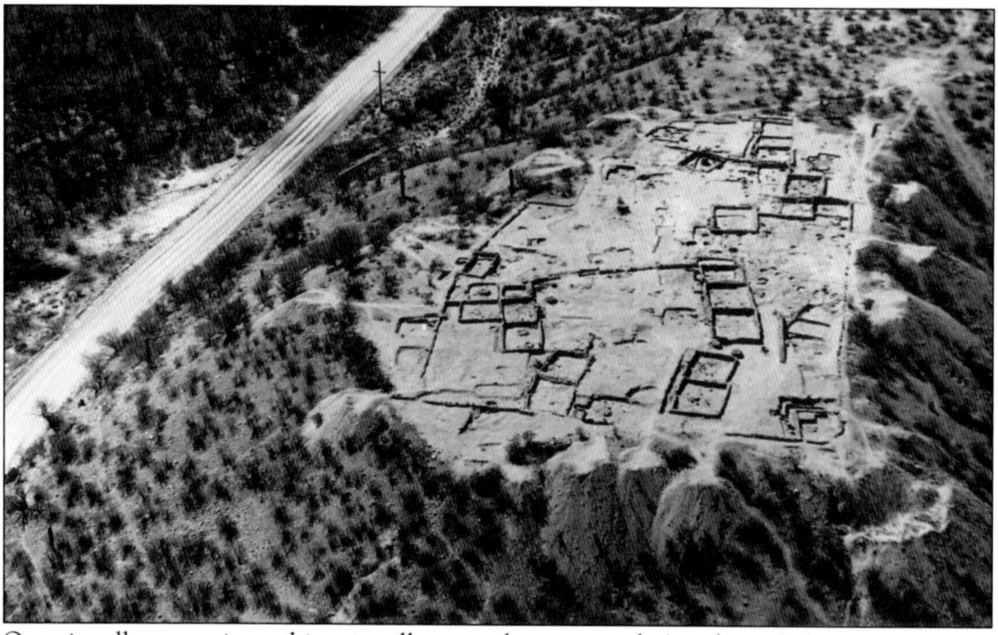

Occasionally, an entire prehistoric village can be excavated. Another ADOT project in the winter of 1969–1970 exposed all of the Second Canyon Site in the San Pedro River Valley, north of Redington. Directed by Laurens C. Hammack and Hayward H. Franklin, the digging revealed Hohokam pit houses (AD 700–1000) under a Salado settlement of adobe surface rooms (AD 1300–1400), which covers the ridge top in this aerial view. A few fire pits represent the final use of the site in early historic times by either Apaches or Sobaipuris. (ASM Accession 2484.)

In 1973, the Continental Oil Company sponsored work at the Escalante Ruin, near Florence. Directed by David E. Doyel, this was the first project in Arizona to completely excavate a late prehistoric (AD 1340–1425) community of adobe surface rooms and a platform mound enclosed by a compound wall. The view in this aerial photograph is looking south, with the platform mound (bisected by a rancher's exploratory trench) in the northwest (lower right) corner of the rectangular compound. For scale, note the roads and, at the top, the modern house. (D.E. Doyel, ASM 36589.)

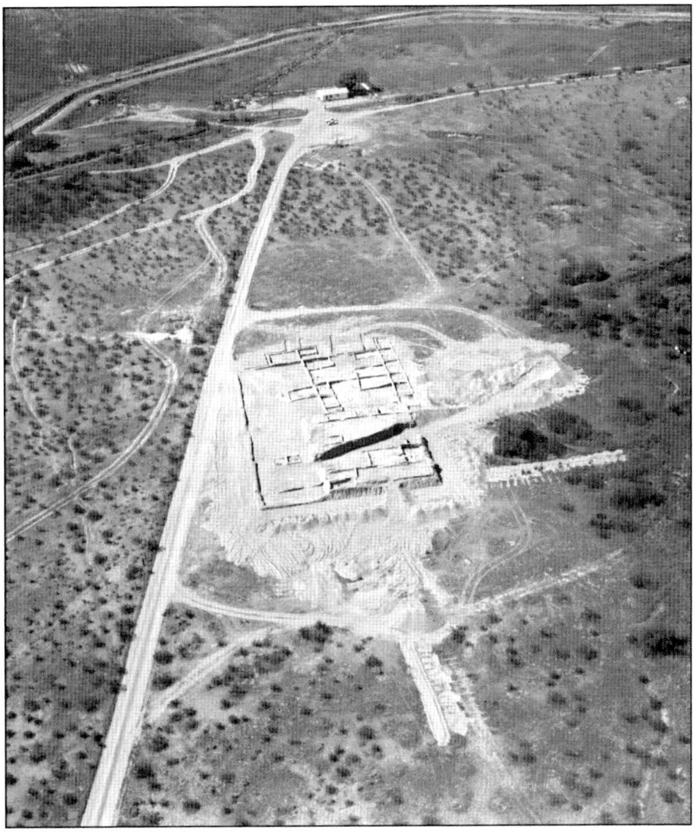

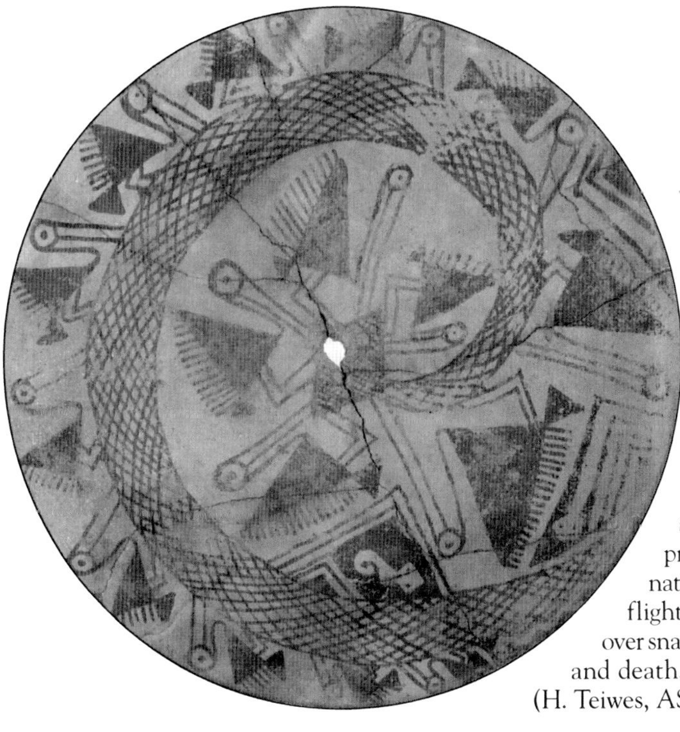

This prehistoric Hohokam pottery plate, dating to around AD 850, displays an elaborate design in red paint of many long-necked birds attacking a snake. It was excavated during the 1965–1966 Punta de Agua Project, sponsored by ADOT, on the San Xavier District of the Tohono O'odham Reservation, south of Tucson. The scene is probably more mythological than naturalistic, with birds, representing flight and the spirit world, ascendant over snakes, representing the underworld and death. The diameter is 13.5 inches. (H. Teiwes, ASM 36229.)

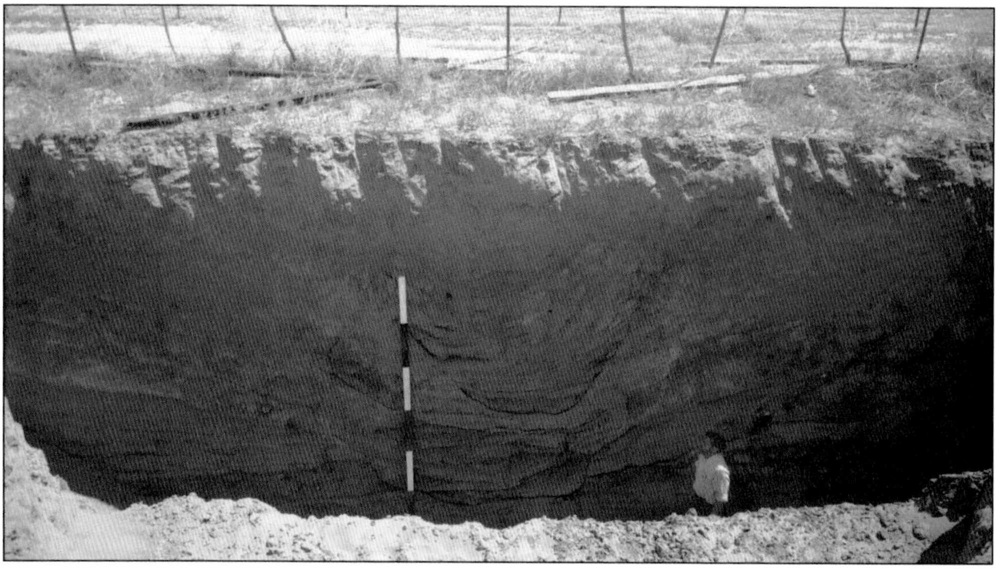

The Hohokam culture is famous for its canal systems, excavated with digging sticks. Head gates on the Salt and Gila Rivers drew water into hundreds of miles of canals leading to communities and fields throughout the Phoenix Basin. In 1975 and 1976, ADOT funded the Hohokam Expressway Project to excavate cross-sections through several large canals southwest of the Pueblo Grande Ruins. The three-meter-tall scale (and field director W. Bruce Masse) shows these superimposed Hohokam canals were about eight feet deep. (H. Teiwes, ASM 43483.)

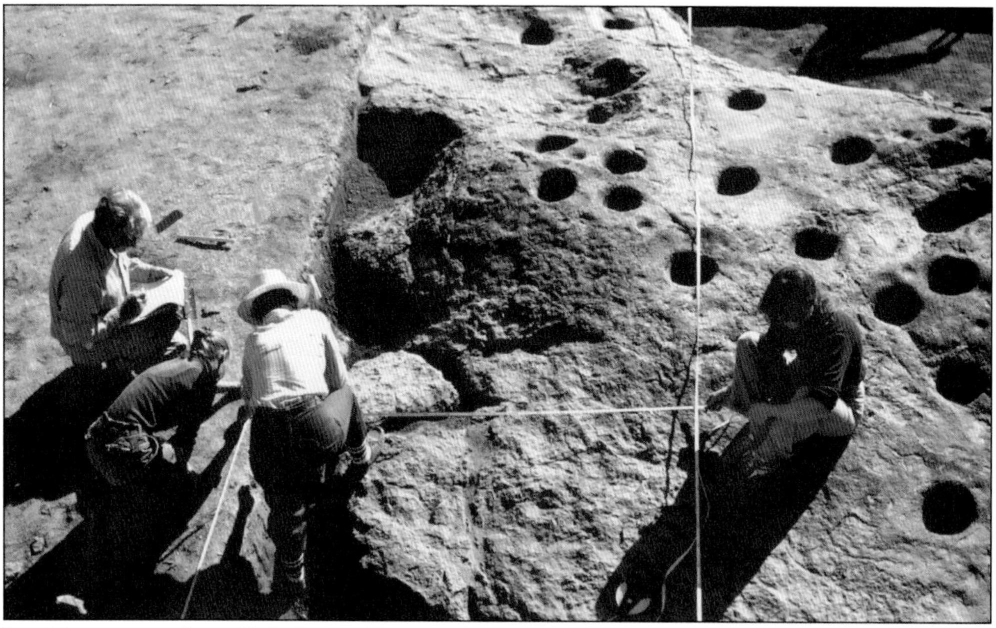

Los Morteros is a large Hohokam village in northwestern Tucson that was partially destroyed by old farming and new urban growth. From 1979 to 1983, excavations were variously carried out at the site by an ASM project, a UA archaeological field school, and a continuing education class. Here, in 1982, volunteers map the bedrock mortars that gave the site its name. Hohokam women used stone or wood pestles to pound up mesquite seed pods in the mortars, discarded the seeds, and ground the pods to flour. (Photograph by and courtesy of Richard C. Lange.)

The Sierra Ancha Project was directed by Richard C. Lange from 1981 to 2004. It extensively resurveyed the cliff dwellings in the rugged canyons on the east side of the Sierra Ancha ("Wide Mountain" in Spanish) Mountains in central Arizona. Some sites had originally been explored by Emil Haury in 1930, while he was working for the Gila Pueblo Archaeological Foundation. This photograph, taken in 1969, looks out across the upper reaches of Pueblo Canyon from a ruin that was occupied around AD 1300. (H. Teiwes, ASM C-3764.)

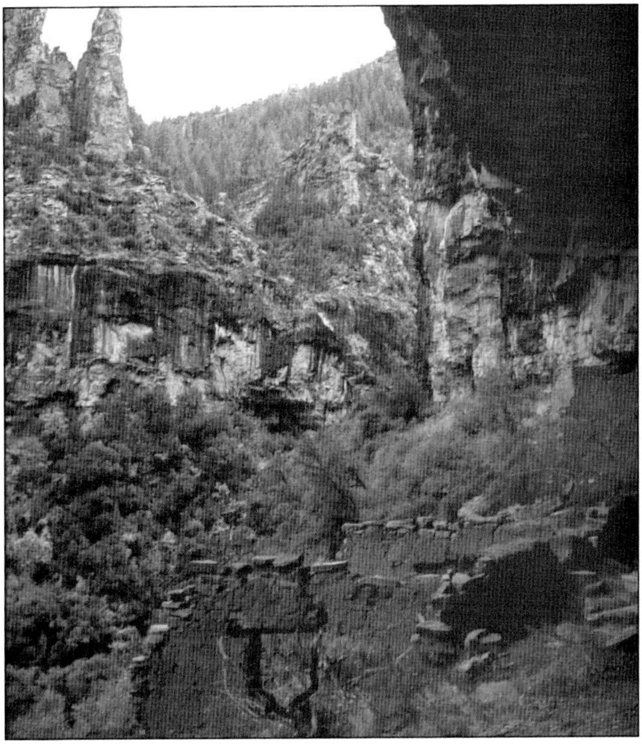

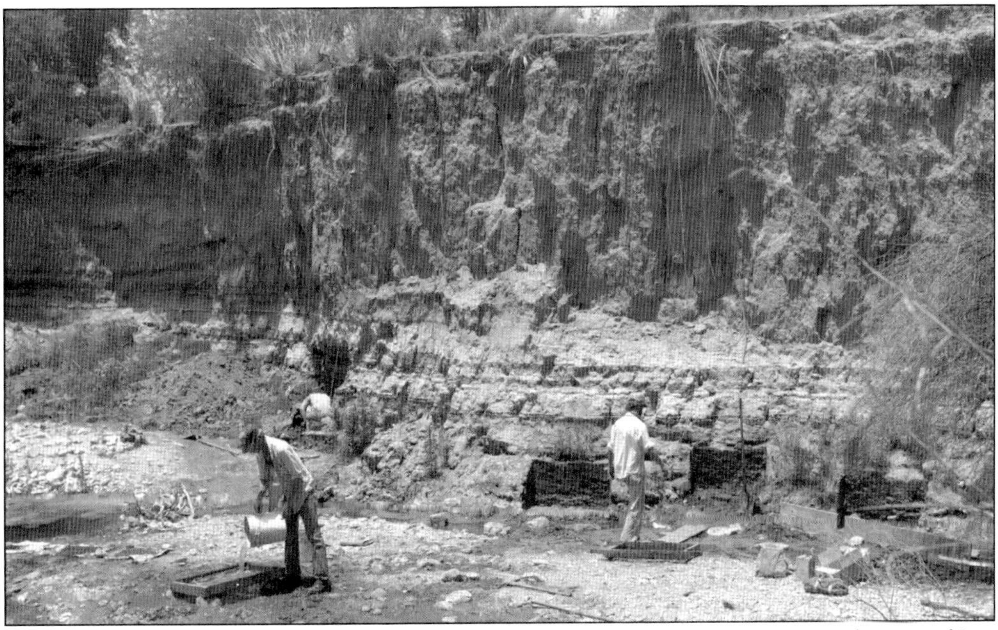

In 1983, ASM archaeologist Bruce B. Huckell directed limited excavations at the site of Los Ojitos ("Little Springs" in Spanish) in Matty Canyon, southeast of Tucson. In the approximately 2,000 years since it was occupied, it had been buried under nearly 15 feet of sediments. Martyn D. Tagg (right) walks toward the small test pits dug at the foot of the bank to recover burials threatened by flooding. Kenneth J. Rozen (left) water-screens the dirt for artifacts. (B.B. Huckell, ASM Accession 2001-178.)

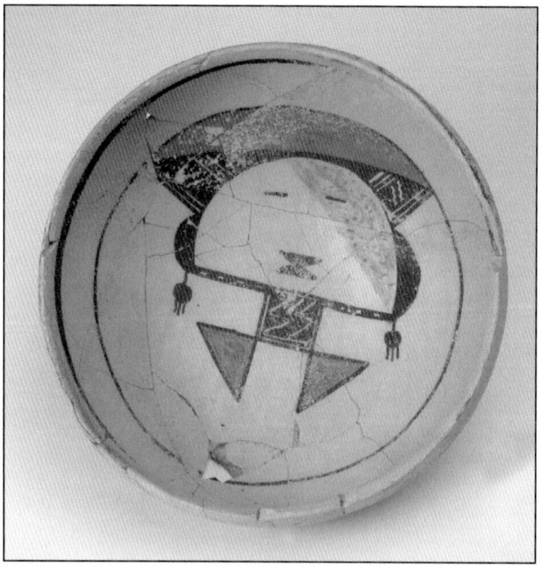

This prehistoric bowl was excavated during the Homol'ovi Research Program, directed by E. Charles Adams and Richard C. Lange from 1984 to 2010. The project investigated six ancestral Hopi pueblos in the vicinity of modern-day Winslow. Decorated with what may be a representation of a Snow Maiden katsina, this bowl demonstrates not only prehistoric trade between the Hopi mesas and Homol'ovi area, but participation by Homol'ovi area villagers in the katsina religion. The diameter is about eight inches. (J. Weakly, ASM.)

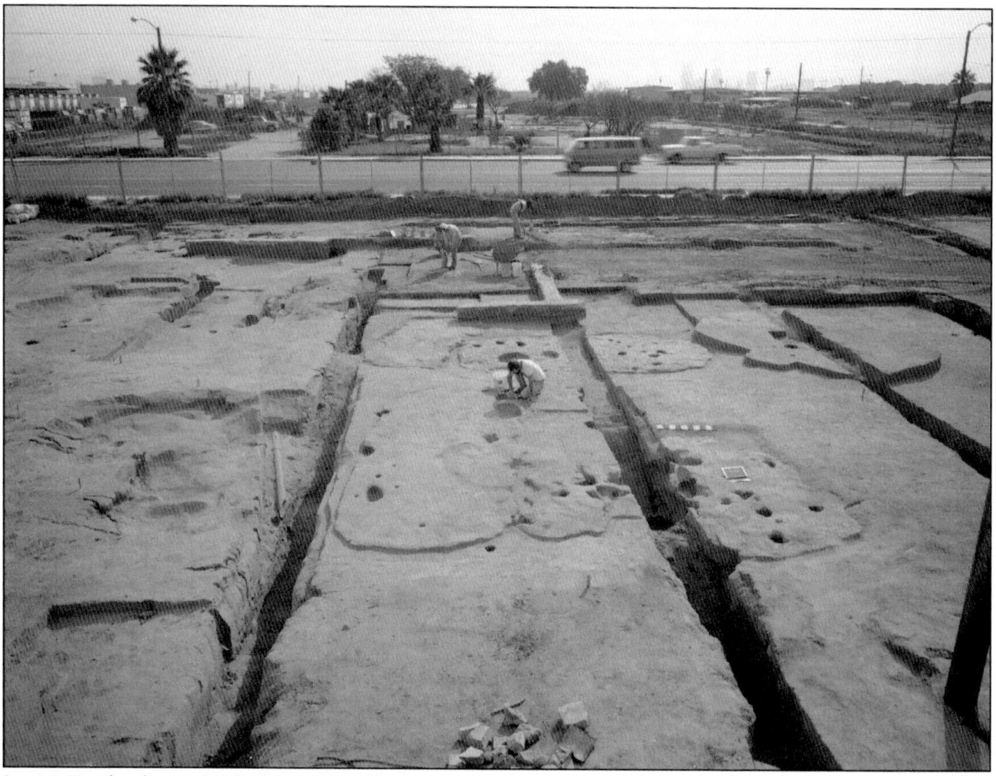

In 1968, the large Hohokam site of Las Colinas ("The Hills" in Spanish) lay in the path of Interstate 10 through Phoenix, and ADOT sponsored testing directed by ASM State Highway archaeologist Laurens C. Hammack. In 1982–1984, with construction finally imminent, David A. Gregory conducted more extensive data recovery. The view in this photograph is looking due east down the construction corridor, with excavated pit houses in the foreground, across Twenty-seventh Avenue, and skyscrapers in downtown Phoenix visible at the upper right. (H. Teiwes, ASM Accession 1985-23.)

Between 1939 and 1979, vocational archaeologist Norton Allen excavated, with permission, at numerous Hohokam sites in the Gila Bend area. Most were being destroyed by the expansion of cotton fields. Norton's lifelong goal had been to preserve these materials for the edification of both archaeologists and Tohono O'odham descendants of the Hohokam. He and his wife, Ethel, accomplished this with the donation to ASM of thousands of documented artifacts, including over 500 whole pots, between 1994 and 2013. (K. Matesich, ASM 87726.)

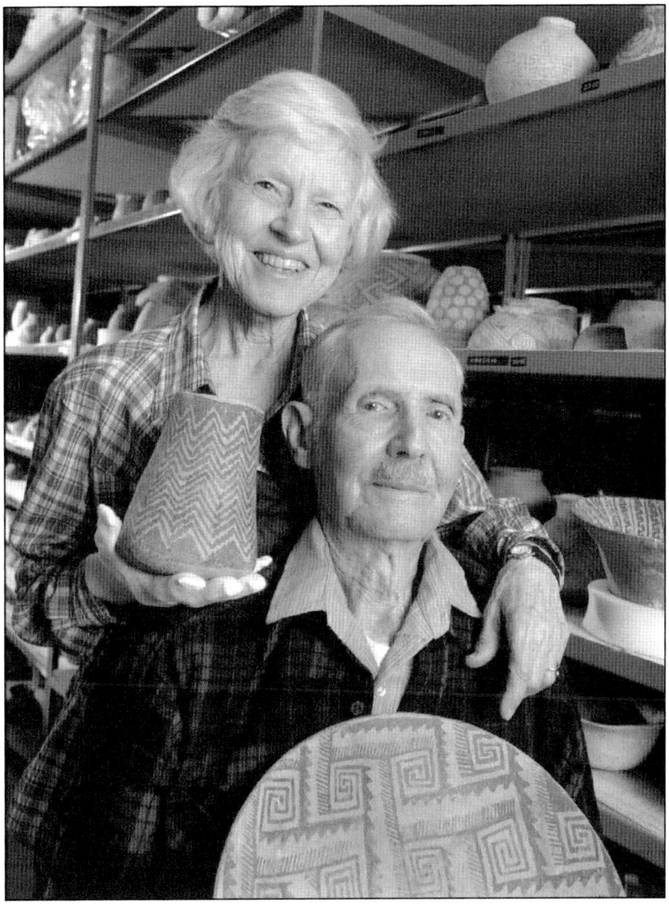

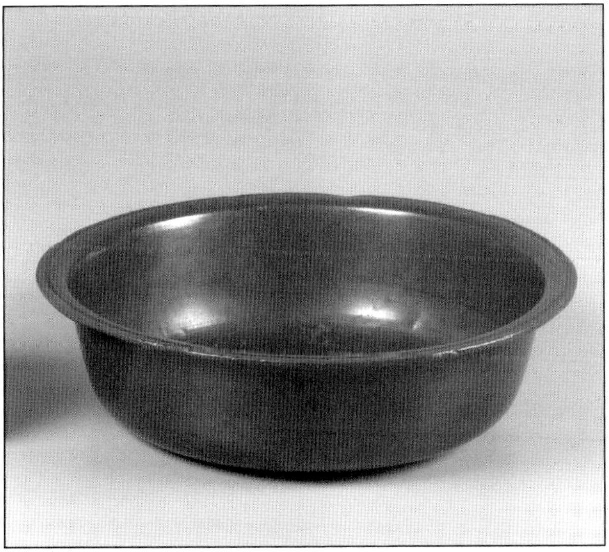

Through the years, numerous researchers have mapped finds of early historic artifacts, hoping to shed light on the locations of trails used by Spanish Colonial explorers. This spun-metal, leaded-bronze bowl, about two inches deep and seven inches in diameter, was found about 1928 by James Dees in the Peloncillo Mountains of southeastern Arizona. ASM state archaeologist John H. Madsen worked to document the discovery with Dees's son Thomas E. Dees, who donated the bowl to ASM in 1994. It dates to between 1700 and 1800. (J. Weakly, ASM.)

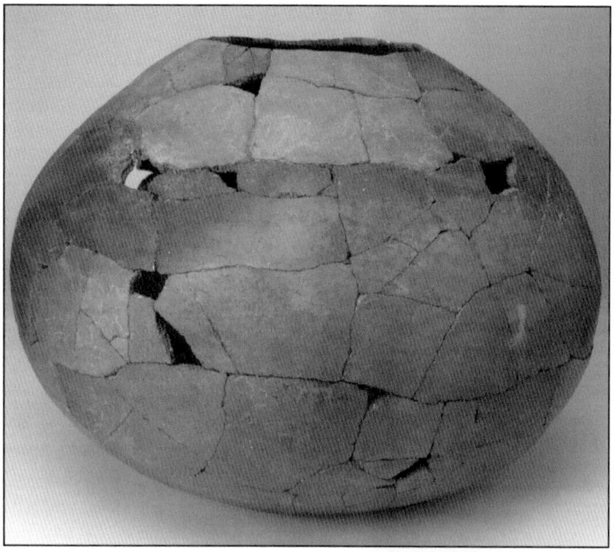

This plainware jar is the oldest whole pottery vessel known from southern Arizona. It was found on the floor of a pit house, which burned in about AD 450, at the Stone Pipe Site, in Tucson. From 1993 to 1995, ADOT contracted with Desert Archaeology, Inc., to excavate archaeological sites in the path of improvements to Interstate 10. There are older unfired and fired clay figurines and pinch-pots, but no earlier utilitarian ceramics. This jar was likely used for storage of food or water. It measures 11.75 inches high and 12.25 inches in diameter. (J. Weakly, ASM.)

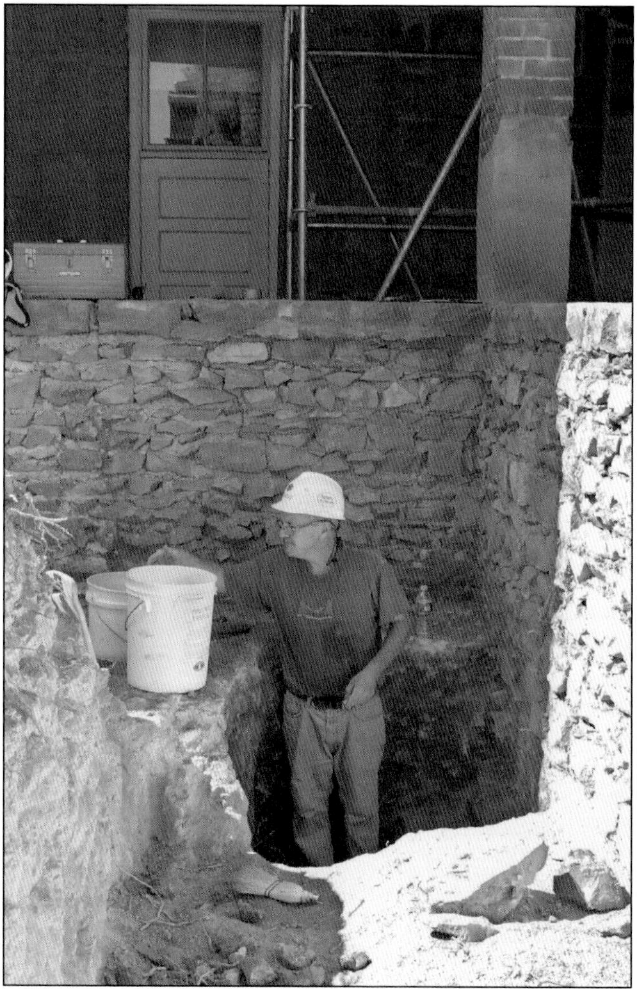

Old Main, the first building on the UA campus and ASM's first home (see page 16), underwent comprehensive renovation in 2013–2014, during which numerous abandoned features of the structure were rediscovered. John H. Madsen, retired state archaeologist from ASM, is standing in and excavating a leaching well found outside the retaining wall, which was used for waste disposal between 1891 and 1909 by the mineralogy chemistry laboratory, located in the northeast room of the first floor. The most common artifacts recovered were fragments of small crucibles used in teaching assay techniques. (Photograph by the author, courtesy of John H. Madsen.)

Five

University of Arizona Archaeological Field Schools

First at the University of Utah and then at the University of Arizona, Byron Cummings took students out nearly every summer between 1907 and 1930 to explore, survey, and excavate archaeological sites in southern Utah and northern Arizona. At UA, students in Cummings's classes often participated in local digs staged on weekends or holidays during the semesters, as opposed to formal field schools. Calling a particular excavation a seminar activity, a field school, an expedition, or a project, was, and still is, somewhat arbitrary. One could argue that a project is a field school if (a) it calls itself one, and (b) it gives academic credit for participation.

There was no field school in the summer of 1938, when Cummings retired and Emil Haury became ASM director. The Forestdale Field School, on the Fort Apache Indian Reservation, ran from 1939 to 1941, was halted by World War II, and was then concluded with cleanup work by staff in 1944. Haury spent the summer of 1945 scouting the high country of the San Carlos Indian Reservation, and he started the Point of Pines Field School in 1946. It continued for 15 summers, excavated in 33 sites of all available time periods, and trained some 300 students, including many who would become leaders in the field of archaeology over the courses of their careers. Raymond Thompson took over as field school director in 1957, and Point of Pines closed down in 1960. There was no field school in 1961. In 1962, the field school moved to a location in southern Arizona, to the western slopes of the Chiricahua Mountains, and operated out of the El Coronado Ranch. The El Coronado Field School lasted one season, and is better known by the name of the one site excavated, the Ringo Site, named after outlaw Johnny Ringo, said to be buried nearby. A field trip in the fall of 1962 to Grasshopper Pueblo, on the Fort Apache Indian Reservation, convinced Haury and Thompson that this was the ideal locale for a new, long-term field school. The Grasshopper Field School was directed by Thompson from 1963 to 1965, by William A. Longacre from 1966 to 1978, and by J. Jefferson Reid from 1979 to 1992—a total of 30 field seasons. Subsequent field schools have been of shorter duration, have increasingly partnered with other groups, and often morph from field school to project and back again.

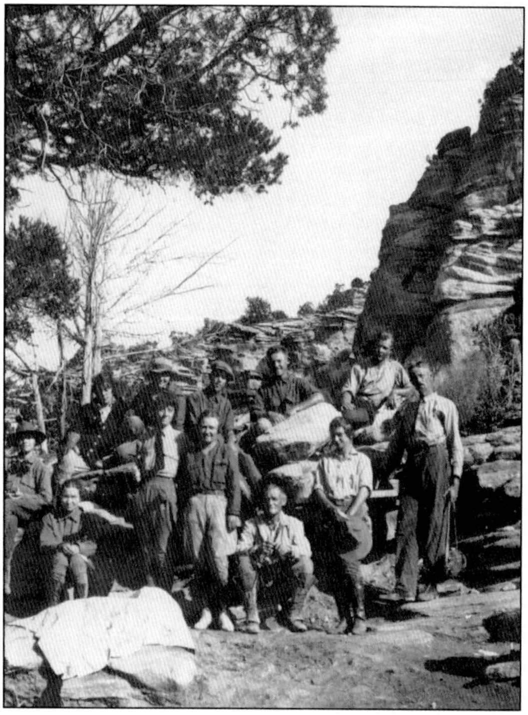

Summer classes for credit were first offered by the University of Arizona in 1918. The first formal UA archaeological field school consisted of Byron Cummings taking 14 men and women to far-northern Arizona for six weeks in July and August 1919 to excavate in Ancestral Pueblo sites, with optional field trips at the end, including visiting ceremonial dances at the Hopi village of Walpi. The students' names were recorded, but they cannot be matched with this group photograph, taken on the south slope of Navajo Mountain. (Byron Cummings, AHS 73179.)

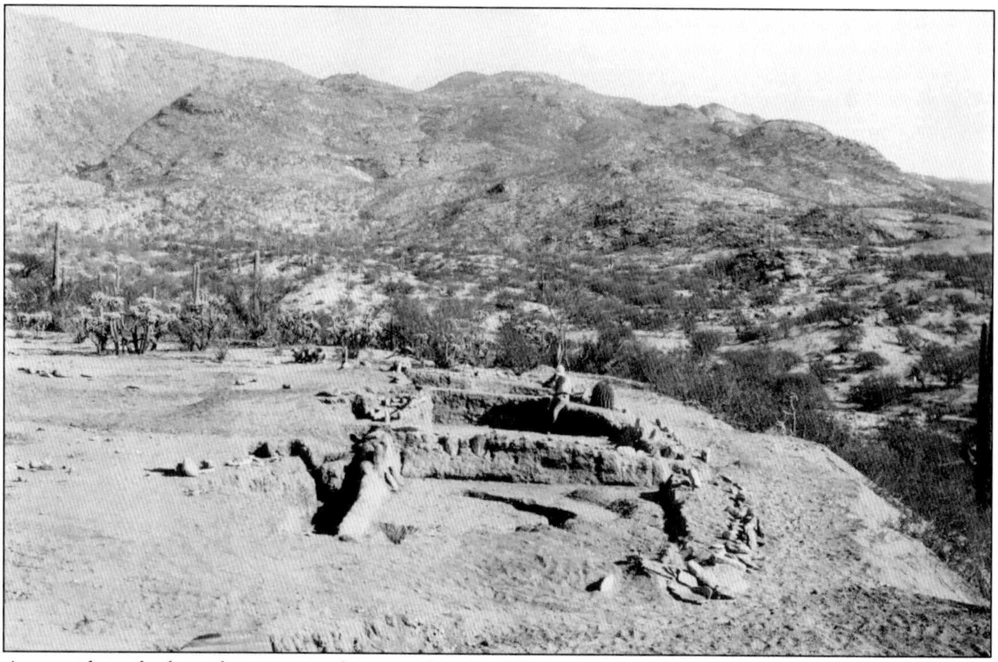

An unidentified student is standing in the middle of three excavated, contiguous, stone-and-adobe-walled rooms at the Tanque Verde Ruin in the eastern Tucson Basin. This Hohokam culture village was excavated sporadically from 1925 to 1927 by UA students taking archaeology courses from Byron Cummings, including some who would become famous in their own right: Clara Lee Fraps (later Tanner), Lyndon Hargrave, Emil Haury, Florence Hawley (later Ellis), John McGregor, and Edward Spicer. (Frank Jenny, ASM 409.)

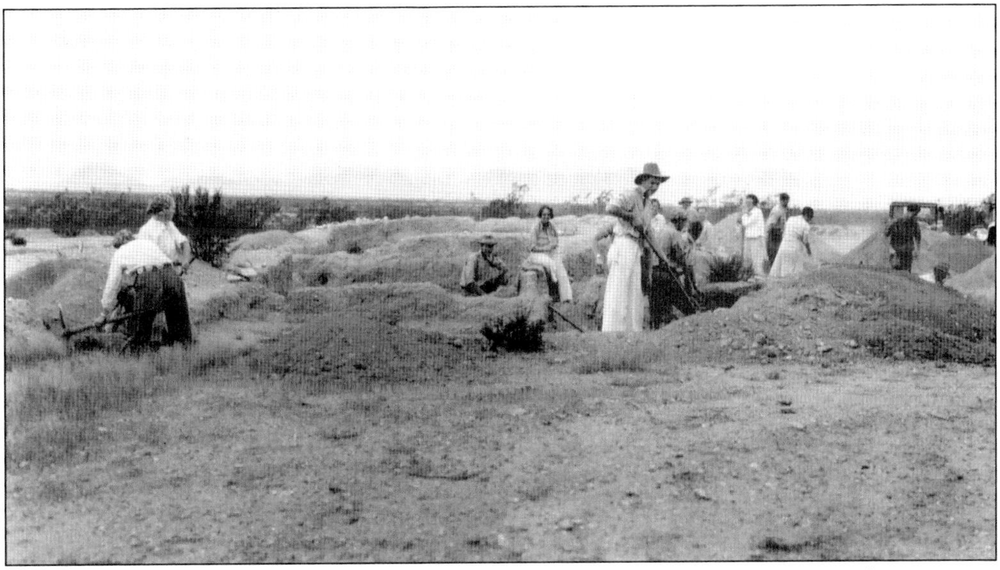

UA students excavate in aboveground adobe-walled rooms at the University Indian Ruin in this October 1932 photograph, looking west toward the Tucson Mountains. This late Hohokam culture site was donated to UA by Dorothy A. Knipe in 1930 to serve as an easily accessible field laboratory. Cummings dug there with anthropology seminar students repeatedly from 1931 to 1937. Additional work was done again in 1940 and 1941 (see page 104), and yet again from 2010 to 2014 by professors Paul and Suzanne Fish and their students. (AHS PC29/Box 6B/F.21A/AJ.)

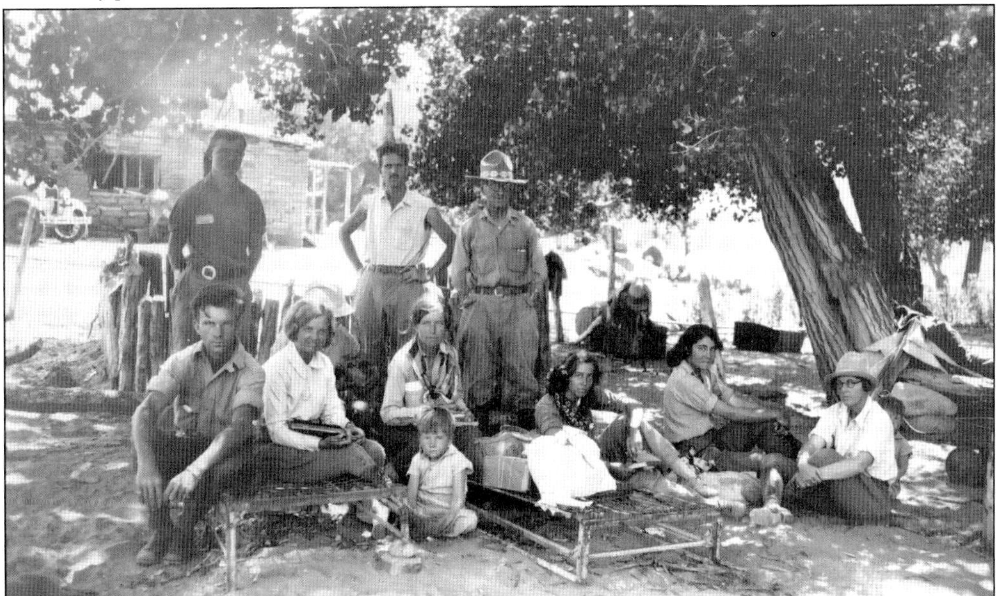

A field school in all but name, Cummings's summer trip with students to northern Arizona in 1930 included his standard regimen of archaeological work punctuated with visits to Hopi and Navajo communities. The group is posed in its base camp at Ben Wetherill's Navajo Mountain Trading Post, on the southeast flank of Navajo Mountain in Utah. Cummings is standing (in hat). Former student, and now fellow anthropology instructor, Clara Lee Fraps (seated behind boy) filed seven lively newspaper articles with the *Arizona Daily Star*. (ASM.)

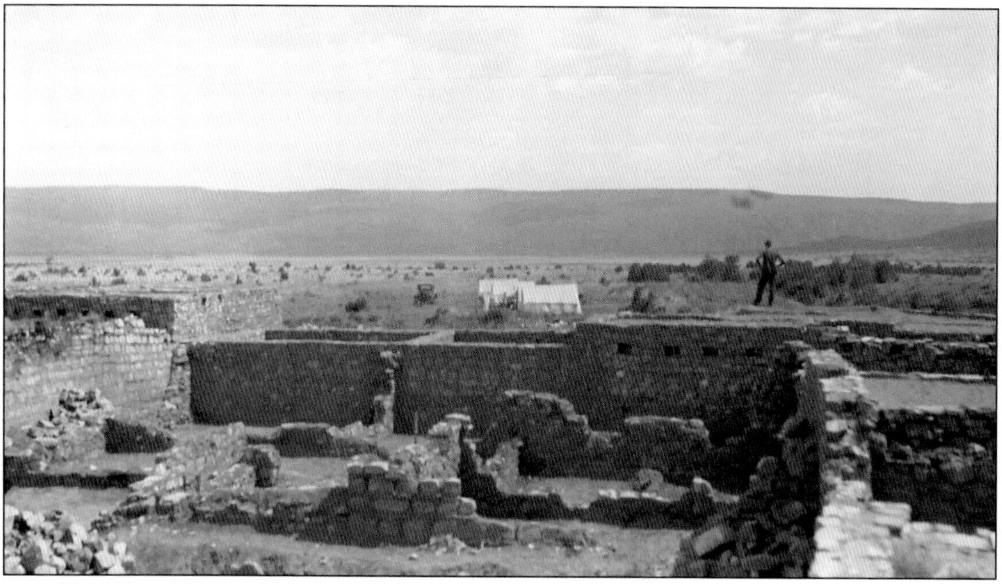

Kinishba ("Brown House" in Apache) is a late prehistoric stone pueblo of some 600 rooms, partly two-story, on the Fort Apache Indian Reservation. Byron Cummings worked there from 1931 to 1946, with the 1934–1937 summers being official field schools. Many rooms were reconstructed in the hope that it would become a national park for education of the public and an economic resource for the White Mountain Apache tribe. It can still be visited, but it has not become a major attraction. (Tad Nichols, ASM.)

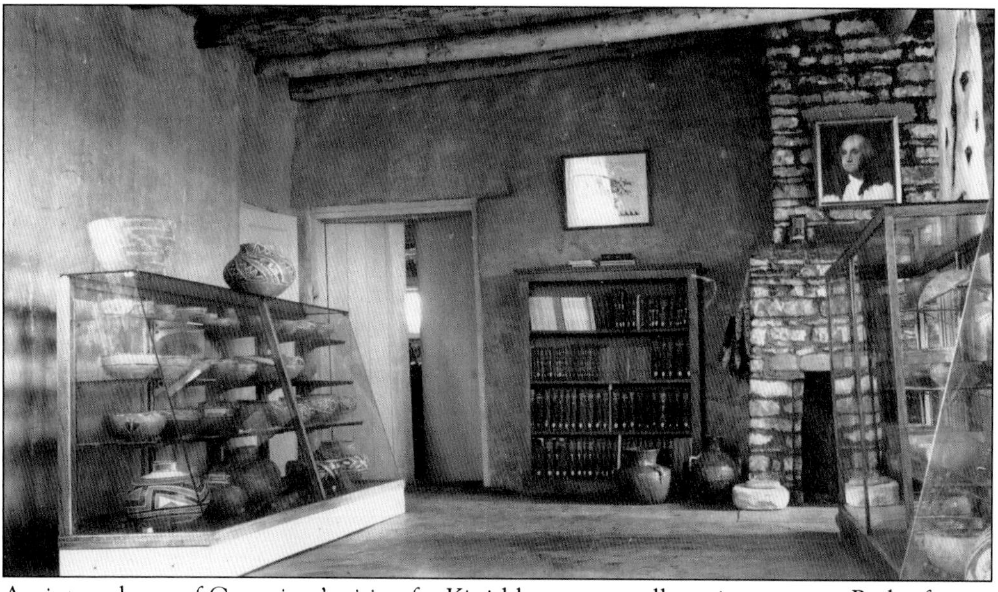

An integral part of Cummings's vision for Kinishba was a small on-site museum. Built of stone from the ruin, it was completed in 1939 and dedicated on April 26–27, 1941. Looking northwest, this view shows exhibit cases holding pottery and artifacts from the excavations. The caretaker's quarters (where Cummings lived until 1946) were beyond the backlit double doors. Sales of local Apache crafts were planned, and two Apache pine-pitch-coated baskets are on the floor, left of the fireplace. With no support, the museum closed in 1955, and the building eventually burned in 1994. (AHS PC29/Box 4/F.4/A.)

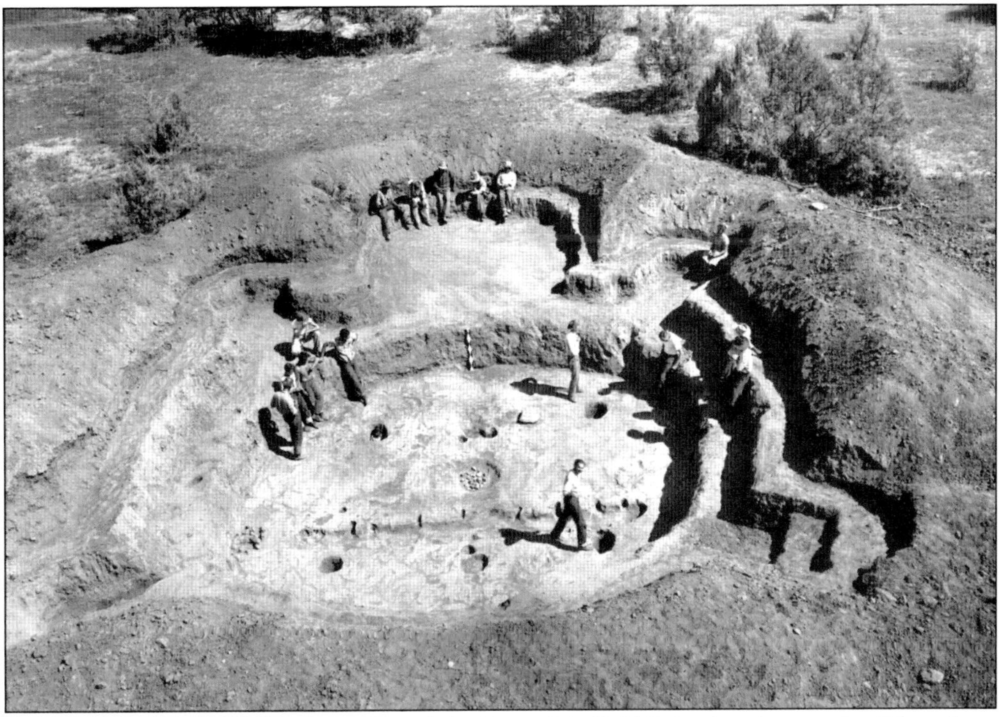

From 1939 to 1941, Emil Haury conducted the Forestdale Field School at sites south of Show Low, primarily the early Mogollon pit house villages at the Bear Ruin and the Bluff Site, and the early stone pueblo of Tla Kii ("Many Rooms" in Apache). Here, students and Apache laborers stand in the large ceremonial kiva at Bear Ruin, dating around AD 600–700. The floor measured nearly 30 feet in diameter. A fire pit is visible in the center, and four large postholes show the former locations of massive wooden roof supports. (E.W. Haury, ASM 481.)

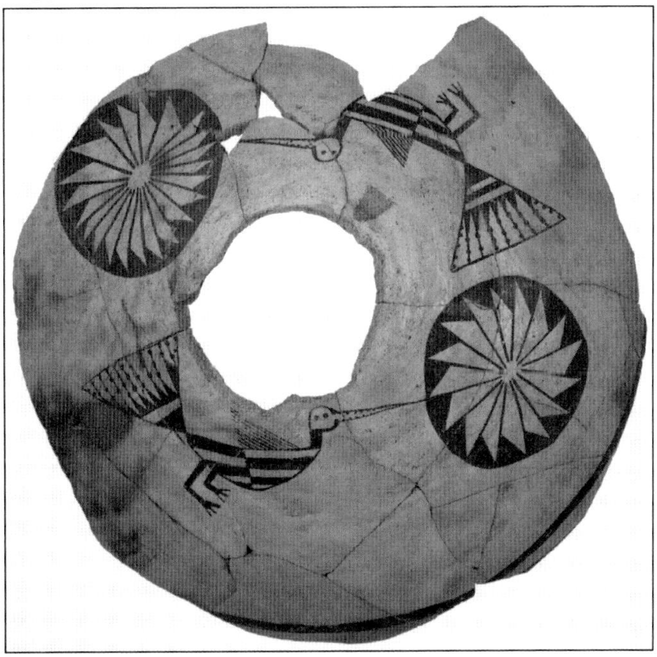

This view is looking down on the upper portion of a broken pottery jar that was thrown as trash into an abandoned storage pit at Tla Kii, sometime around AD 900–1000. The neck and mouth and lower body are gone, but the shoulder is decorated in black paint with an unusual design that strongly suggests hummingbirds feeding at flowers. All of the other pottery at the site is decorated with only geometric designs, and this jar may have been made elsewhere and traded in to Tla Kii. The diameter is 13.5 inches. (H. Teiwes, ASM 53943.)

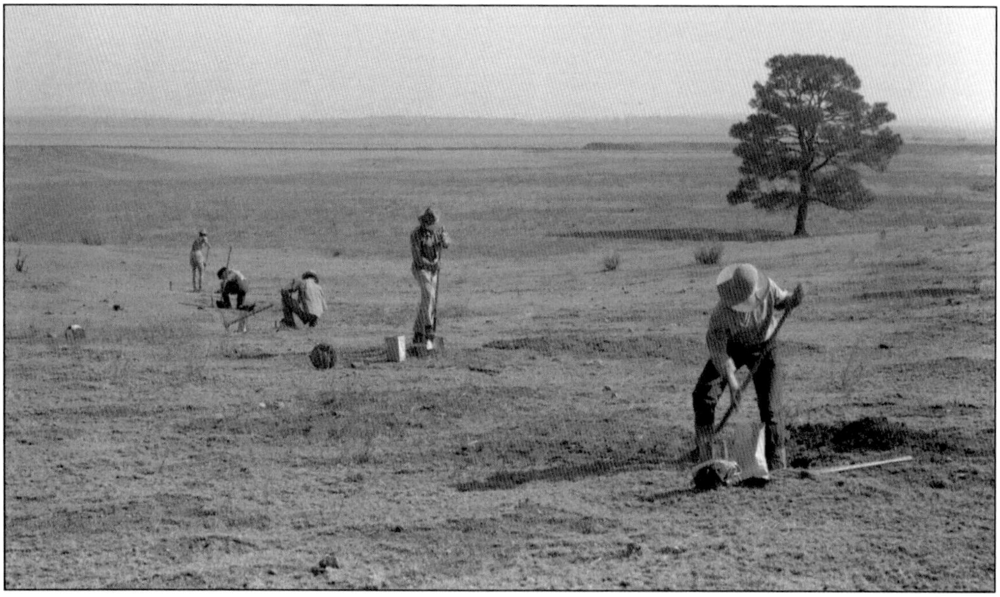

Aside from an abundance of potsherds, the modern surface of Circle Prairie, on the San Carlos (Apache) Indian Reservation, exhibited few clues to the wealth of prehistoric architecture and artifacts that lay buried. Much is said about the "romance of archaeology," with abundant references to the use of trowels and paintbrushes, but, before that, there generally comes a good deal of pick-and-shovel work. Above, on June 12, 1946, students at the Point of Pines Field School start digging. What was revealed usually looked something like the scene below: contiguous rectangular masonry rooms making up an "apartment complex" with dozens, or even hundreds, of rooms. This living room has a central, rectangular, slab-lined cooking hearth and stone tools scattered across the floor. Storage rooms had no hearths but often contained several, or many, storage pots, sitting where they had been left 500 years ago. (Above, ASM 1578; below, ASM 2644.)

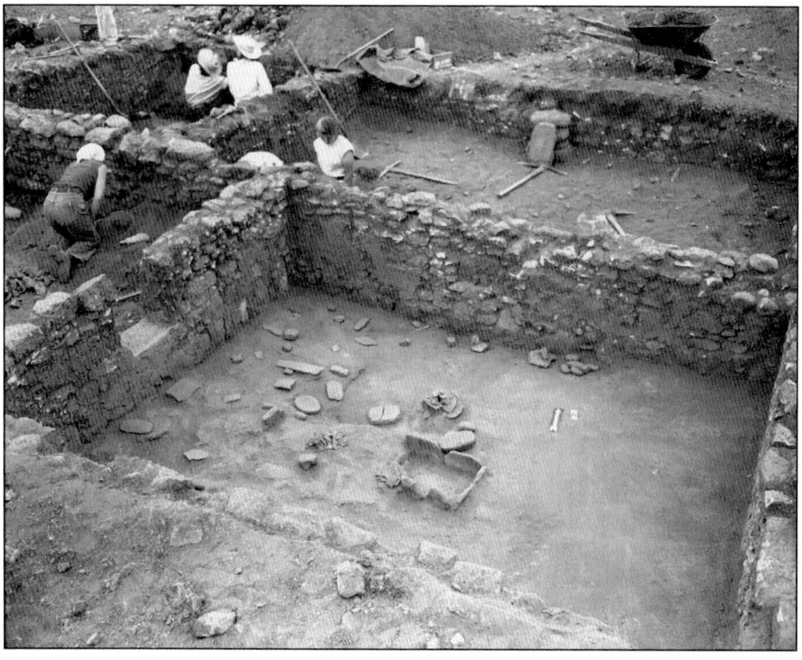

Student Carol Gifford stands in the mouth of Red Bow Cliff Dwelling, a small set of masonry rooms roughly contemporaneous with the Circle Prairie pueblos but about six miles to the southwest, set in a nearly inaccessible rock shelter in the south-facing cliff of the Nantack Ridge. Excavations here in 1955 yielded abundant perishable materials not generally preserved in open sites, including fragments of basketry, sandals, textiles, bows, arrows, cane cigarettes, and wood, gourd, and horn tools of various types. (James C. Gifford, ASM.)

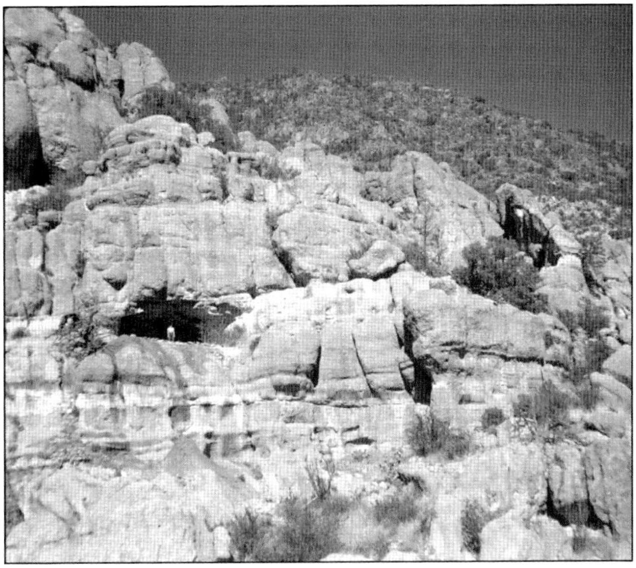

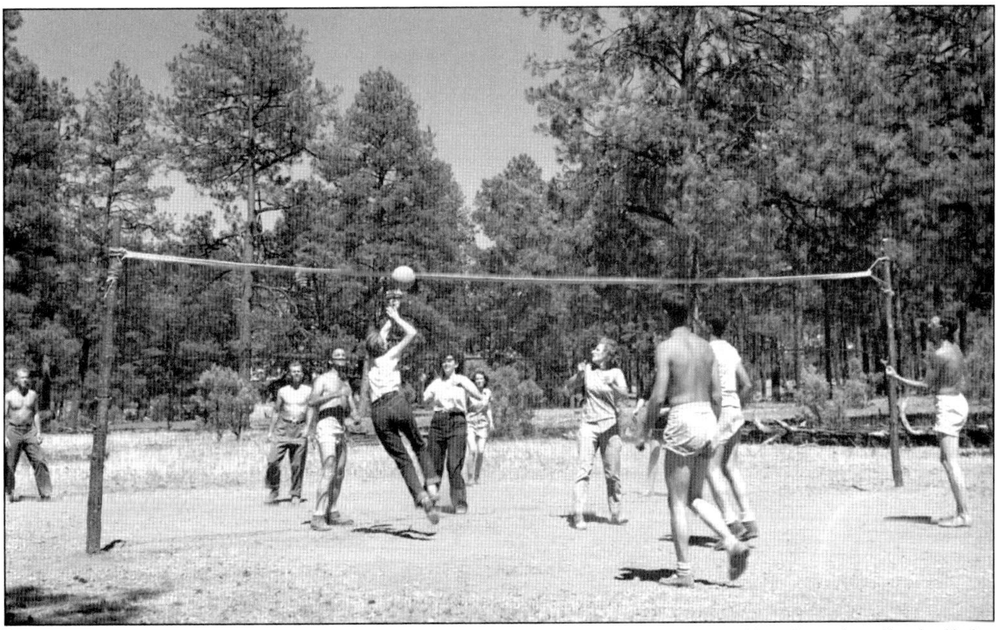

Students at any self-respecting field school in the Southwest generally played volleyball for diversion, such as this game at Point of Pines in the summer of 1947. Games between different field schools were not unknown, with a few ongoing rivalries recorded. Final statistics for the annual struggles between the UA Grasshopper Field School and the Vernon Field School out of the Field Museum of Natural History in Chicago are unknown, as is the whereabouts of the coveted trophy (a prehistoric mano). (E.B. Sayles, ASM 2152.)

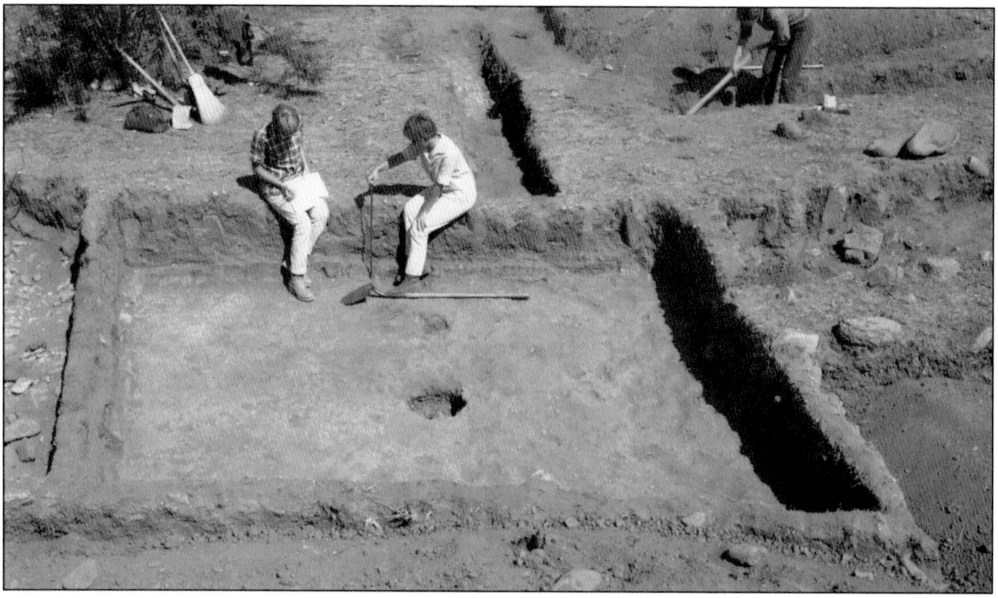

Work at the Ringo Site included excavation in two compounds with contiguous adobe rooms and enclosed plazas, dated to about AD 1250–1325. Here, in July 1962, Roxanne L. Peterson (left) and Mary Susan Green map an excavated room, while, beyond them, Janet A. Gibson digs a trench in the plaza. Deposits were shallow, and most of the potsherds had been reduced to a very small size as a result of the area having been a horse pasture. (A.E. Johnson, ASM 7959.)

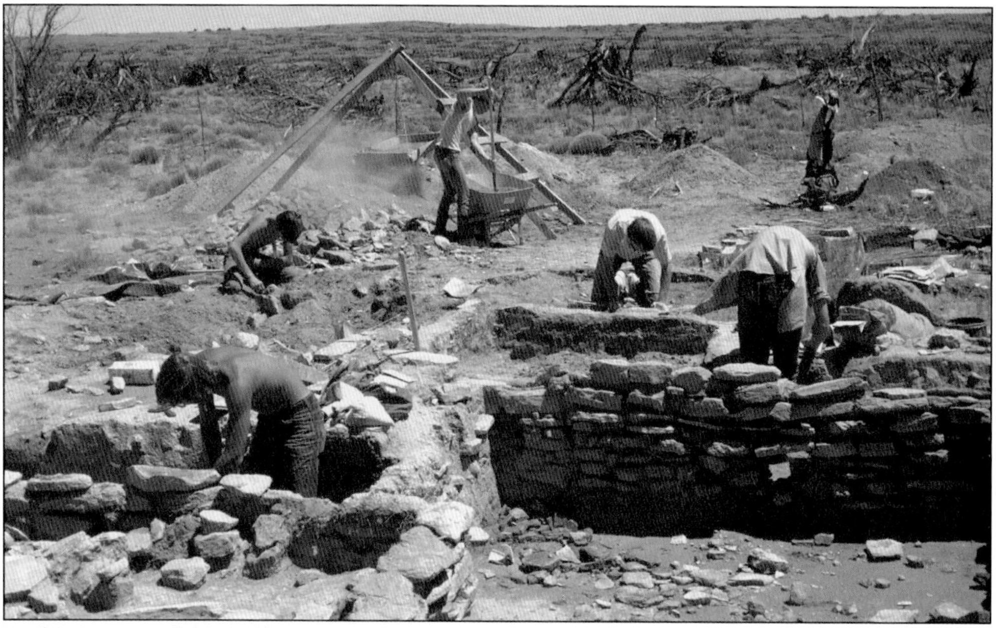

Paul S. Martin of the Field Museum in Chicago directed a field school based in Vernon, Arizona, from 1956 to 1973. He retired to Tucson only to pass away halfway through a two-year project. In the summer of 1974, undergraduate UA students completed the project, with doctoral student David R. Wilcox supervising work at the Swannie Site pueblo (shown here), and Allen E. "Gene" Rogge at the Connie Site pit house village. This wrap-up season was known informally as the Snowflake Undergraduate Field School. (D.R. Wilcox, ASM Accession 1974-14.)

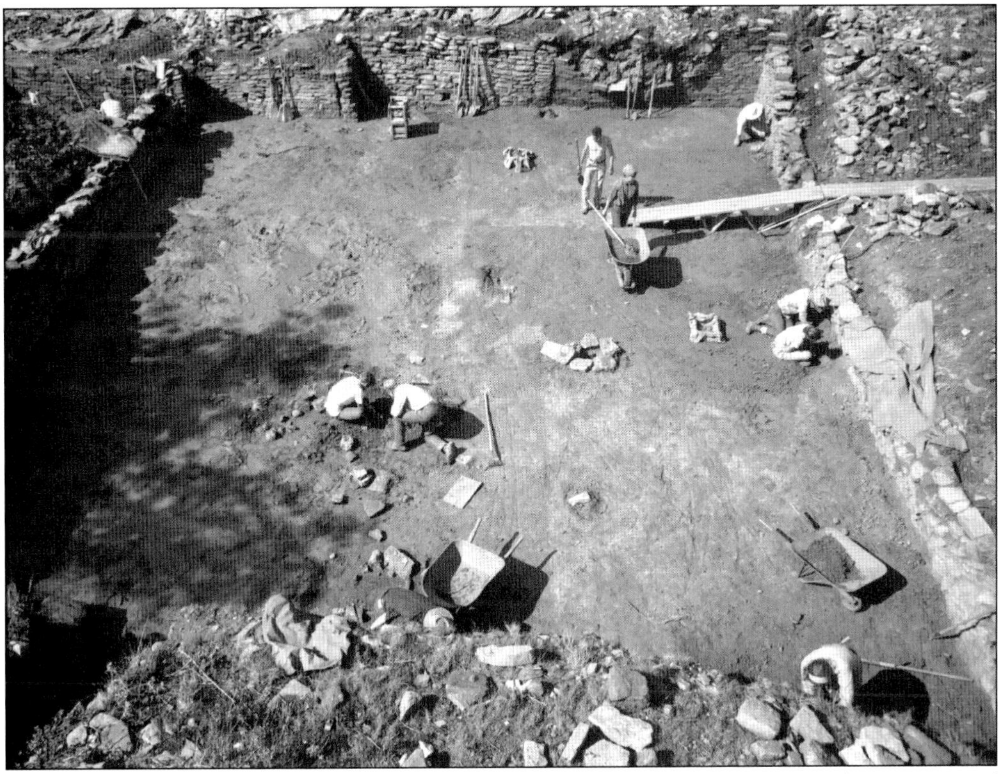

Grasshopper Pueblo had around 500 rooms, some of which were two-story, and was occupied during the late 1200s to the late 1300s. In the summer of 1964, a large rectangular plaza enclosed by the pueblo was explored by trenching around the interiors of the walls, down to the floor. A backhoe then removed the fill from the center of the room to just above the floor. Shown above, students then carefully excavated the floor with shovels, trowels, and whisk brooms. Dirt was wheelbarrowed up and out on the ramp at right. With the floor cleaned, it became clear (below) that, in the 1330s, 10 massive posts were set into the ground (in the holes next to each student) and the entire area, measuring nearly 40 by 50 feet, was roofed over to serve as a great kiva. This large ceremonial room would have hosted religious rituals for the residents of Grasshopper Pueblo and probably surrounding communities as well. (Both, Marion Parker; above, ASM 10518; below, 10523.)

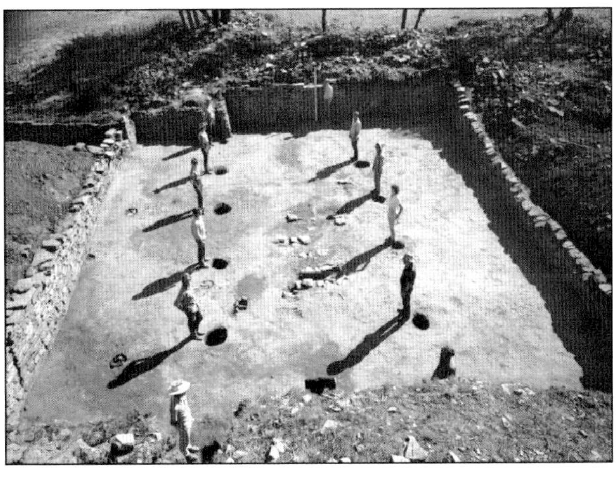

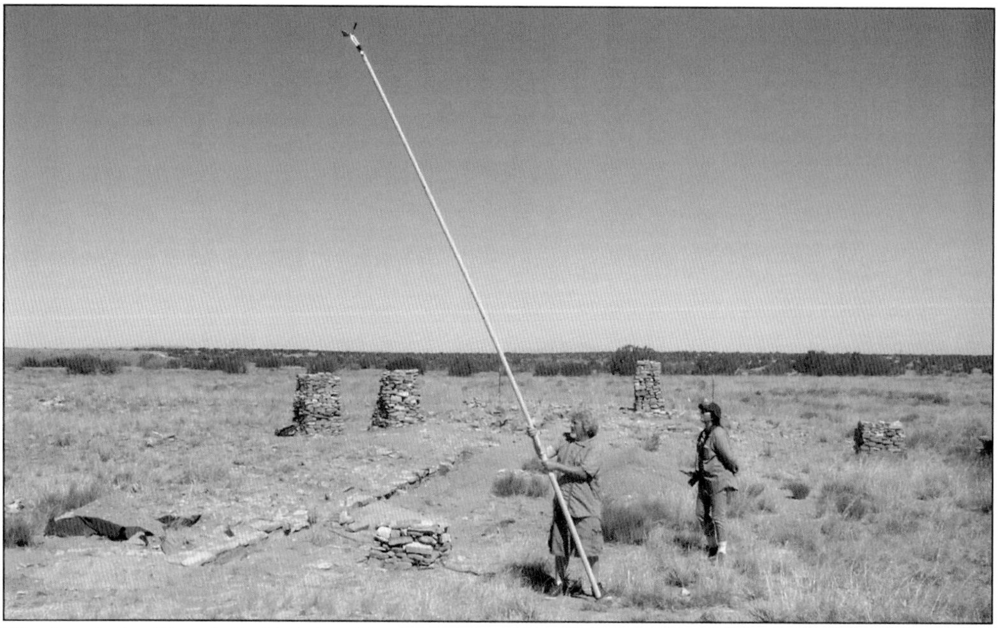

The Rock Art Ranch Field School began in 2011, exploring Ancestral Pueblo sites southwest of Joseph City, under the direction of E. Charles Adams and Richard C. Lange. Here, Douglas W. Gann takes overhead photographs of excavated stone walls using a digital camera atop a pole, and Alicia Vega takes additional oblique views of the same walls. Later combinations of images and measurements allowed Gann to create a virtual digital "pueblo" that can be viewed and explored on the ASM website. (Richard C. Lange, ASM.)

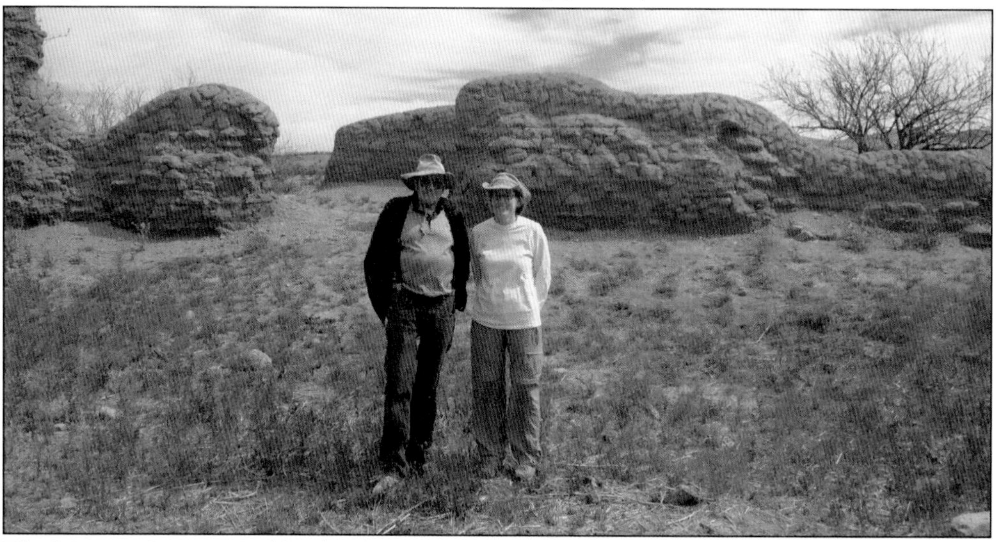

The Mission Guevavi Field School began in 2013 to obtain additional information about the 18th-century Jesuit mission, located north of Nogales. On March 22, 2014, field school director Barnet Pavao-Zuckerman (right) stands in front of the adobe brick walls of the *convento* with Bernard L. "Bunny" Fontana, who, with William J. Robinson, J. Cameron Greenleaf, and James E. Ayres, directed excavations at the site 50 years earlier (1964–1966) with Arizona Archaeological and Historical Society volunteers and UA students. (Photograph by J. Homer Thiel, courtesy of Barnet Pavao-Zuckerman.)

Six

Exhibits and Public Programs

All museum exhibits are temporary, including those referred to as "permanent." Some exhibits and programs are created for a specific purpose, with a predetermined lifespan. Others stay until they become dated in content or appearance. Some exhibits in the ASM South Building lasted over 50 years, but the preference now is for more exhibits of shorter duration. This chapter looks at a sample of ASM's exhibits.

Early exhibits at ASM were fairly static: Artifacts were displayed with a minimal amount of information. With the acquisition of its own building in 1936, ASM's exhibits became more formal and more informative, and specific topics or cultures were examined. In 1952, ASM hired its first exhibits curator, Robert G. Baker, whose job it was to fabricate anything needed in the museum's own shop. In recent decades, public expectations are more sophisticated, preservation of the items displayed is given greater consideration, and the ASM staff has shrunk. As a result, construction of cases and preparation of graphics is increasingly outsourced, with museum staff retaining control of content and consulting with the groups whose stories are told.

Exhibits now are not simply masses of intriguing objects, although that is still what most visitors come to see: actual, original, real cultural treasures of the state of Arizona. It is ASM's privilege and duty to preserve these collections, but, equally as important, to share them with the public and to educate visitors about them. Naturally, making research and artifacts in the museum more accessible has evolved through the years. Public outreach has expanded from open house night and the occasional newspaper article or lecture to a substantial presence on the Internet, which debuted in 1996 with online resource materials and exhibits at www.statemuseum.arizona.edu. School groups still come to tour the museum, as they have since its inception, and programming specifically for children continues to be an integral part of the museum's educational mission. For adults, "Learning Expeditions" led by ASM curators were started in 1997, followed by "Archaeology & History Summer Camp" programs in 2000.

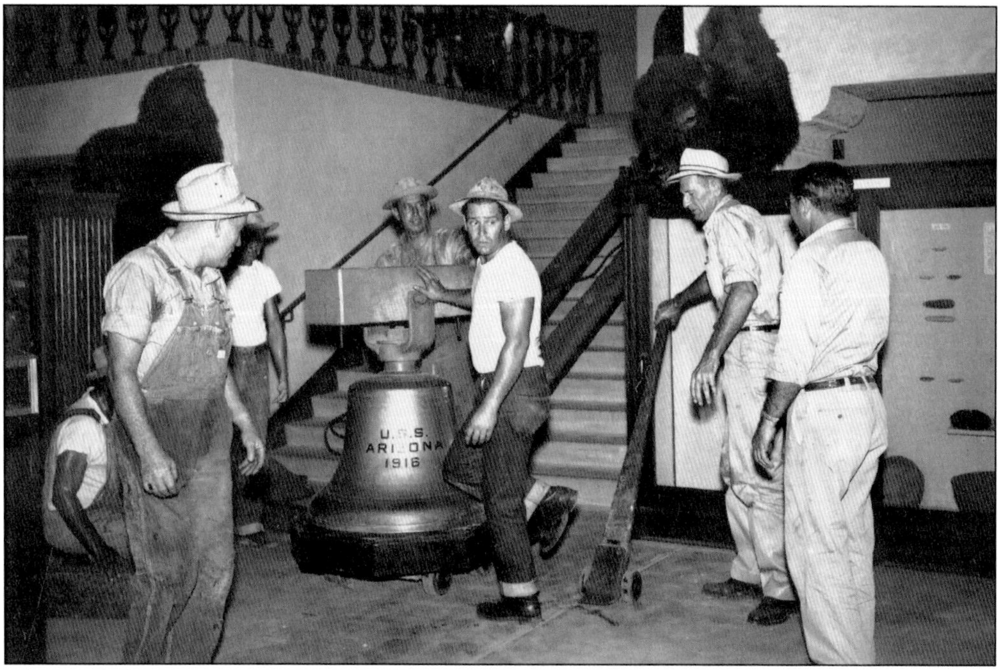

The battleship USS *Arizona* was sunk at Pearl Harbor in 1941. In 1946, R. Bill Bowers, a UA alumnus, found one of the *Arizona*'s bells at the Bremerton Shipyards in Washington State. The US Navy donated the bell to UA, where it was displayed on the mezzanine of ASM South. Here, in August 1951, the bell has just been slid down wooden planks to the main exhibit floor, headed for installation in the newly finished first Student Union building. Removed in 2000, it was hung in the bell tower of the new Student Union in 2002. (UASC N-420a.)

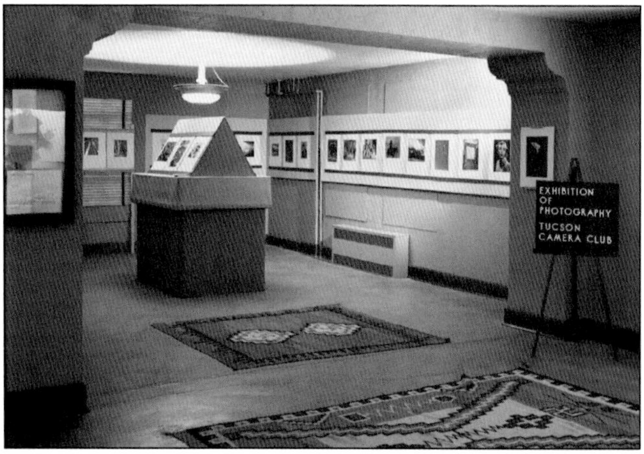

ASM curator E.B. Sayles was one of the founders of the Tucson Camera Club, and doubtless facilitated its annual shows at ASM, starting in 1946 and continuing through at least 1958. Many shows were exhibited in the northeast alcove of the exhibit floor of ASM South. The overhead light fixture visible here during the 1952 show was replaced by adjustable spotlights no later than 1955. (E.B. Sayles, ASM 2909.)

ASM's American bison ("buffalo") was part of the state herd in House Rock Valley, north of the Grand Canyon. Shot in the fall of 1927 and mounted that winter, it arrived at ASM in early 1928. Whether it was ever in Agriculture Hall is unknown. However, once the museum was under the West Stadium, it greeted visitors there from 1930 to 1935. After 1936, it migrated around ASM South (see pages 21 and 22), where it was a favorite of children. Since 2001, it has been on display in the UA Veterinary Science and Microbiology Building. (L.F.H. Lowe, ASM 4039.)

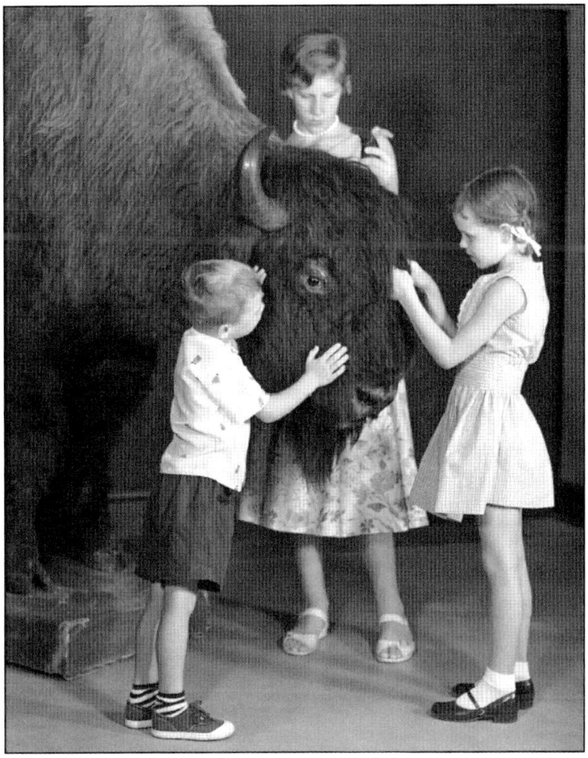

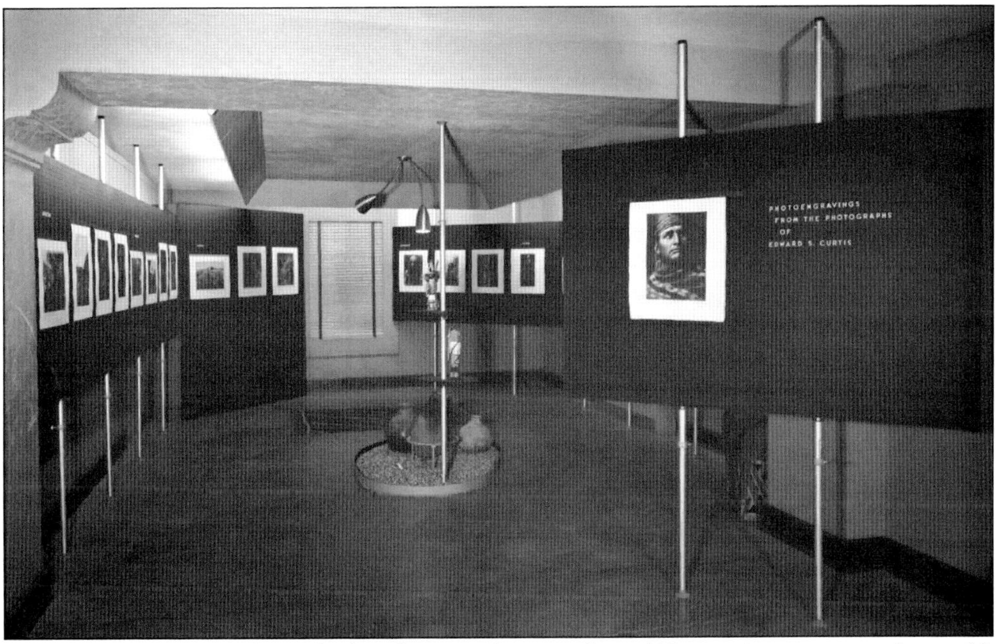

Edward S. Curtis is perhaps the best-known photographer of Native Americans in the world. Between 1907 and 1930, he published 222 complete sets of his 20-volume North American Indian series of books and their accompanying portfolios. ASM owns a set of both and periodically puts portions of the sets on exhibit. The first known occasion, shown here, was a 1958 display in ASM South, in the northeast alcove of the main floor. (L.F.H. Lowe, ASM 4559b.)

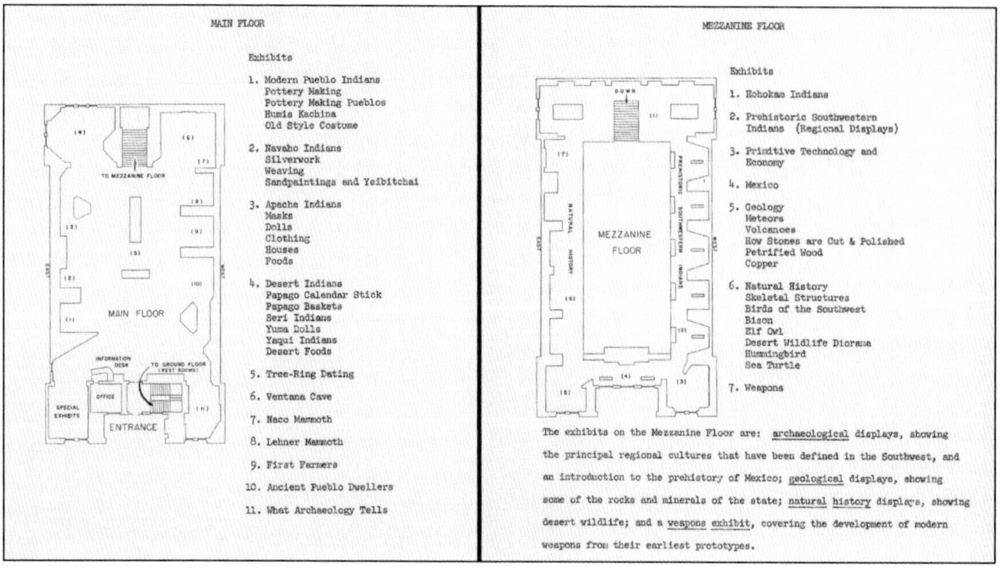

ASM director Emil Haury typified his predecessor's view of museum exhibits as "a clear case of horror vacui" (from the Latin for "fear of empty space"), with all available surfaces occupied by objects (see page 21). Early in his tenure, Haury reorganized the museum's exhibits, delegating different subjects to specific areas. These 1956 plans of the ASM South main exhibit floor and mezzanine document his decisions and reflect the arrangement of exhibits once the museum's windows had been covered (see page 22). (ASM.)

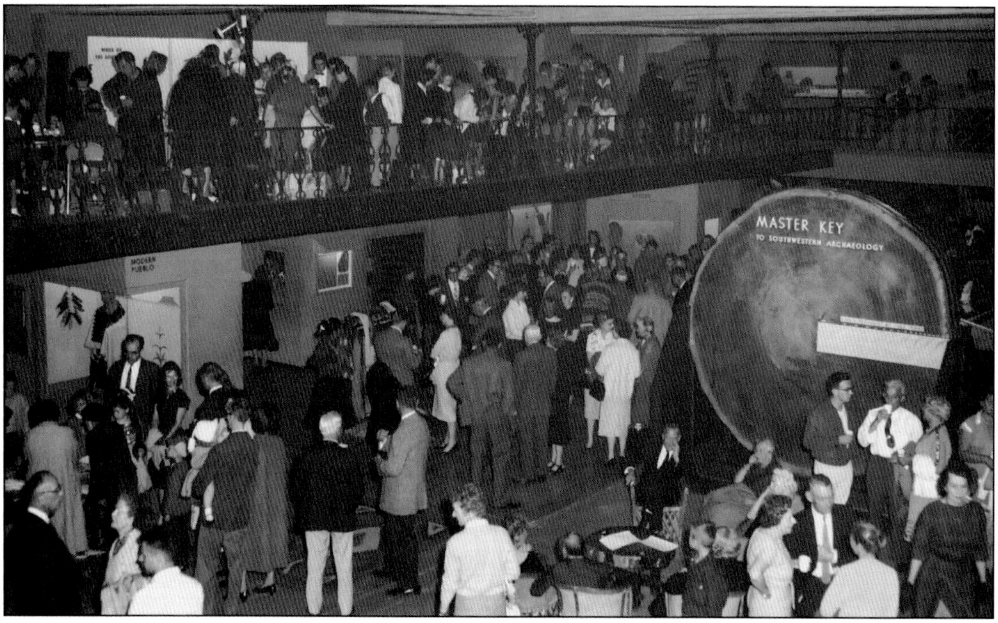

The first ASM open house, another of Haury's ideas, was held on January 15, 1941. For many years thereafter, open houses were usually held on weekends or evenings in the fall or spring. Storage rooms and laboratories were opened, with staff answering questions. Crafts demonstrators, musicians, and dancers often performed. The likely acme of open houses was on February 10, 1961, in ASM South, attended by 1,061 visitors. Open houses have largely been replaced by SWIAF (chapter 7) and, since 2011, smaller open houses directed at UA students. (G. Bartell, ASM 6928.)

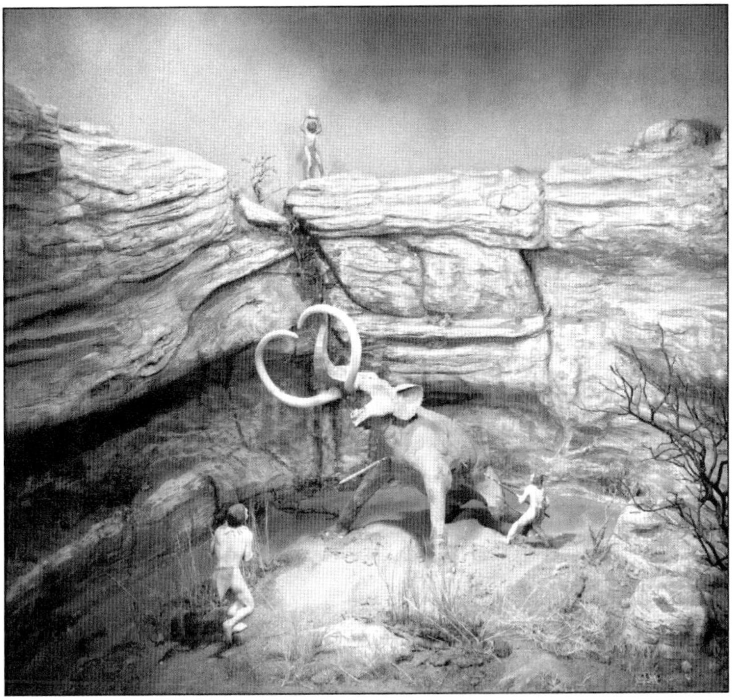

In the ASM South Building, along with the bison (see page 83), perennial favorites among children were the miniature dioramas that depicted life in the ancient Southwest. Although piles of large bones and stone spear points in the exhibit about the Naco and Lehner Sites might be interesting (see page 59), ASM preparator Robert G. Baker's lifelike depiction of an attack on a 10-inch-tall mammoth was far more memorable. (H. Teiwes, ASM 18509.)

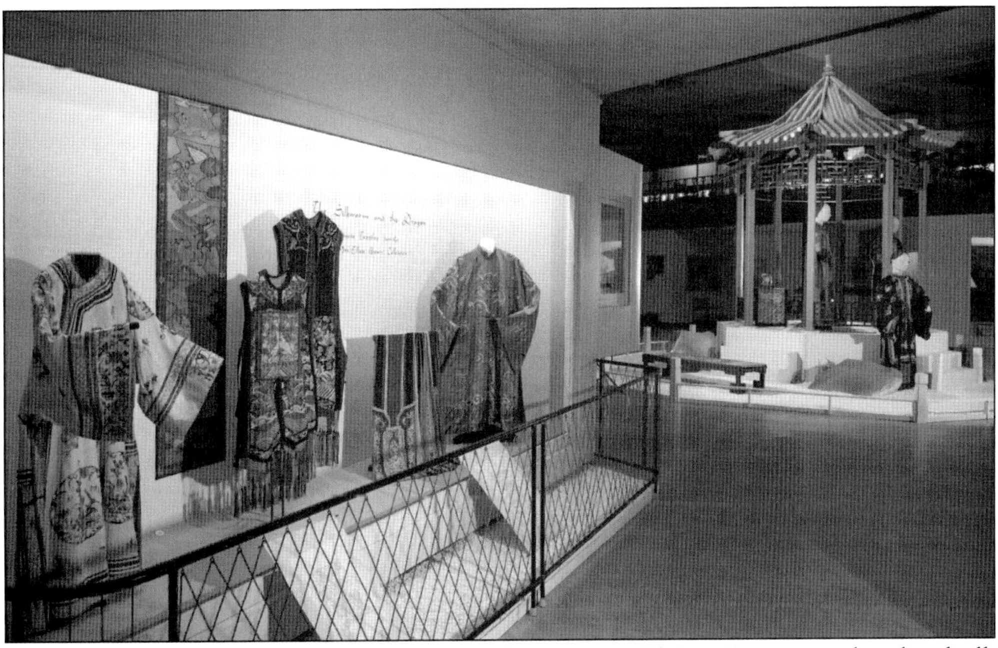

ASM has a small but exquisite collection of Chinese Late Chi'ing Dynasty embroidered silk garments, donated by the estate of Grace B. Brown. In 1968–1969, curator of exhibits Ernie Leavitt created an exhibit and booklet of the same name, *The Silkworm and the Dragon*. The case at left is opposite the sales desk in the northeast corner of the exhibit floor in ASM South, and the pagoda is in the middle of the floor. (H. Teiwes, ASM 20977.)

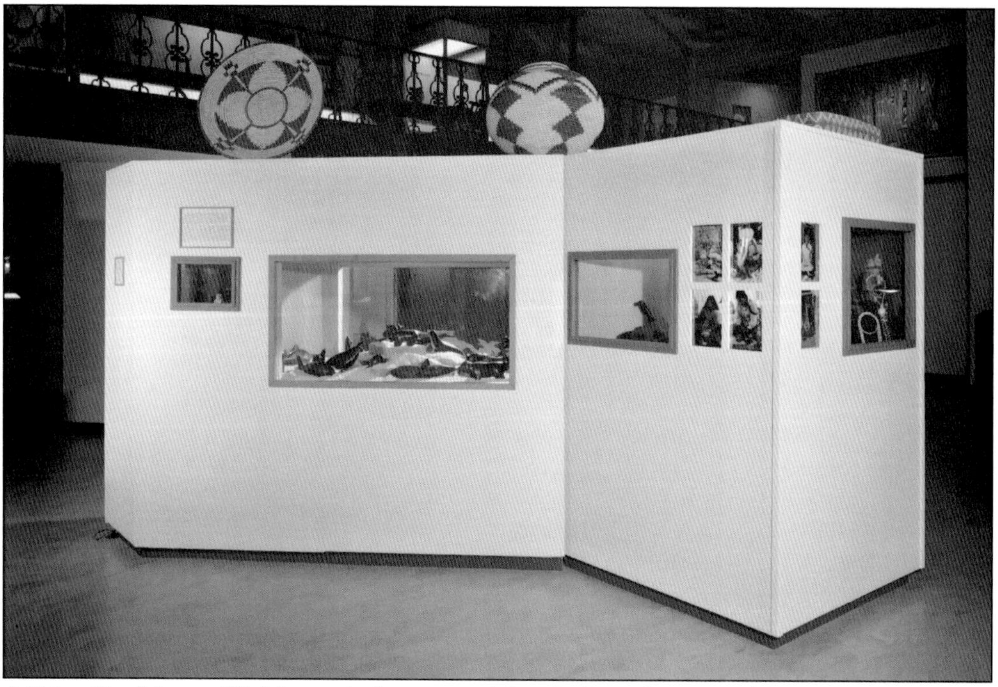

ASM utilized James W. Manson's donation of Seri Indian objects and his photographs from Sonora (see page 48) to stage a major exhibit on Seris in 1970–1971. *Kunkaak: The People* was in ASM South, built under the mezzanine on the east side, with large exhibit cases extending into the center of the exhibit floor. (H. Teiwes, ASM 28317.)

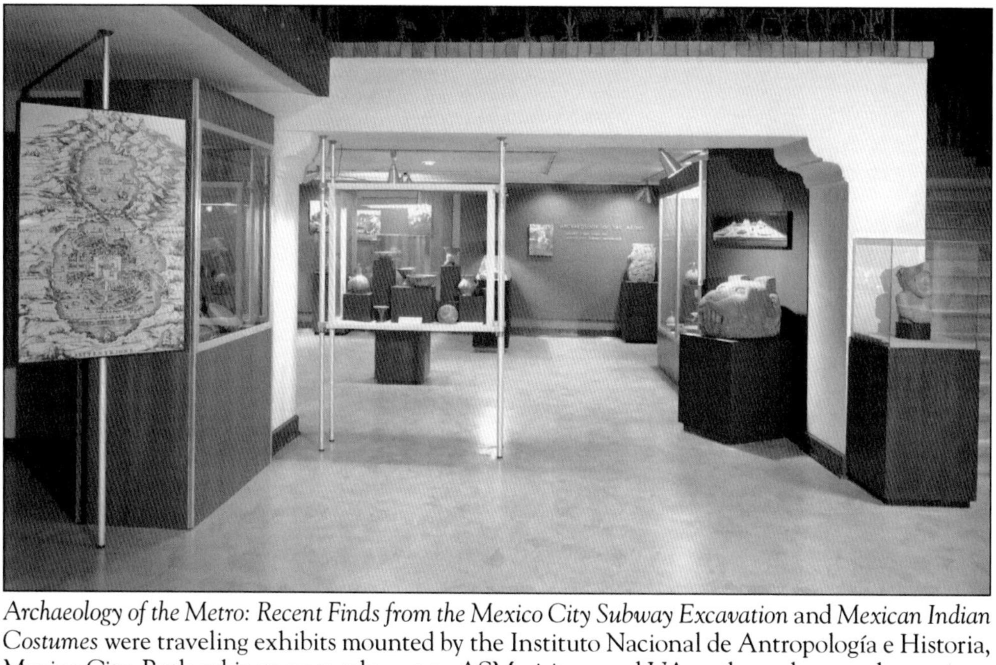

Archaeology of the Metro: Recent Finds from the Mexico City Subway Excavation and *Mexican Indian Costumes* were traveling exhibits mounted by the Instituto Nacional de Antropología e Historia, Mexico City. Both subjects were relevant to ASM visitors and UA anthropology students, since the Southwest of the United States is also Mexico's Northwest. The Metro exhibit was displayed in the southeast alcove of the main floor in ASM South in 1973–1974. (H. Teiwes, ASM 38159.)

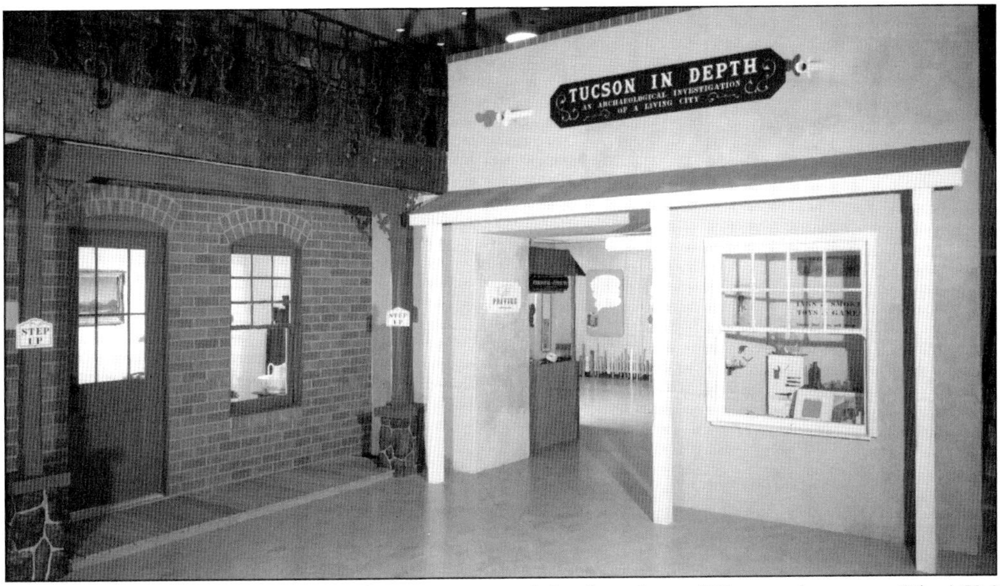

In 1975, to coincide with the 200th anniversary of the founding of Tucson (see page 59), ASM created the exhibit *Tucson in Depth*, featuring a microcosm of building fronts representing different eras in the city's history. Materials from the recently concluded TUR Project in downtown Tucson (see page 63) were used to show how archaeologists work with artifacts, historical records, maps, and photographs to flesh out history. (H. Teiwes, ASM 41156.)

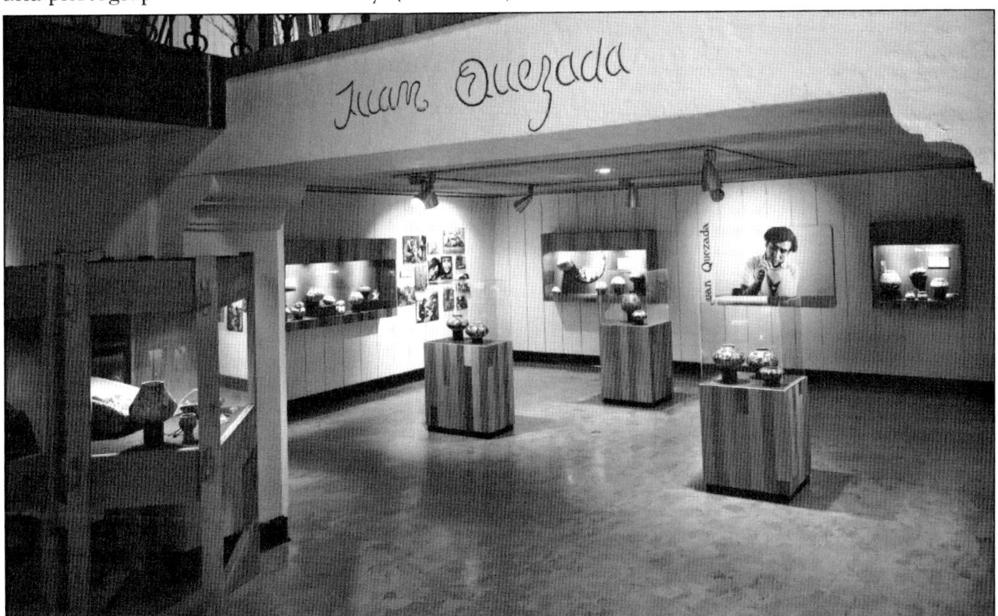

Self-taught Mexican potter Juan Quezada modeled his initial efforts on prehistoric Native American pottery of the Casas Grandes and Mimbres cultures. Now world-famous, Quezada was "discovered" in 1976 by anthropologist Spencer MacCallum, who helped Quezada hone his craft and promoted Quezada and the burgeoning community of potters in his hometown of Mata Ortiz, Chihuahua. Quezada's very first show was at ASM in the winter of 1977–1978, in the southeast alcove of the main floor in ASM South. (H. Teiwes, ASM 45375.)

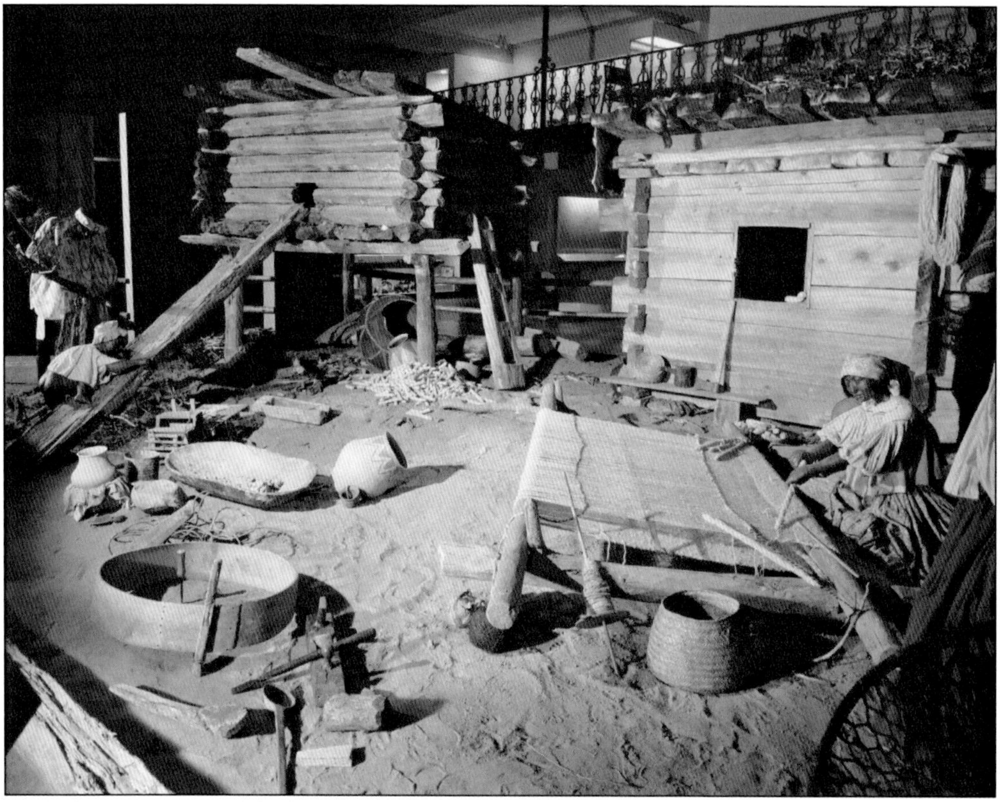

With the acquisition of the largest modern collection of Tarahumara Indian objects in the world (see page 50), ASM built a major exhibit in ASM South. *Los de la Sierra: The Tarahumara Indians of Chihuahua* (open 1979–1983) included a wooden house, a granary, a chicken coop, a loom, and mannequins in the center of the main floor, as well as a rock shelter built of imitation stone tucked under the west mezzanine. Tarahumaras attended the opening to demonstrate weaving, pottery making, and dancing, accompanied by their own musicians. (H. Teiwes, ASM 50132.)

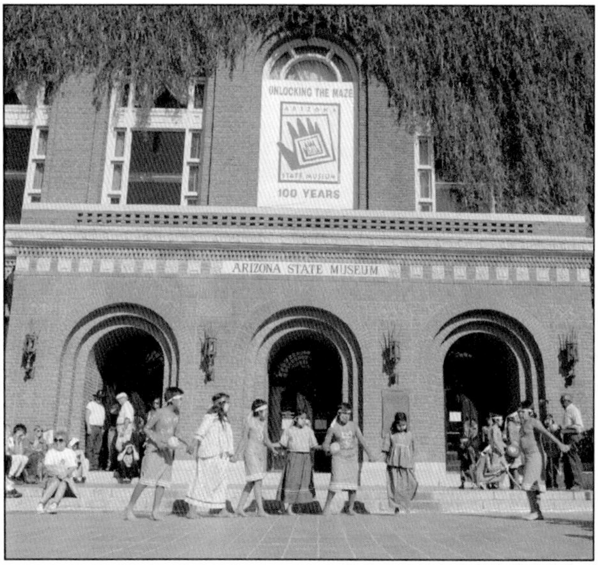

Partially opened in 1993 and completed in 1995, *Paths of Life: American Indians of the Southwest* is the museum's largest exhibit, with sections on the origins, history, and contemporary life of the Native American groups in Arizona and northwestern Mexico. Here, during the 1993 opening, a Tohono O'odham youth dance group performs in front of ASM North. The banner hung in the center window was the first of many to come, used to announce new shows. (H. Teiwes, ASM 87382.)

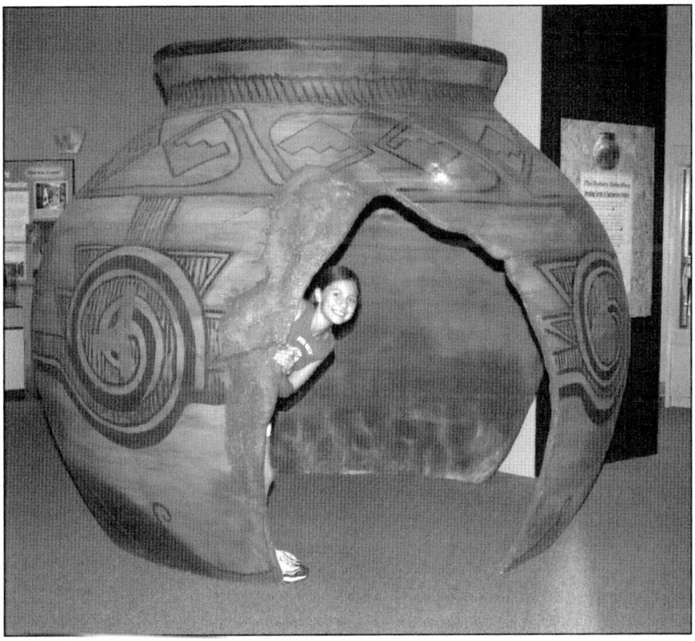

ASM head of Collections Suzanne Griset curated *Pottery Detectives: Decoding Secrets of Southwestern Pottery* (open 2003–2004). As Morgain Ghost demonstrates, its most noticeable feature was an eight-foot-high fiberglass jar, painted and textured to illustrate the many ways pottery can be decorated, be damaged, and deteriorate through use and discard. Smaller displays gave specific examples of how archaeologists tease information from mute potsherds. (J. Weakly, ASM.)

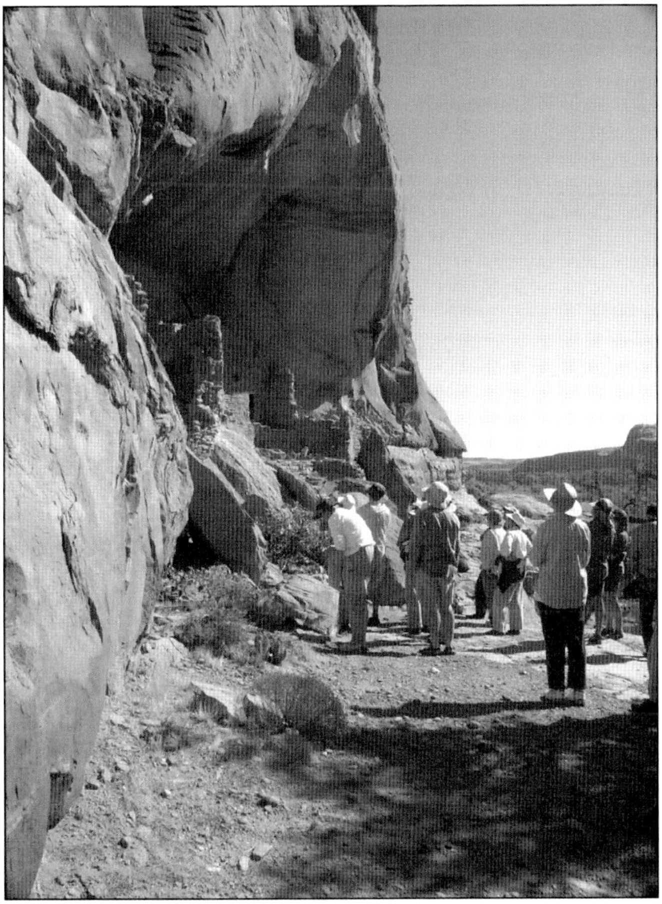

Tour participants on a 2004 Four Corners Learning Expedition trip through Arizona, New Mexico, Colorado, and Utah with ASM archaeologists E. Charles Adams and Richard C. Lange pay a visit to River House Ruin, an Ancestral Pueblo site so named because it is easily accessible from the San Juan River, downstream from Bluff, Utah. The site is also known as Snake House because of a large snake, or *awanyu*, pictograph on the back wall of the shelter. (Photograph by and courtesy of Richard C. Lange.)

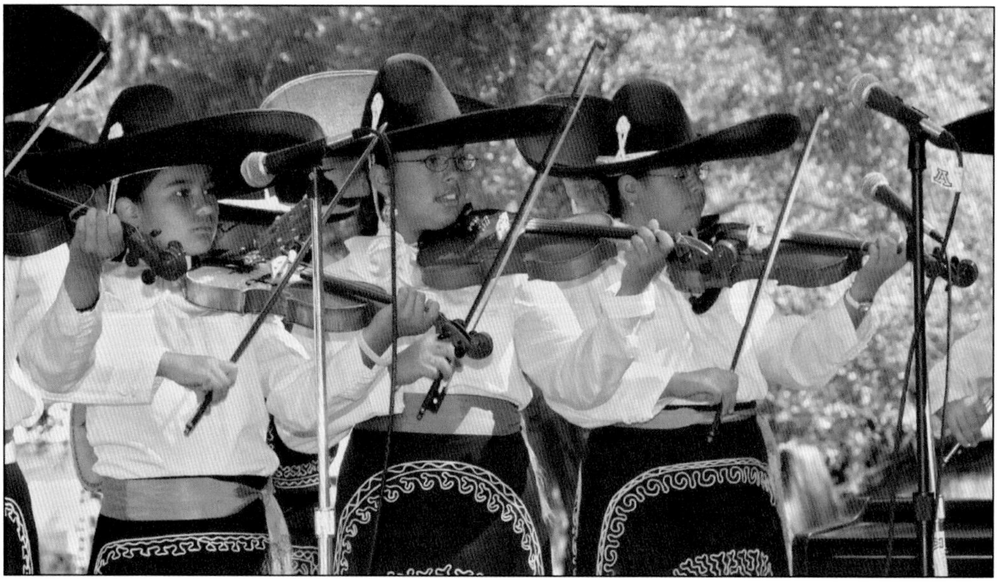

Exhibits and programming related to Hispanic heritage in the Southwest have increased through the years, with photographic displays by Agustín Víctor and Miguel Casasola, José Galvez, and Alejandra Platt; paintings by Daniel Martin Diaz, Xavier Garza, and Salvador Corona; and discussions of border and immigration issues, Frida Kahlo, the Treaty of Guadalupe Hidalgo, and the enduring presence of Hispanic culture and history in the Southwest. Here, internationally famous youth mariachi group Los Changuitos Feos de Tucson ("Tucson's Ugly Little Monkeys" in Spanish) performs at an ASM Hispanic arts and crafts festival in 2004. (J. Weakly, ASM.)

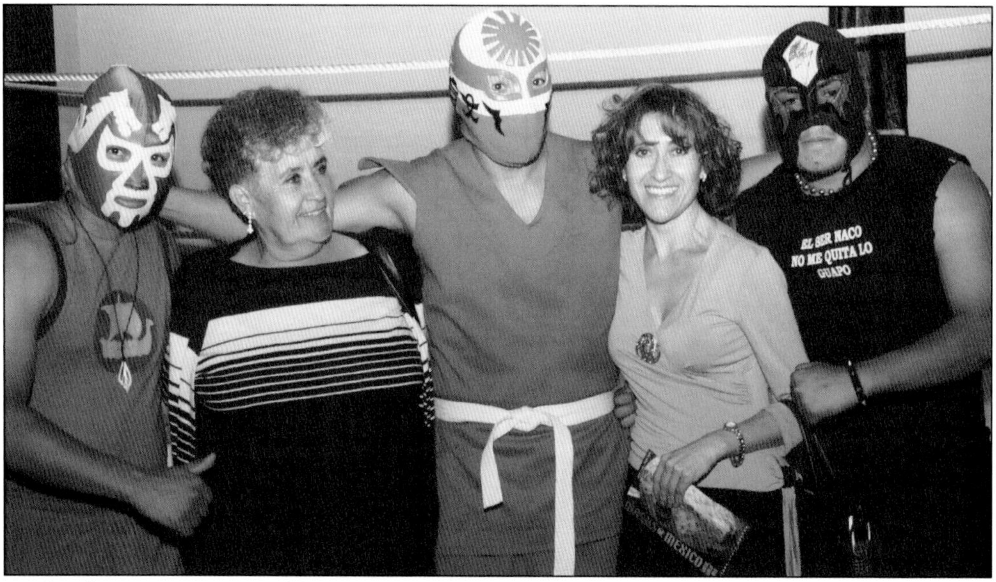

Masks of Mexico: Santos, Diablos y Más (open 2005–2007) featured a history of the use and meaning of masks in Mexico from prehistoric times to the present. Included were archaeological stone masks; religious and folk art masks from the Donald and Dorothy Cordry collection (see page 49); and videos, costumes, and masks of modern-day *luchador* professional wrestlers. Opening night featured *Lucha Libre* wrestling matches in a ring on the ASM lawn with Sol de Oriente (center) and friends. (J. Weakly, ASM.)

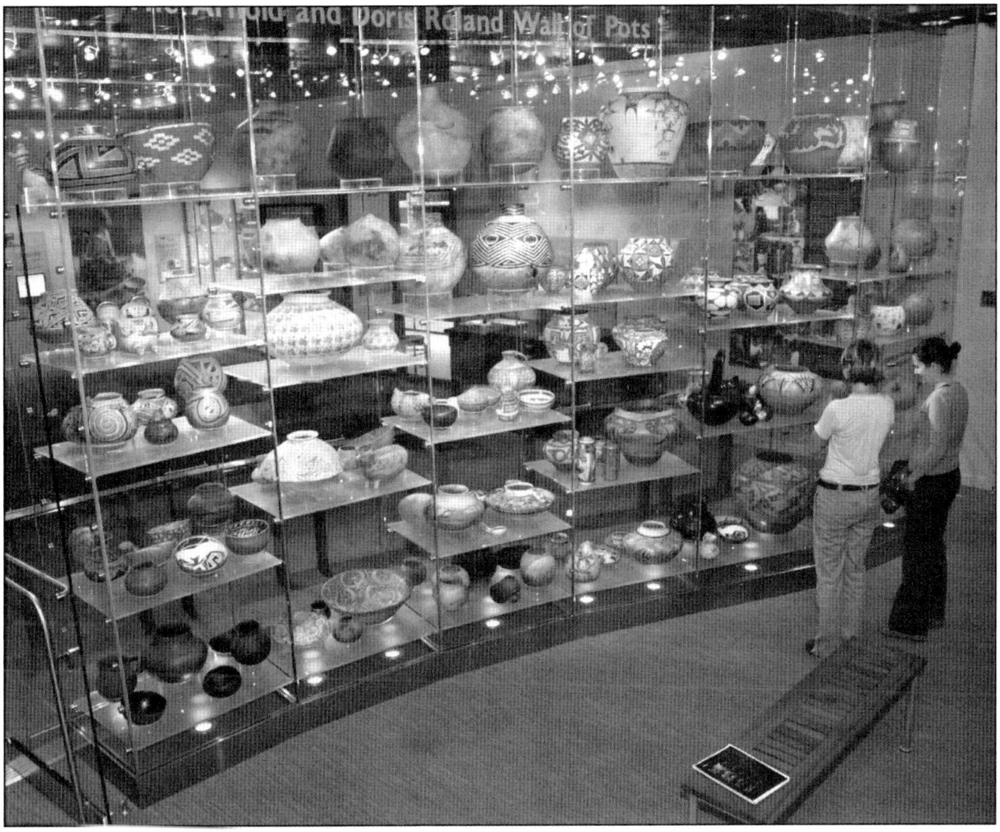

Outside of the ASM pottery vault (see page 36) are exhibits and videos that explain how pottery is made, its various forms and functions, and contemporary trends. Rachael Freer-Waters (left) and Gina M. Watkinson, from the ASM Conservation Laboratory, browse the floor-to-ceiling *Arnold and Doris Roland Wall of Pots*. It contains 150 pots selected by ASM curators to illustrate continuity and change over nearly two millennia of pottery making in the various cultural areas of the Southwest. (J. Weakly, ASM.)

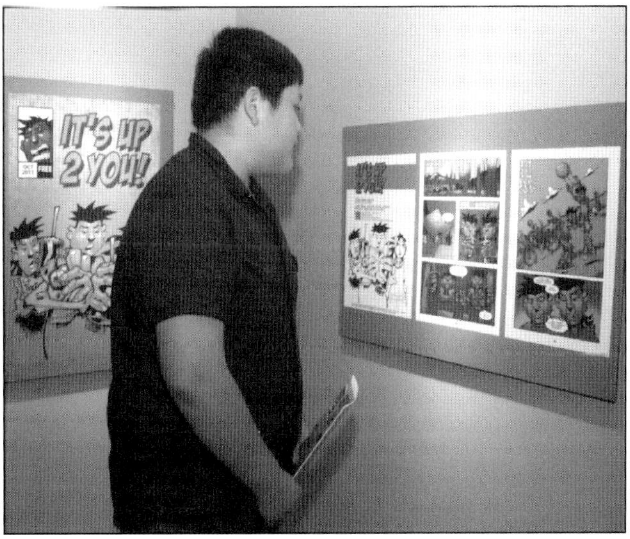

In 2011–2012, ASM curator of Education Lisa Falk sponsored *Through the Eyes of the Eagle: Illustrating Healthy Living*, a combination of exhibits, videos, and family activities aimed at educating young people about diabetes prevention from a Native American viewpoint. Here, a visitor examines artwork from *It's Up 2 You!*, a free comic book illustrated by artist and educator Ryan Huna Smith (Chemehuevi/Navajo) designed to show how diet choices can affect a person's health and life. (Alanah Tupponce, ASM.)

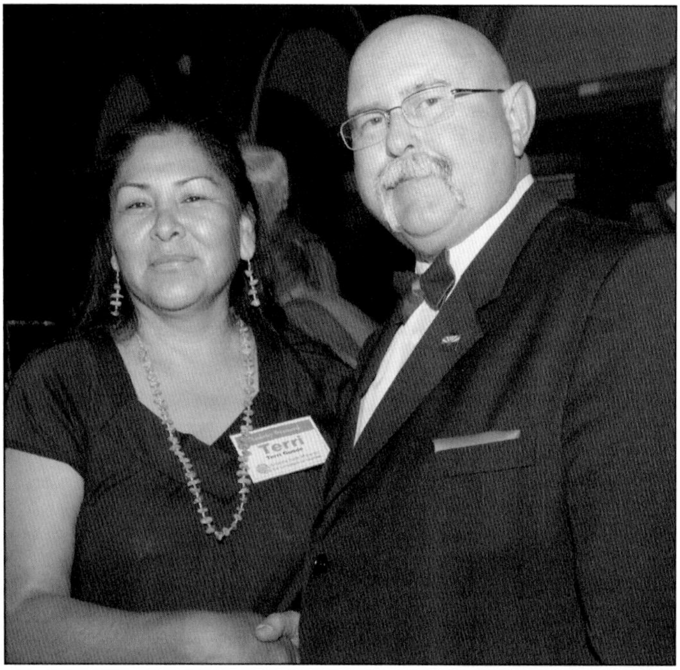

In anticipation of building interpretive exhibits for the new basketry vault (see page 37), the *Basketry Treasured* exhibit (open 2012–2014) displayed 500 of the most beautiful and interesting baskets and fiber artifacts from ASM's collection. At the opening, San Carlos Apache basket weaver Terri Goode (left) met Arizona's first governor, George W.P. Hunt (impersonator Don Shields), who made an early donation of baskets to ASM (see page 42)—and looks good for his age (see page 12). (J. Weakly, ASM.)

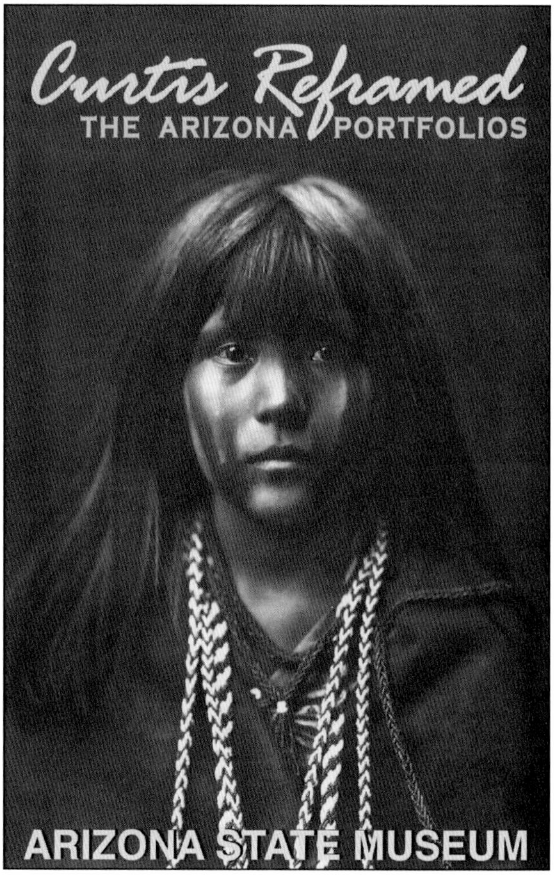

Although Edward S. Curtis (see page 83) documented the Native American cultures he photographed, he sometimes also romanticized and misrepresented them. His work is constantly reexamined from different perspectives. In 2013–2015, ASM photographer Jannelle Weakly mounted *Curtis Reframed* (with this publicity image from 1903 of Mósa, a Mohave girl), featuring commentary by contemporary Native Americans. During 2014–2015, it was accompanied by pieces of new artwork in various media, by Native American artists inspired by, and in response to, Curtis's photographs. (Photograph by Edward S. Curtis, publicity image courtesy of ASM Photographic Collections.)

Seven

Southwest Indian Art Fair

Although the Southwest Indian Art Fair (SWIAF) is one of ASM's many public programs, it has become ASM's signature event every spring. The Native Americans and visitors it attracts over the course of a weekend make up about 20 percent of the museum's total annual visitation.

SWIAF began when Jan Bell, head of the ASM Collections Division, proposed holding a fair at ASM to showcase contemporary Native American potters, as part of the museum's 100th-anniversary celebrations. Planning began in 1992, with the American Indian Pottery Fair taking place on February 26–27, 1994 (not 1993, as is sometimes stated). It included more than 100 potters from 16 tribes in Arizona and New Mexico, as well as lectures, demonstrations, and children's activities. Tables filled the lobby inside ASM North and extended to a few tents on the lawn out front. Potters were charged a $25 fee, and sales were between potters and the public, with no ASM commission. Originally planned as a one-time event, the fair proved so popular with potters and visitors alike that, for 1995, the program was incorporated into ASM's Public Programs Division, where it has remained. Its scope was expanded to include additional media, and it was accordingly renamed the Southwest Indian Art Fair (SWIAF), with the 1994 Pottery Fair considered to have been the first SWIAF. Coordinators have been Jan Bell (1994), Dawn Cromwell (1995–2002), Sherri Raskin (2003–2007), Angelo Joaquin (2008–2009), the SAACA (2010; see page 95), Martin Kim (2011–2012), and Daniel Vander Ploeg (2013–2014). The goals of SWIAF have remained essentially unchanged since its inception: to support and encourage Native American artists and craftspeople from Southwestern communities by providing an outlet for their work; to create educational opportunities for the public by sponsoring a venue in which to interact with the artists; and to provide public visibility for the Arizona State Museum and its programs.

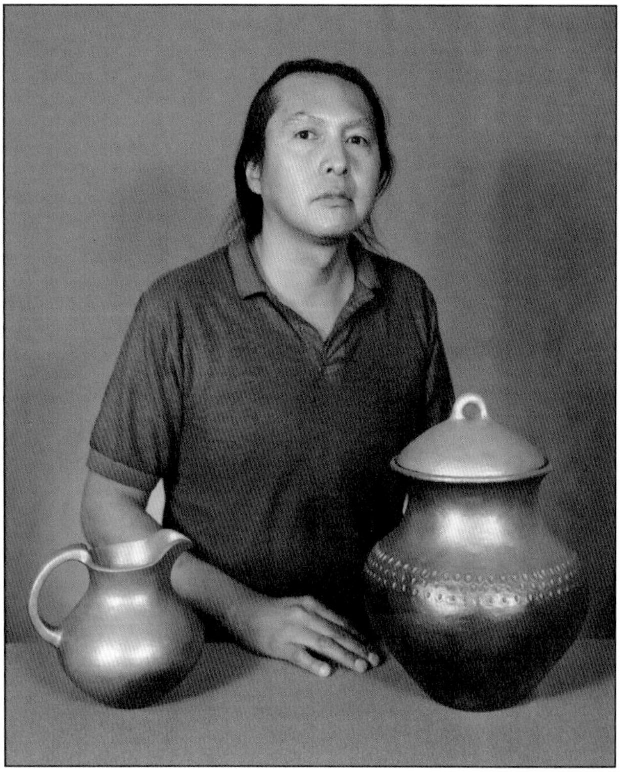

Anthony Durand, a potter from Picuris Pueblo in New Mexico, attended ASM's 1994 American Indian Pottery Fair, which turned out to be the first Southwest Indian Art Fair (SWIAF). Anthony had learned from his grandmother Cora Durand to make the gold-colored micaceous pottery that has been created at Picuris since prehistoric times. Cora, in her 90s, was also at the fair. The next year, *The First Micaceous Pottery Market* was held in Santa Fe, New Mexico, and micaceous pottery began to rival painted wares in sales. (K. Matesich, ASM 87708.)

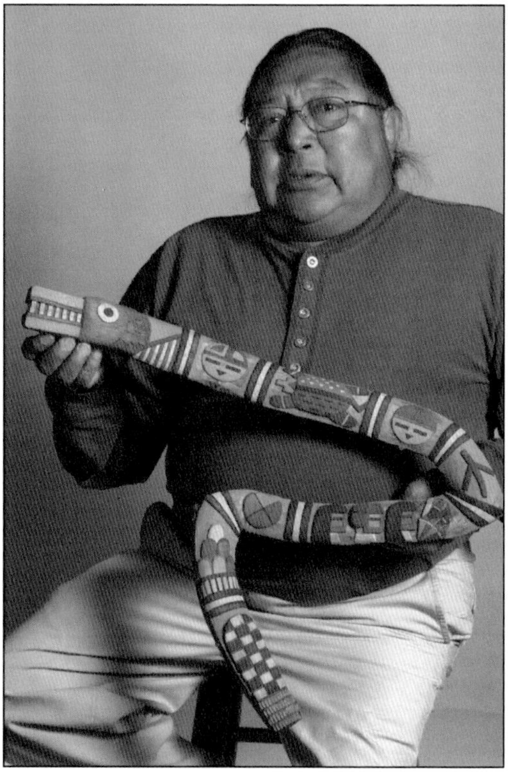

Delbridge Honanie is from Shungopavi Village, Second Mesa, on the Hopi Indian Reservation in northeastern Arizona. At the 2006 SWIAF, he holds his entry, *Ancient Water Serpent*, a carved and painted, naturally shaped cottonwood root, which won the Judge's Choice Award. Honanie has been a regular participant at SWIAF through the years, and he won a Lifetime Achievement Award in 2013. (J. Weakly, ASM.)

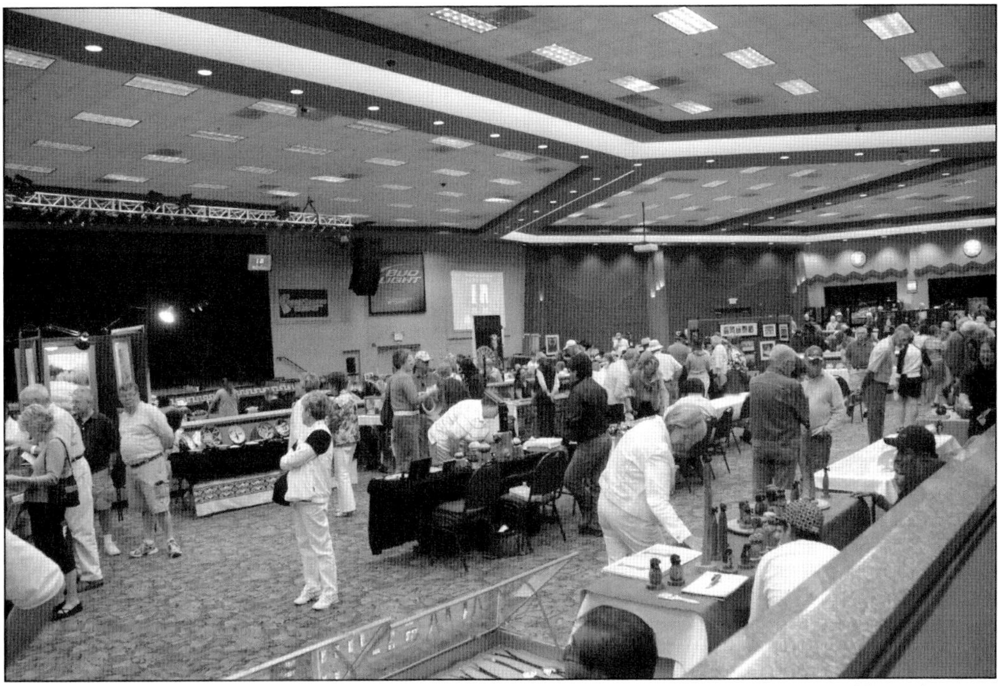

The 2010 SWIAF was canceled because budget cuts and layoffs left ASM unable to host it. However, ASM Advisory Board members, community members, and award sponsors rallied. The Southern Arizona Arts & Cultural Alliance (SAACA), a nonprofit dedicated to creating opportunities for artists, ran the fair. It took place on schedule, in March 2010, indoors, in the conference center of the Desert Diamond Casino, just south of Tucson, provided free by the Tohono O'odham Nation. With this invaluable bridge, SWIAF was able to return to ASM in 2011. (J. Weakly, ASM.)

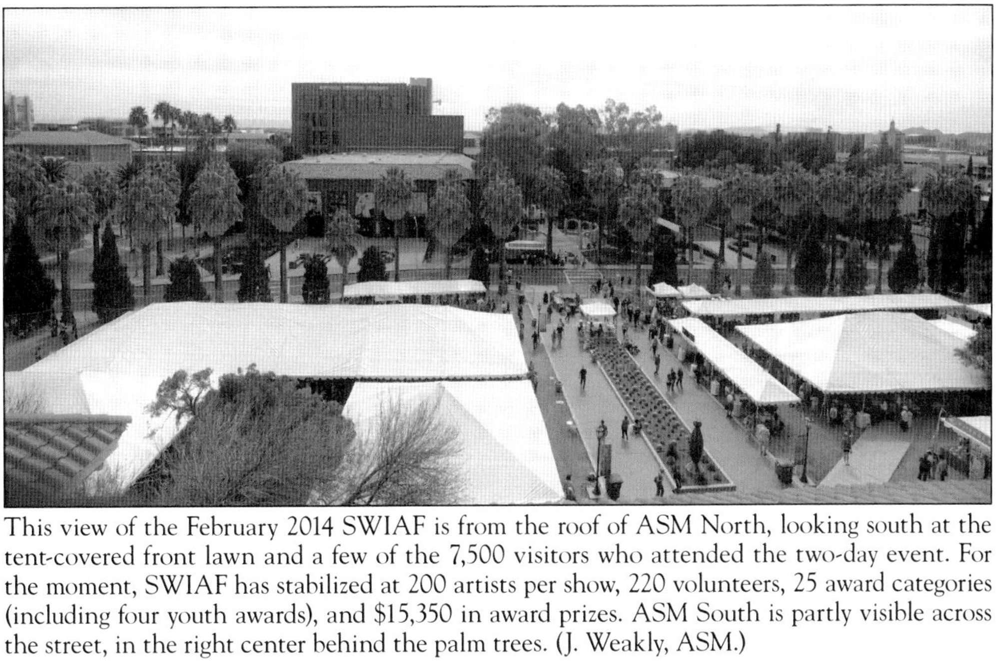

This view of the February 2014 SWIAF is from the roof of ASM North, looking south at the tent-covered front lawn and a few of the 7,500 visitors who attended the two-day event. For the moment, SWIAF has stabilized at 200 artists per show, 220 volunteers, 25 award categories (including four youth awards), and $15,350 in award prizes. ASM South is partly visible across the street, in the right center behind the palm trees. (J. Weakly, ASM.)

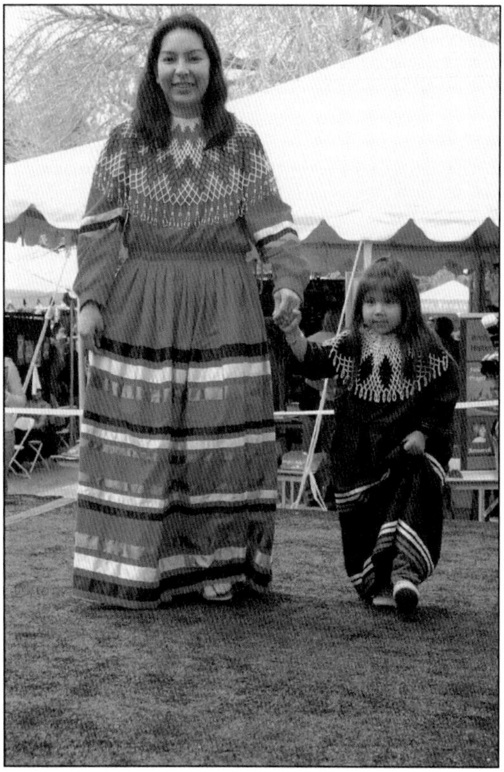

A fashion show was added to SWIAF events in 2014. Here, Reylynne Williams (left), from the Gila River Indian Community, and an unidentified young Tohono O'odham friend model traditional but newly designed Hualapai dresses made by Monique Mahone-Alvirez (Hualapai/Navajo). She markets her line of Yaha Wear Designs from her home in Peach Springs, on the Hualapai Indian Reservation. (Lisa Falk, ASM.)

The 2014 SWIAF was the first year that Seri Indians traveled from Sonora, Mexico, to attend the fair. Four women brought baskets, ironwood carvings (a craft invented by Seris in the early 1960s), stone carvings, and jewelry made mostly from plant and animal materials. Here, Maria del Carmen Moreno Lopez holds one of her baskets, in the Seri booth on the lawn in front of ASM North. (J. Weakly, ASM.)

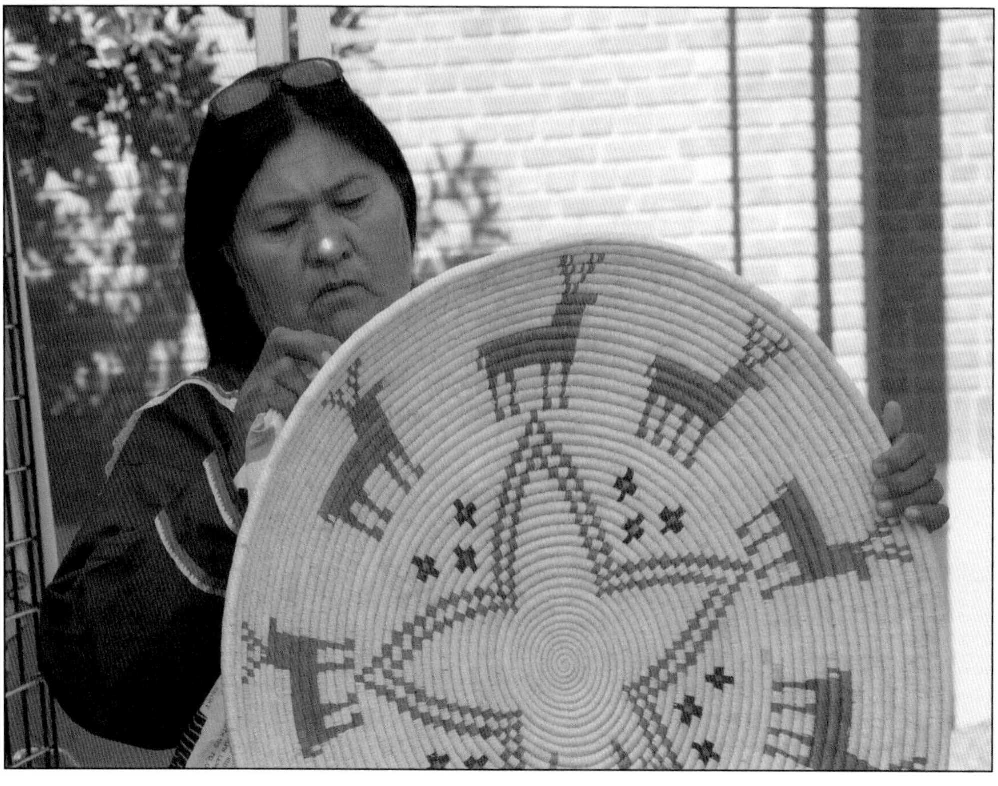

Eight

Scientific Spin-offs and Public Partners

One of the oldest and most important of the museum's relationships has been with the Arizona Archaeological and Historical Society (AAHS), which is usually identified as an affiliate of ASM. In early 1916, newly hired ASM director Byron Cummings gave a series of public lectures, stimulating enough enthusiasm (and perhaps competitive spirit) that the Arizona Archaeological Society was formed on April 14, 1916, in Tucson (not to be confused with the current Arizona Archaeological Society, founded in 1964 in Phoenix, which is still based there and has chapters statewide). The competitiveness stemmed from the fact that a similar group had formed earlier in Phoenix, named the Arizona Archaeological and Historical Society, but had been dormant since 1912. It agreed to merge with the Tucson group (and turn over its unused funds) on the condition that the Tucson group adopt the Phoenix group's name. This was done in 1917

In the 1930s, partnerships were often variations on applying for funds from federal relief agencies like the Public Works Administration and the Works Progress Administration. Many partnerships in the 1940s and 1950s were socially oriented, with ASM providing space for meetings or an exhibit venue for such groups as the Tucson Audubon Club, the Tucson Camera Club (see page 82), the Tucson Gem and Mineral Society, the Tucson Natural History Society, and the Tucson Stamp Club.

Emil Haury, as ASM director and head of the Department of Anthropology, was in a position to foster a staggering amount of interdisciplinary cooperation and synergy, being personally involved in the founding of the Laboratory of Tree-Ring Research (1937), Bureau of Ethnic Research (1952), the Radiocarbon Laboratory (1958), and the University of Arizona Press (1959), as well as encouraging research in archaeomagnetic studies in the Department of Geosciences (1960s).

More recently, partnerships have focused on building permanent endowments, internships (like the Norton Allen Native American Indian Internship Fund, started in 2000), and funding sources (like Friends of ASM Collections, 2005, and the ASM Director's Council, 2013) to offset decreases in support from granting agencies and the State of Arizona.

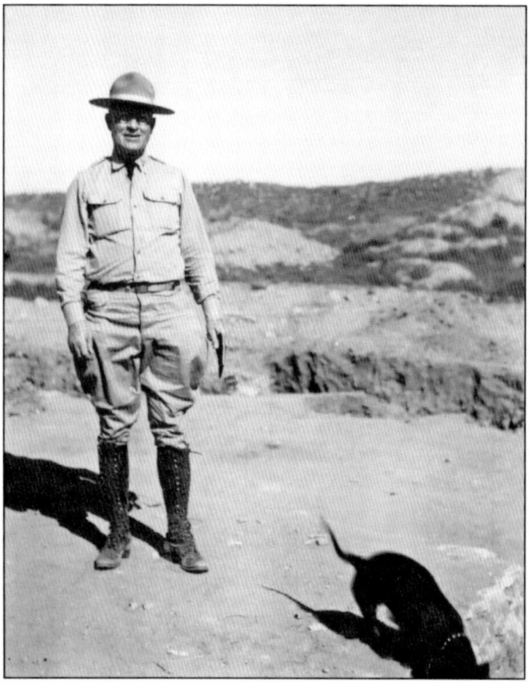

One of the most important contributions to Southwestern anthropology made by AAHS was, and is, the publication of the quarterly journal known from 1935 to 1988 as *The Kiva,* and since then simply as *Kiva*. Publishing current research from the region, *Kiva* reaches the profession and the public, near and far. The creation of Harry T. Getty, Thomas Hale, and Rev. Victor Rose Stoner, the journal's first issue appeared on May 16, 1935. Stoner edited the first three volumes. Here, Stoner and Gus the dachshund visit Awatovi in 1938. (Watson Smith, ASM.)

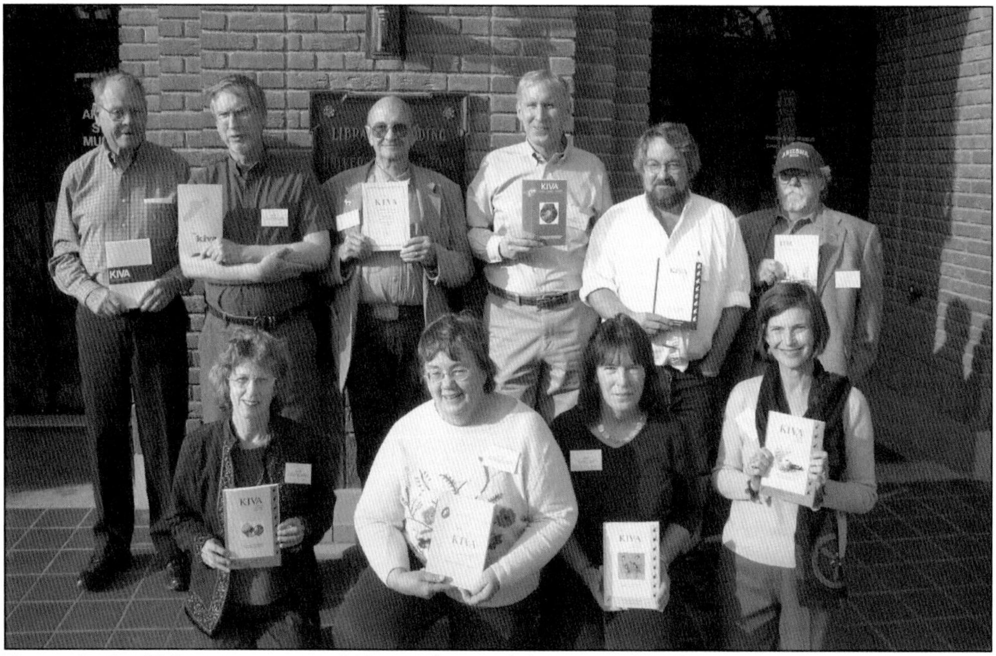

To mark the 75th anniversary of *Kiva*, editors of the journal gathered in front of ASM North on March 5, 2010, for a group photograph. The editors, with the years during which they served indicated, are, from left to right, (kneeling) Gayle Harrison Hartmann (1991–1995), Linda M. Gregonis (1988–1991), Tobi L. Taylor (1996–1998), and Nancy Bell Rollings (1995–1996); (standing) Alexander J. Lindsay Jr. (1957–1958), Richard V.N. Ahlstrom (1985–1987), Bernard L. Fontana (1958–1960), Stephen H. Lekson (2007–2011), Ronald H. Towner (1999–2006), and Mike Jacobs (1980–1985). (Photograph by and courtesy of Andrew L. Christenson.)

From 1958 to 1963, William J. Robinson, Bernard L. Fontana, and volunteer UA Anthropology students conducted excavations next to Mission San Xavier del Bac, south of Tucson. The goal was to explore the late prehistoric and early historic period in southern Arizona, as well as to garner information about construction of the church, which was completed in 1796. That dig was published in *The Kiva*. More small-scale volunteer excavations have been conducted through the years, including this one in 1972, with Fontana in the background. (H. Teiwes, ASM 34245.)

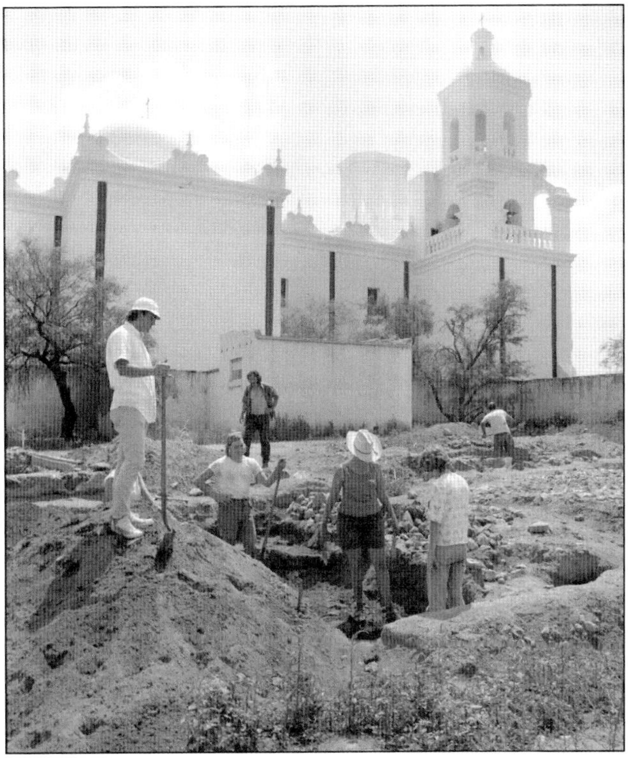

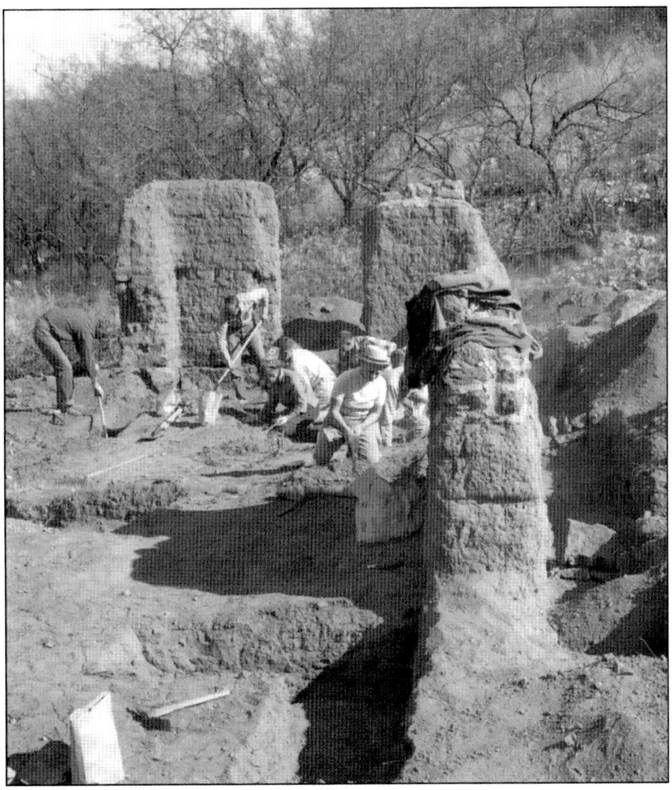

The excavation of Johnny Ward's Ranch in the winter of 1960–1961 is the gold standard of AAHS projects. It was instigated by AAHS president Bernard L. Fontana, carried out by AAHS volunteers, analyzed in collaboration with colleagues at UA and ASM, and published fully and promptly in *The Kiva*. It was also the very first project issued an excavation permit by ASM under the Arizona Antiquities Act of 1960. Here, volunteers have begun excavating the interior of what remained of this adobe ranch house from the late 1800s. (Hiram Parent, ASM 10050.)

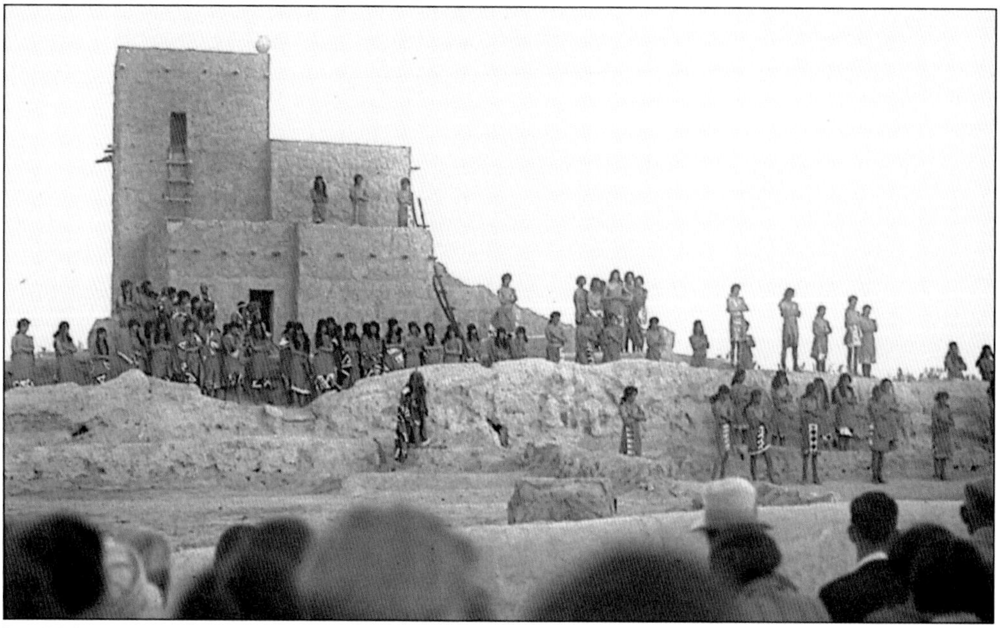

In 1926, to promote interest in Casa Grande Ruins National Monument, a "historical" pageant was held there, ostensibly portraying the lives of local Native Americans. With a three-story, "adobe pueblo" stage made of wood that was built on the ruin and covered with "Indian" actors, as shown here, it was a huge success. ASM director Byron Cummings wrote the 1929 and 1930 scripts, and actual Hopis, Navajos, and Pimas performed dances. Thankfully, this UA-NPS partnership was short-lived. (Photograph by Edwin F. Carpenter, courtesy of Roger E. Carpenter.)

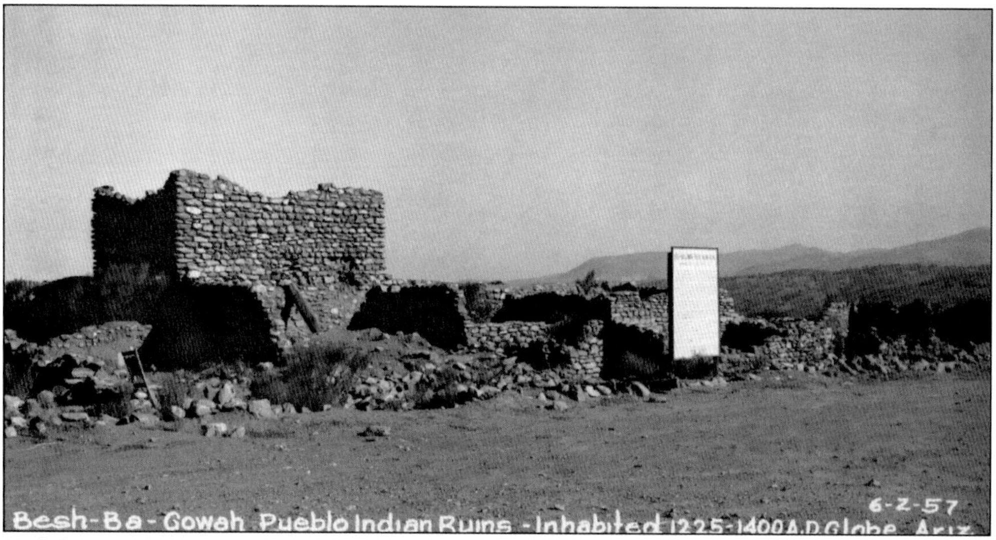

Besh-ba-gowah ("Metal Camp" in Apache) is a large, late prehistoric, masonry pueblo owned by the City of Globe. Excavations (1938–1940) there were incorporated into a Works Progress Administration (WPA) project sponsored by the Gila Pueblo Archaeological Foundation and overseen by ASM. The entire site was dug, and a few rooms were rebuilt. By 1957, as this postcard shows, the site was falling into ruin again. Another resurrection in the 1980s and a new, on-site museum have made it a valued part of Globe. (ASM Accession 1983-90.)

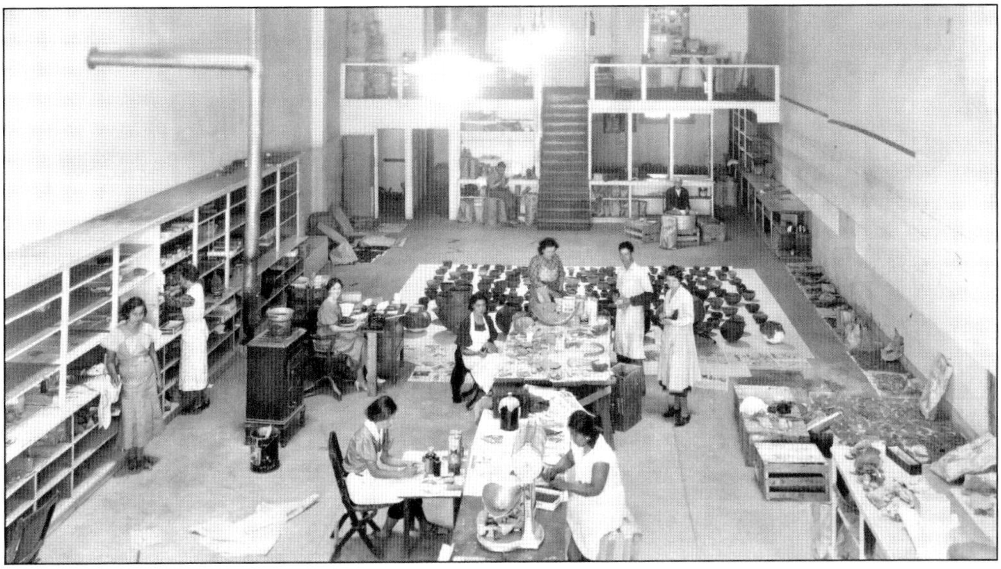

Tuzigoot ("Crooked Water" in Apache) is another large, late prehistoric masonry pueblo near Clarkdale. Grace M. Sparkes and the Archaeological Committee of the Yavapai County Chamber of Commerce secured Federal Emergency Relief Administration (FERA) and Civil Works Administration (CWA) funds to work at the site. Supervisory archaeologists Louis R. Caywood and Edward H. Spicer worked there with logistical support from ASM director Byron Cummings. During 1933 and 1934, the pueblo was completely dug and rebuilt. A laboratory under the direction of Caywood was set up in the empty Hydrosia Distilled Water Company store in Clarkdale (above). Workers can be seen washing, reconstructing, labeling, and cataloging the artifacts. Exhibit cases were built, and the store was converted into a temporary museum (below). Tuzigoot was made a national monument in 1939. (Both, ASM Accession 96-183.)

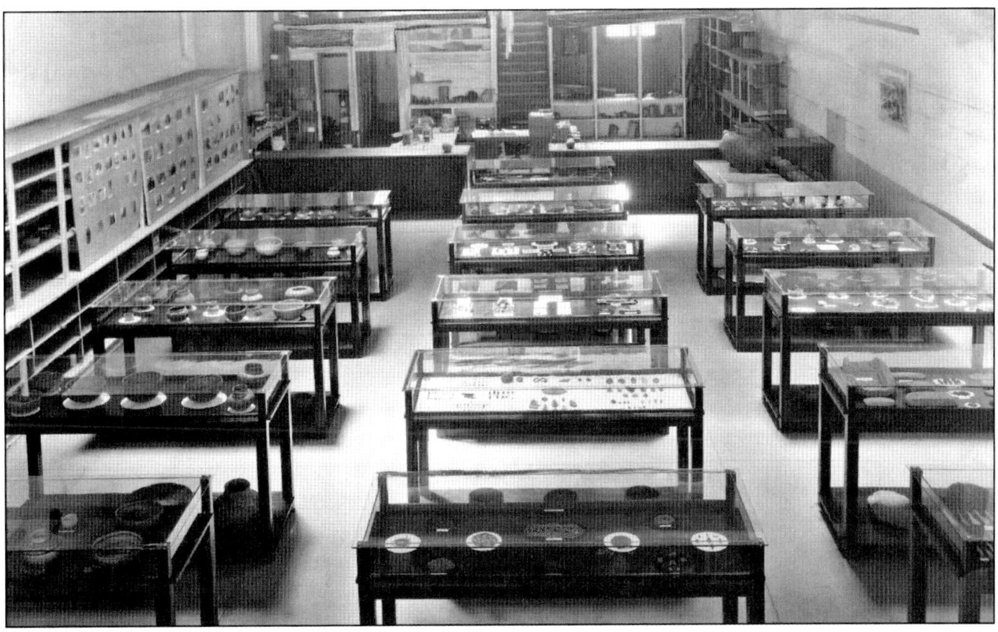

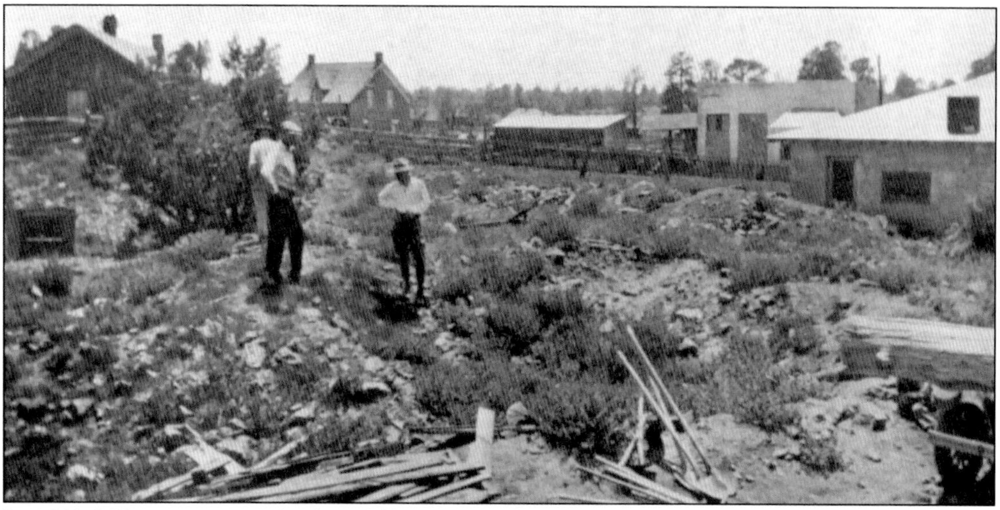

In 1919, UA astronomer Andrew Ellicott Douglass realized that the annual growth rings of individual trees could be correlated with each other, and that by overlapping series of these rings, a dating technique could be developed. The National Geographic Society funded searches of prehistoric ruins for ancient timbers that could fill a gap in Douglass's series. That timber was found on June 22, 1929, by Lyndon Hargrave and Emil Haury in the churned rooms of the Whipple Ruin (also known as the Showlow Ruin), shown here, in the town of Show Low. The science of dendrochronology (tree-ring dating) was now a reality, allowing the precise dating of any site in the Southwest with suitable wood specimens. (E.W. Haury, ASM.)

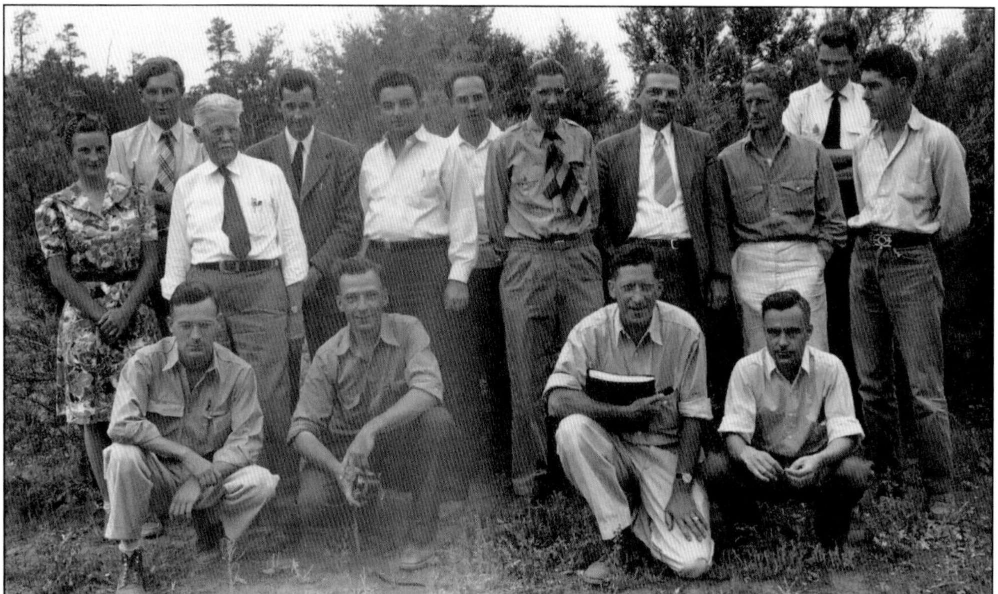

A tree-ring conference held at the Forestdale Field School on July 12–13, 1941, included a who's who of Southwestern dendrochronologists, as well as archaeologists interested in the technique. Pictured, from left to right, are (kneeling) Carleton S. Wilder, Watson Smith, Paul S. Martin, and Harry T. Getty; (standing) Mrs. and Deric Nusbaum O'Bryan, A.E. Douglass, W.S. Stallings Jr., Edmund Schulman, Alfred F. Whiting, Gordon C. Baldwin, John C. McGregor, Erik K. Reed, Robert J. Braidwood, and Edward T. Hall. (E.W. Haury, ASM 661.)

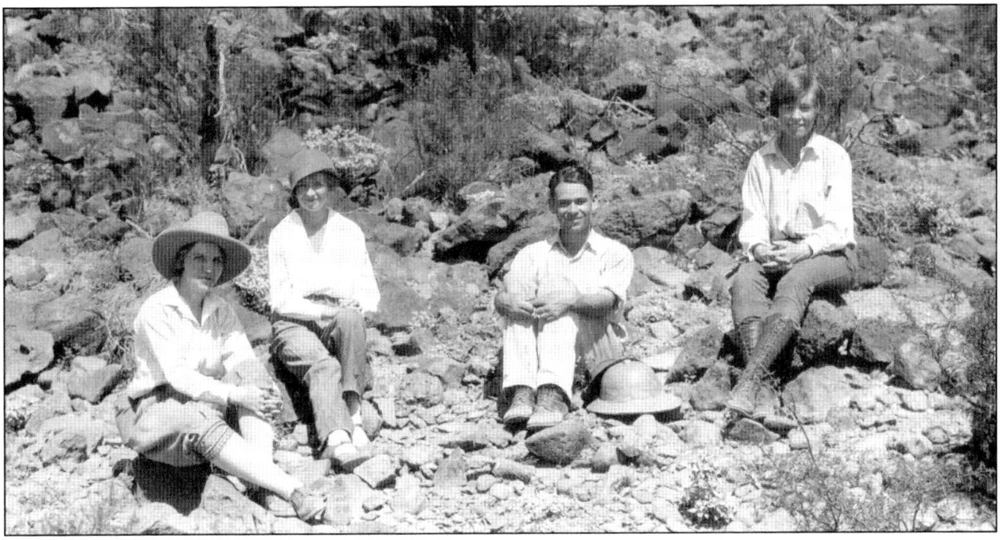

In the spring of 1930, with Haury as his assistant, Douglass taught the first course on tree-ring dating ever offered at UA (or anywhere) to a class of 14 students. In this photograph, probably taken in 1926, are, from left to right, Florence Hawley (Ellis), Gladys Phare, Emil Haury, and Clara Lee Fraps (Tanner). Hawley and Fraps were in that class. The UA Laboratory of Tree-Ring Research was not formally created until 1937. (AHST PC29/Box 6B/F.20/AI.)

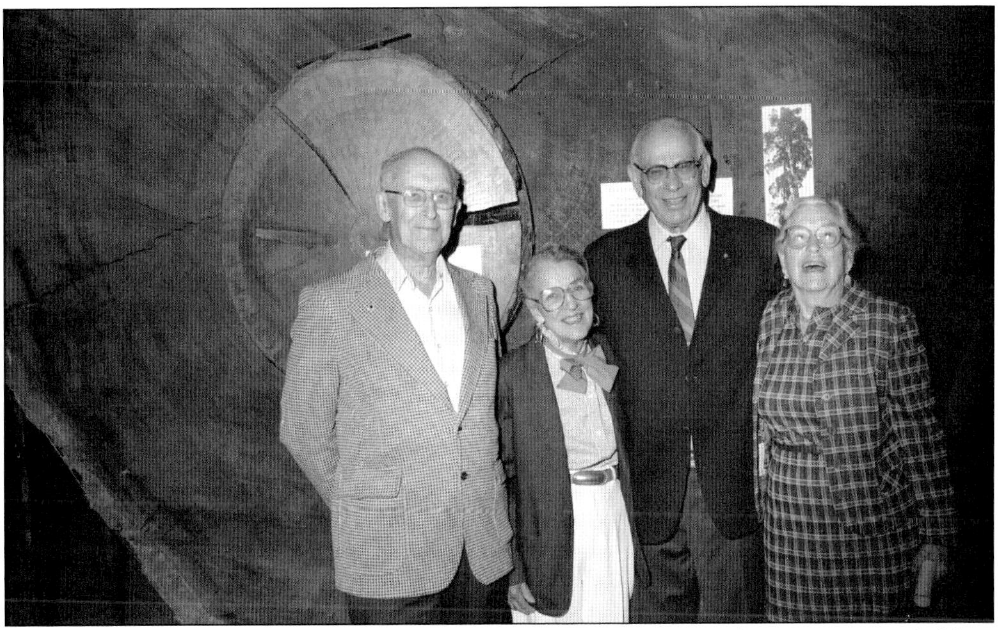

As part of UA centennial celebrations, a 55th-anniversary tree-ring class reunion was held on the main exhibit floor of ASM South. Here, in February 1985, are, from left to right, Waldo R. Wedel, Florence Hawley Ellis, Emil Haury, and Clara Lee Tanner. Wedel, a boyhood friend of Haury's from Newton, Kansas, became the leading authority on Plains archaeology. Ellis became the preeminent scholar of archaeology and ethnology in New Mexico. Tanner taught in the UA Department of Anthropology for 50 years. (H. Teiwes, ASM 64569.)

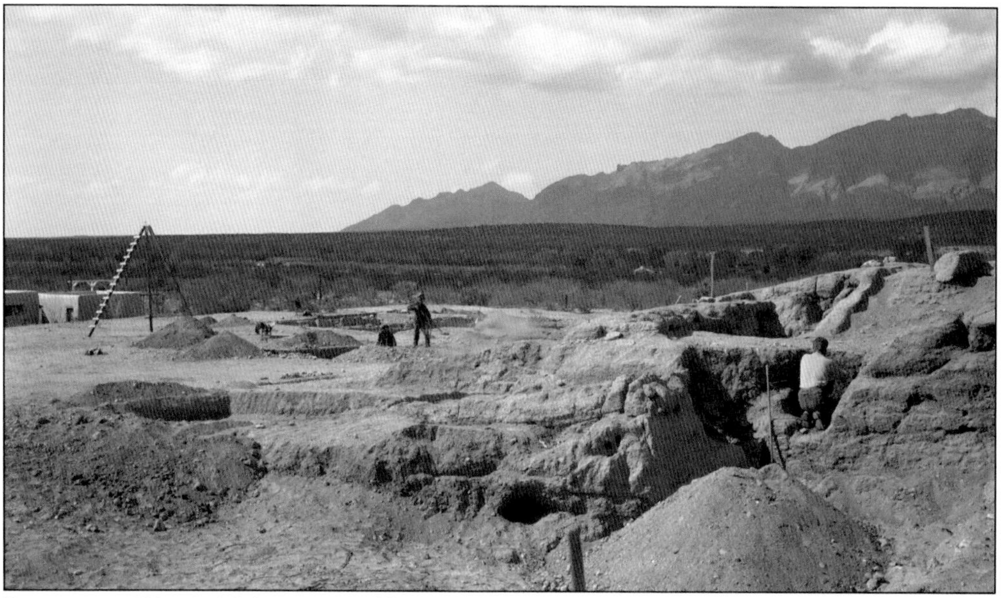

During its 1933–1942 lifespan, in addition to building parks, buildings, and roads, the Civilian Conservation Corps (CCC) sponsored some archaeological work. Julian Hayden, who had supervised work at Pueblo Grande in Phoenix, was put in charge of similar excavations at the UA-owned University Indian Ruin in Tucson. This 1940 view looking northwest toward the west end of the Catalina Mountains shows a CCC laborer digging in the platform mound at right, with the caretaker's house and a wooden photography tower at left. (E.W. Haury, ASM 421.)

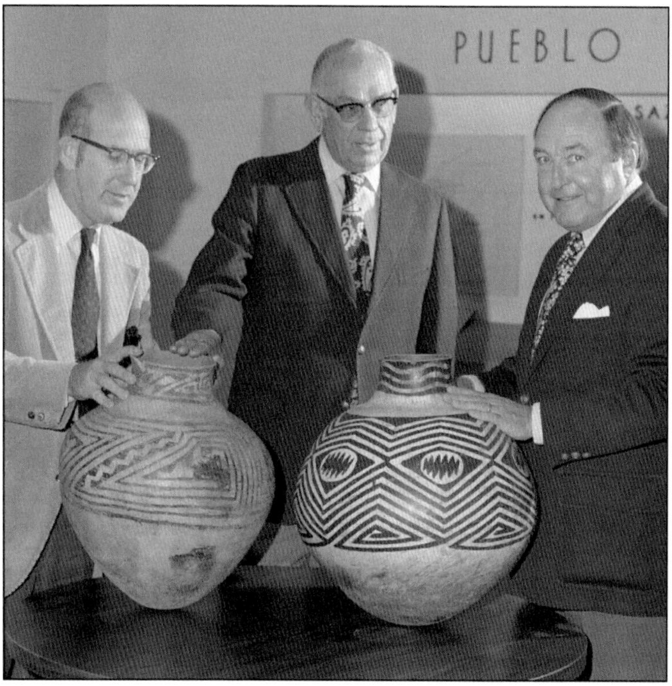

In 1975, the "Twin Pots" from Turkey Cave, in northern Arizona, were reunited in ASM South. Pictured, from left to right, are Raymond H. Thompson and Emil Haury of ASM and Robert Euler of the National Park Service. These black-on-white jars had been buried inches apart, but the left one was found by Byron Cummings around 1915 and came to ASM. The one on the right was found by Harold Gladwin in 1929, taken to Gila Pueblo, and loaned to NPS. Since ASM inherited the Gila Pueblo collections, Haury persuaded Euler to transfer the jar to ASM. (H. Teiwes, ASM 41181.)

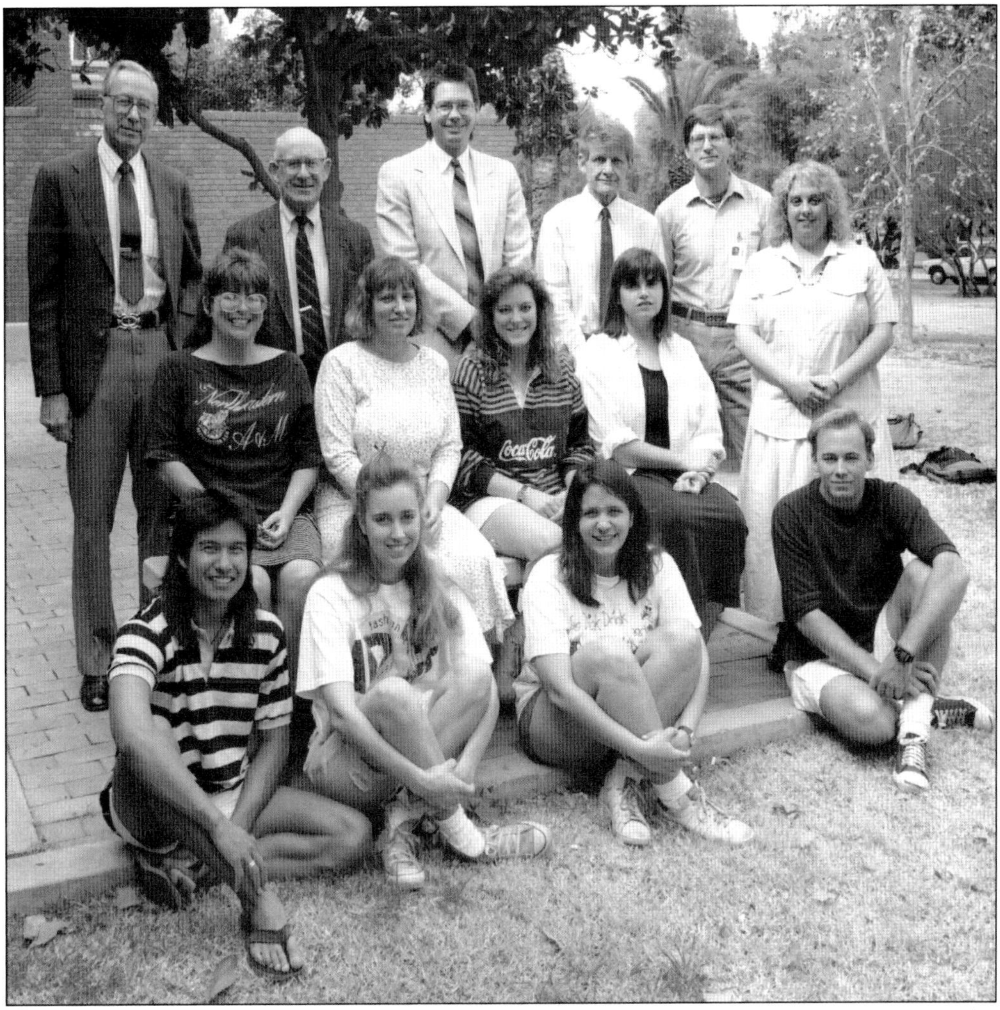

The Central Arizona Project Repository (CAPR) was a cooperative agreement among the Bureau of Reclamation (BOR), the National Park Service (NPS), and ASM. From 1986 to 2004, it gathered together in Tucson the archaeological collections resulting from work in the path of the Central Arizona Project Canal, and processed and inventoried them for curation. Ultimately, collections from Ak-Chin Indian Community lands were placed with the Ak-Chin Him-Dak Eco-Museum; collections from the Tonto Basin went to the Archaeological Research Institute at Arizona State University; all other collections (primarily Hohokam) went to the Huhugam Heritage Center at the Gila River Indian Community; and the CAPR was disbanded, its job completed. Here, on the north lawn of ASM North in March 1990, are the administrative and curatorial staffs and the UA anthropology student employees of the CAPR. They are, from left to right, (front) Albert Morales, Chandra Spence, Gina Moore, and David Hostetler; (seated) Martha Sowerwine, Linda Brown (computer specialist), Audrey Freiman, and Dorothy Jones; (standing) George S. Cattanach Jr. (NPS), Raymond H. Thompson (ASM director), Thomas R. Lincoln (BOR), R. Gwinn Vivian (ASM associate director), Alan Ferg (curator), and Donna Fesselmeyer (archivist). Later employees most responsible for the success of the program were curator Marcia Donaldson (1993–2004), archivist Chris Cleary (1991–2003), and computer specialist Peter In-Albon (1995–2004). (ASM.)

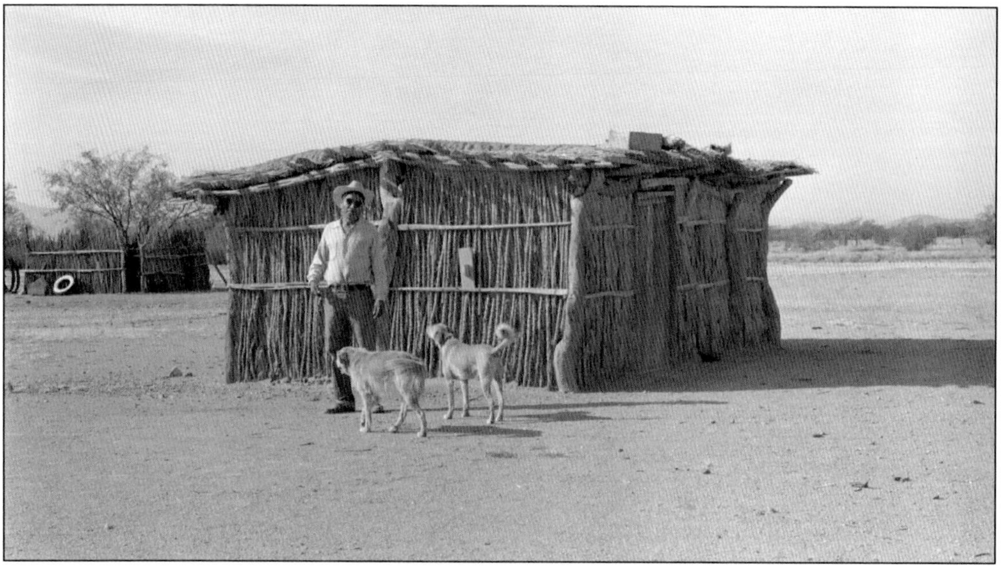

Discussions between William H. Kelly and Emil Haury resulted in the establishment in 1952 of the Bureau of Ethnic Research (BER), renamed the Bureau of Applied Research in Anthropology (BARA) in 1982. BER gathered information that would help Arizona tribes gain better access to medical and educational resources. UA student Richard D. Jones, working on a census, photo-documented his work at his own expense. Typical of the photographs he donated to ASM is this one, taken in Komelik on January 16, 1963, of Augustine Pablo with his storage shed made of ocotillo stalks, full of squash and tools. (Richard D. Jones, ASM Accession 2012-429.)

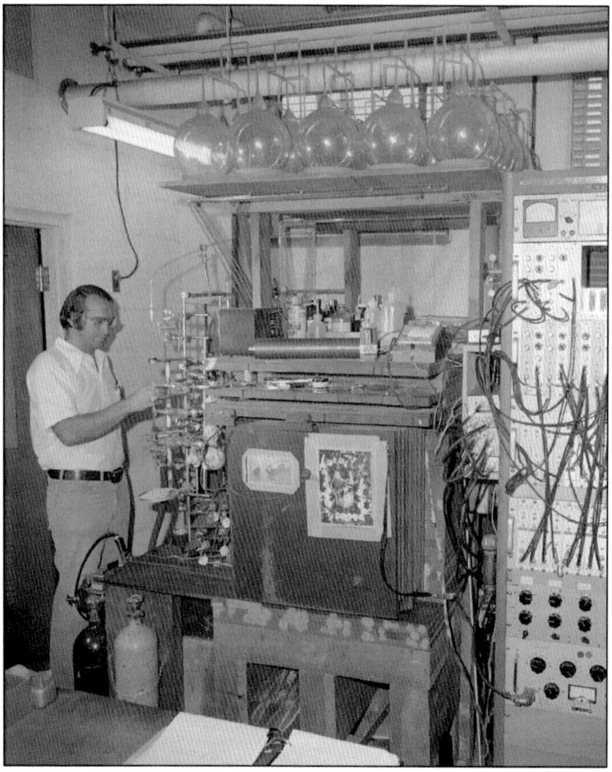

Emil Haury, excited by the prospect of having another dating technique for the archaeologist's toolbox, oversaw the creation of the radiocarbon-dating laboratory at UA from 1951 to 1957. He obtained a Research Corporation grant for equipment in 1952, and, by 1955, actual dating runs were being conducted. The first results of dating archaeological samples from Arizona sites were published in 1957, and the Radiocarbon Laboratory became a department within UA in 1958. Here, in 1974, Larry Arnold monitors the equipment. (H. Teiwes, ASM 38694.)

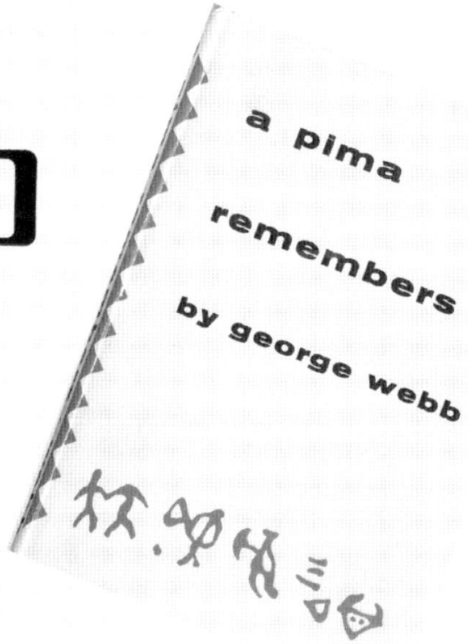

The University of Arizona Press came into being on September 1, 1959, upon approval by the Arizona Board of Regents of a proposal written primarily by Emil Haury, Edward Spicer, and Raymond Thompson. The first book it published was *A Pima Remembers*, a slender volume of reminiscences by George Webb, a Pima born about 1893 on the Gila River Indian Reservation. Its cover, decorated with mnemonic glyphs from a calendar stick, is shown here, along with the earliest logotypes of the University of Arizona Press. Webb's original manuscript resides in the ASM Archives. (Digital scans of logotypes, photograph of book cover by J. Weakly.)

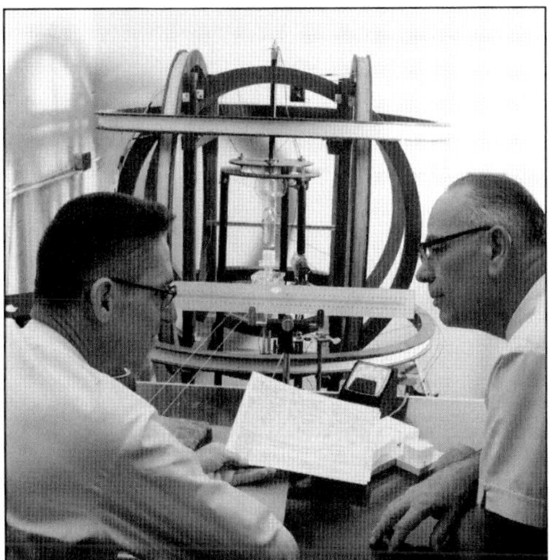

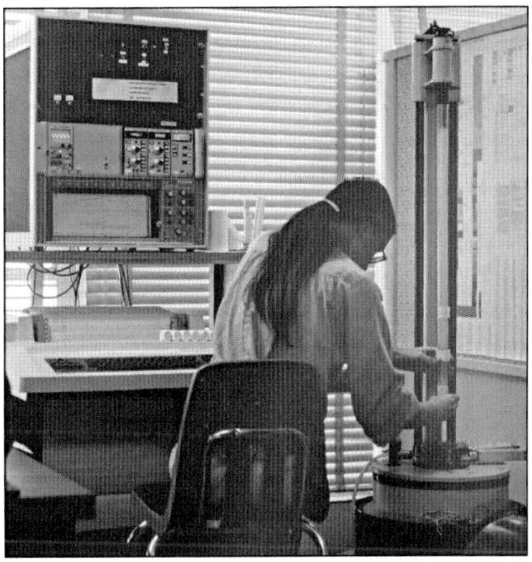

Archaeomagnetic dating of archaeological samples was pioneered in the 1960s at UA by Robert L. DuBois, but he has been universally criticized for never releasing his raw data. On the left, DuBois (left) shows Emil Haury how samples from the 1964–1965 excavations at Snaketown will be measured. On the right, Barbara A. Murphy of the ASM Archaeomagnetic Program measures samples with a cryogenic magnetometer in the UA Department of Geosciences laboratory in 1982. (Left, H. Teiwes, ASM 79908; right, photograph by and courtesy of Richard C. Lange.)

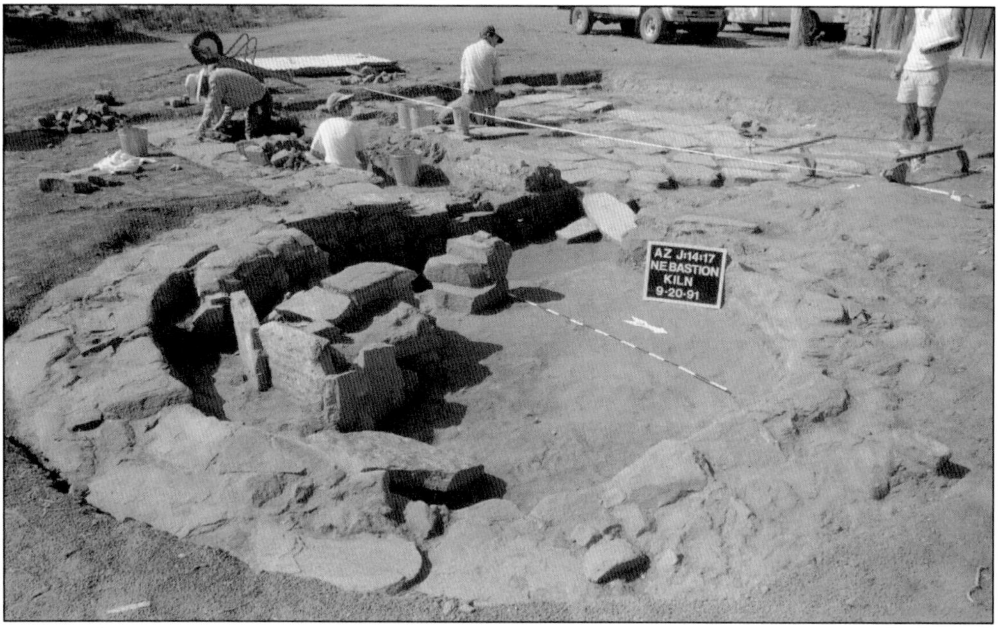

ASM archaeologists, most notably Richard C. Lange and E. Charles Adams, have worked frequently with avocational archaeologists from the Arizona Archaeological Society (AAS), lecturing, teaching, and supervising field projects. Each fall from 1991 to 1996, the author supervised AAS volunteers exploring Brigham City, a Mormon fort occupied from 1876 to 1881 and located in present-day Winslow. Here, the crew excavates a potter's kiln and workshop attached to the circular bastion in the foreground. (Photograph by Richard and Florence Lord, courtesy of the author.)

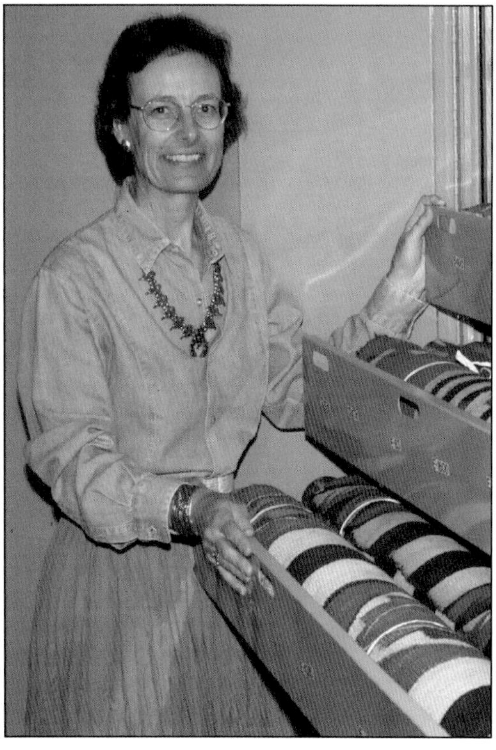

In 1977 and 1978, Ann Lane Hedlund helped catalog ASM's textiles. In 1997, she became director of the Gloria F. Ross Center for Tapestry Studies, Inc., and forged a cooperative agreement with UA. The center was located in ASM from 1998 to 2013, changing its name to the Gloria F. Ross Tapestry Program in 2010. Hedlund completed several center-sponsored books while at ASM, coordinated the creation of the Joe Ben Wheat Southwest Textile Database on the ASM website, and retired in 2013. (J. Weakly, ASM.)

ASM benefits from the presence of a Mexican consulate in Tucson. The consulate has arranged the loan of traveling exhibits, such as the *Talavera Contemporánea* exhibit of modern Mexican ceramics in 2012. Here, Consul de Mexico en Tucson Juan Manuel Calderón Jaimes visits with Sonoran photographer Alejandra Platt-Torres at the opening of her 2013 ASM exhibit *A World Separated by Borders*, which explored shared images of Arizona and Sonora. (J. Weakly, ASM.)

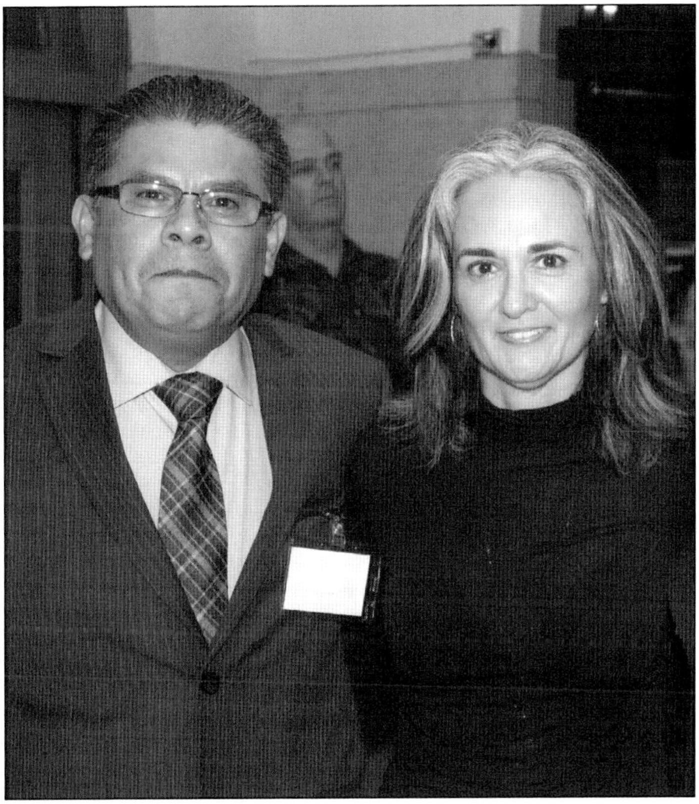

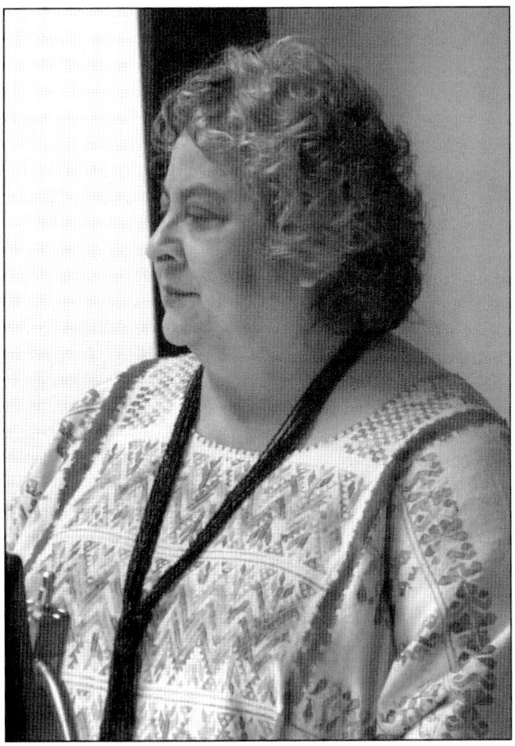

María Elisa Villalpando Canchola, archaeologist from the Instituto Nacional de Antropología e Historia (INAH) for the state of Sonora, Mexico, is seen here at the 2014 opening of *In Flight: Adriel Heisey's Images of Trincheras Archaeology*, which includes beautiful and revealing aerial photographs of prehistoric hilltop sites. Starting in 1979, Villalpando has facilitated decades of collaborative projects among Mexican and US archaeologists, working especially closely with ASM Archaeology curators Suzanne and Paul Fish and their Borderlands Archaeology Program. (J. Weakly, ASM.)

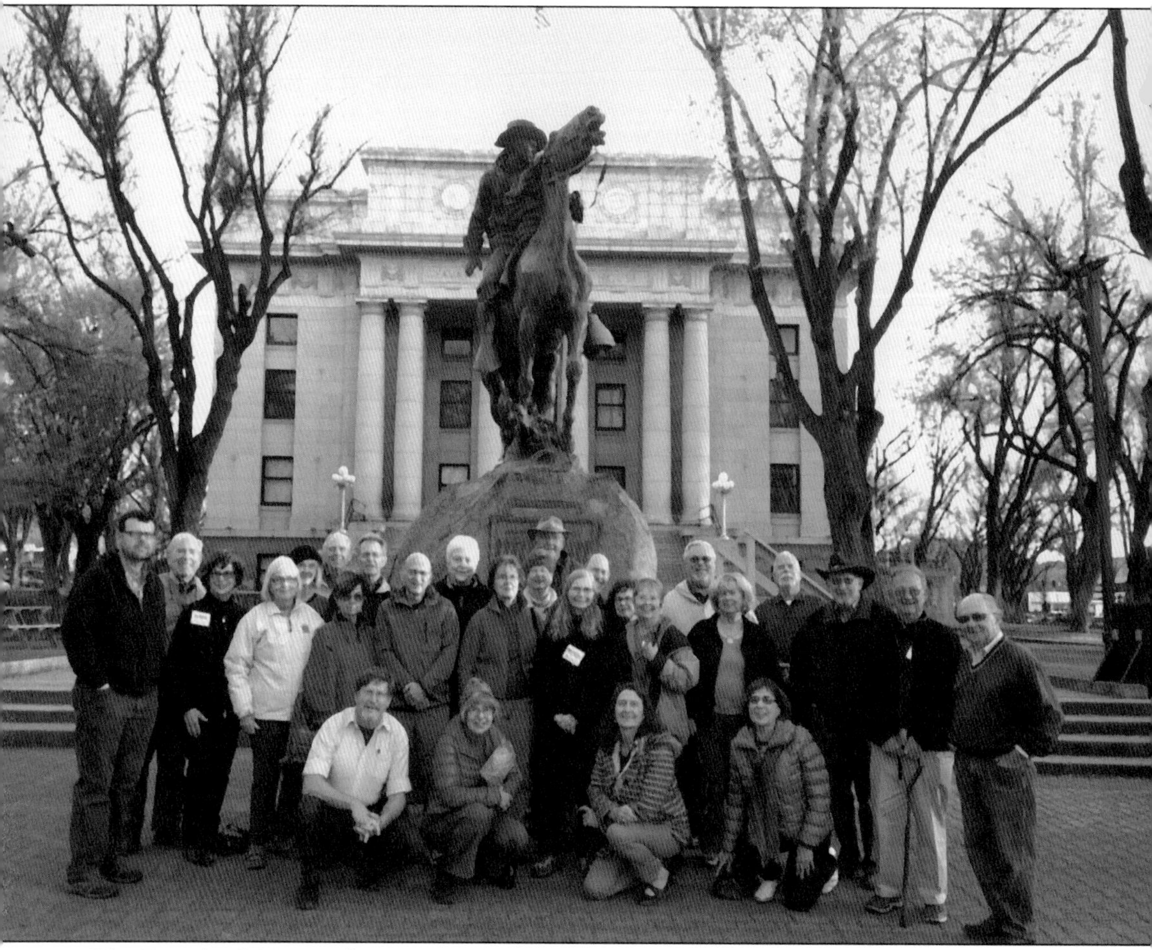

The Friends of ASM Collections are dedicated to strengthening and promoting the world-class ethnological collections of ASM. The brainchild of ASM curator Diane Dittemore, the group was formed in 2005 and raises funds to enable ASM to purchase important pieces of Native American art that are otherwise beyond the museum's resources. Benefits of membership include special receptions, lectures, and travel tours, usually orchestrated by ASM director of Marketing Darlene Lizarraga. Friends' tours typically include museums, galleries, and destinations related to Southwestern art. A three-day "Prescott Adventure" in April 2014 included visits to three museums and a bronze art foundry, lodging in a historic hotel in Prescott, and visits with Hopi artists Al Qöyawayma and Gerry Quotskuyva in their studios. Here, the Friends pose under a statue of "Rough Rider" Buckey O'Neill in the Prescott city square. Pictured, from left to right, are (kneeling) Alan Ferg (ASM curator), Jen Tellman, Diane Dittemore (ASM curator), and Paddy Schwartz; (standing) Patrick Lyons (ASM director), Stuart Beckerman, Susan Beckerman, Susan Smith, Maribeth Morehart, Don Morehart, Pat Hemann, Phil Davis, Larry Gravitz, Ina Gravitz, Nancy Kellett, Linda Van Straaten, Jack Van Straaten, Marilyn Marshall, Bernie Alper, Candace Alper, Jan Pipes, Tom Moulton, Sally Quinby, Matt Jenton (coach driver), Ed Schwartz, John Hemann, and John Danloe. Not pictured are Doreen Burbank, Patricia Danloe, and Darlene Lizarraga. (Photograph by and courtesy of Darlene Lizarraga.)

Nine

Museum Staff

Given that the Arizona State Museum is more than 120 years old, it is clearly impossible to give a full accounting here of the hundreds of employees who have left their mark on this institution. The museum began in 1893 with one employee, curator Herbert Brown, and has expanded to over 60 permanent employees in eight different programs and divisions: administration, business services, collections, development and marketing, operations, preservation, public programs, and research. As impressive as that may sound, decades of annual reports written by every ASM director make clear that the museum has been, and continues to be, chronically in need of more staff if it is to fulfill its legally mandated responsibilities and the preservation and educational goals in its mission statement. Fortunately, ASM has a large, and growing, number of "support groups," who, although not exactly staff (they donate their time), make it possible for ASM to maintain a significantly higher level of public service, collections care, and research than would be possible without them. These include student interns, ASM members, docents, and volunteers from all walks of life—including former employees (which speaks well of the museum). The Friends of ASM Collections are noted in chapter 8 as ASM partners, but the group fits equally well here. In addition, in 2013, director Patrick Lyons established a new ASM Director's Council to assist in fundraising and advocating for the museum's goals.

Although it may sound clichéd, the other silver lining to current conditions is the staff the museum has. ASM staff are historically collegial, intelligent, considerate, and dedicated, which makes for an interesting and enjoyable workplace, as well as long-term, productive working relationships with colleagues in other museums, agencies, and tribes. In recent years, quite a few ASM employees have passed the 30-year mark, but the record as of 2014, with 42 years and counting, is held by curator of Archaeological Collections Mike Jacobs.

The following pages note all of the individuals who have led ASM through the years, and then present a smattering of photographs of faculty and staff. Apologies to all who could not be fit in, and those for whom no photographs could be found.

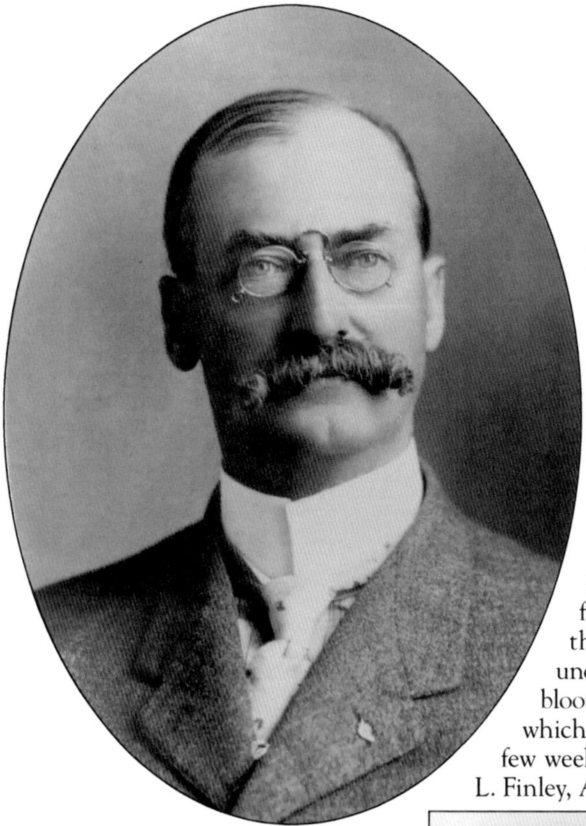

Herbert Brown (born 1848, died 1913) was the museum's first employee and first curator, from 1893 to 1912, at which time he resigned because of illness. Of his many occupations, including newspaperman, peace commissioner, prison warden, and UA regent, Brown may well have enjoyed ornithology more than any of his other pursuits. Here, near Tucson, he was investigating an elf owl nest in a hole, or "boot," near the top of a saguaro cactus that is over 20 feet tall. Photographed on June 13, 1910, the tops of the saguaro arms bear a few unopened flower buds, but almost all have bloomed. Bats pollinated some of the flowers, which have set fruit and will burst open in a few weeks. (Left, AHST 11425; below, William L. Finley, ASM.)

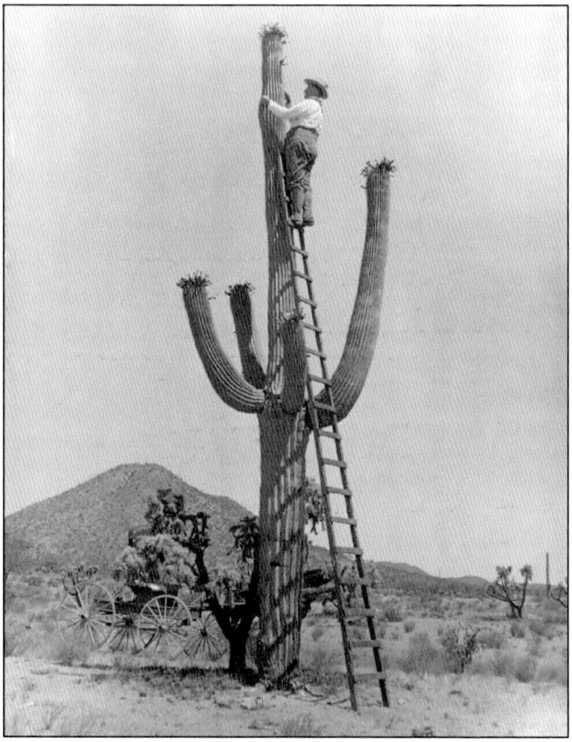

John James Thornber (born 1872, died 1962) had a distinguished career in the UA College of Agriculture (1901–1928). His role in the history of ASM was that of a temporary caretaker. Thornber's wife, Harriet, was, with Herbert Brown, a founder of the Arizona Audubon Society, and Thornber doubtless knew Brown. After Brown resigned from ASM in 1912, the museum's collections were boxed and placed under Thornber's care from 1912 to 1915 (see pages 17 and 18). (UASC N-9949.)

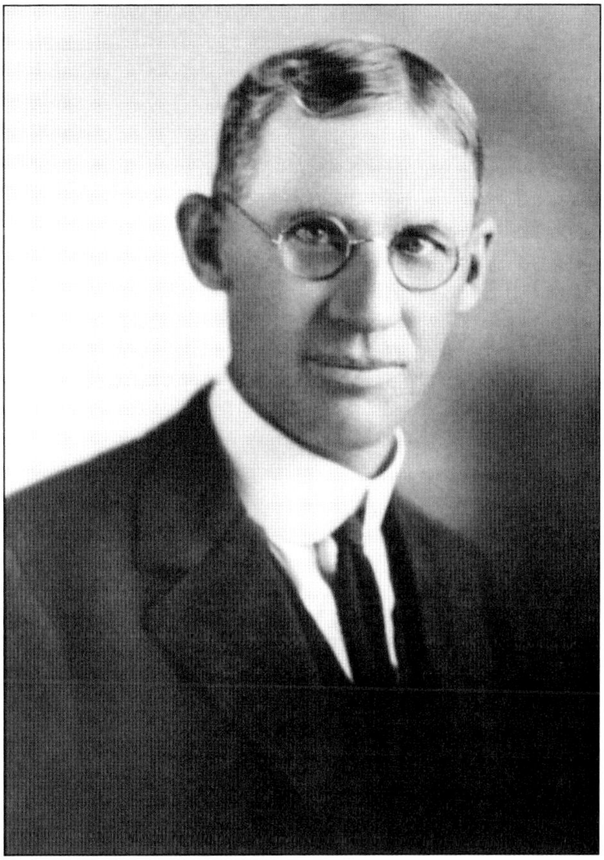

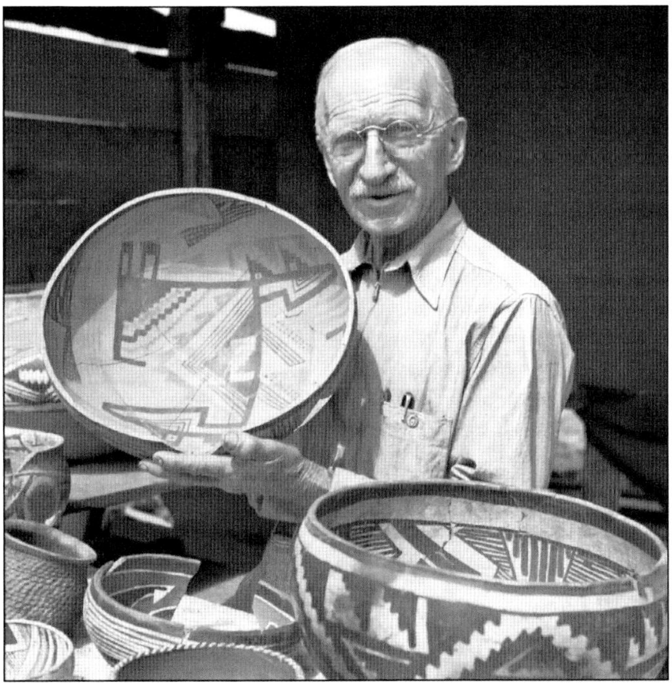

Byron Cummings (born 1860, died 1954) was ASM's first director, from 1915 to 1938. He began his career at the University of Utah in 1893, teaching Latin, Greek, and English, but he became interested in archaeology. In 1915, Cummings was hired at UA as both the head of the Department of Archaeology and the director of the Arizona State Museum. He was forced to retire from them in 1937 and 1938, respectively, but remained director emeritus until his death in 1954. Here, in July 1939, he displays some of the pottery found at the site of Kinishba (see page 74). (Tad Nichols, ASM.)

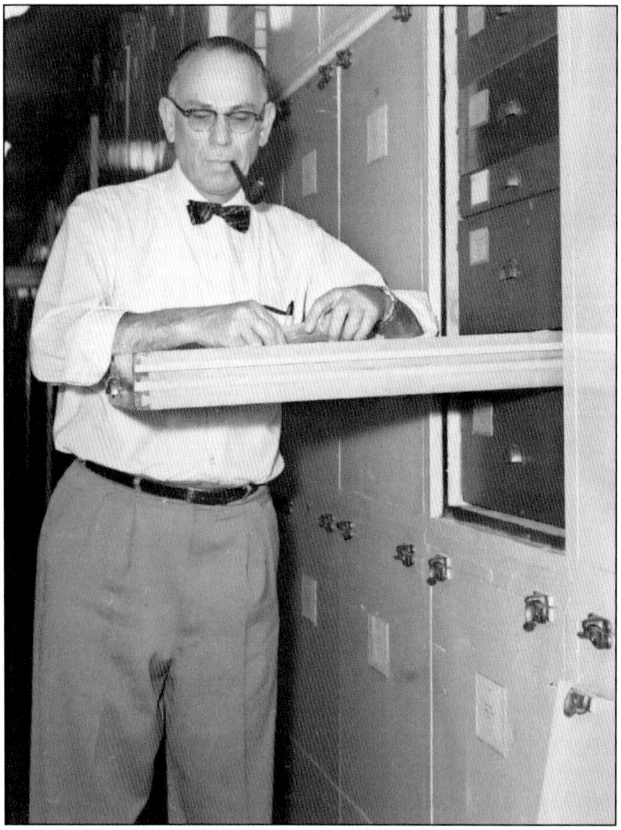

Dr. Emil W. Haury (born 1904, died 1992) had a career that was intertwined with UA from the day he met Byron Cummings in 1924. First a student of Cummings, Haury then worked for Harold Gladwin at the Gila Pueblo Archaeological Foundation (1930–1937), only to have Cummings invite Haury to be his successor. Haury was head of the UA Department of Anthropology from 1937 to 1964 and ASM director from 1938 to 1964. Read Thompson's 1995 article in *American Antiquity* (see page 127) for a synopsis of Haury's career. Haury is seen here at the Smithsonian Institution on March 14, 1958. (ASM.)

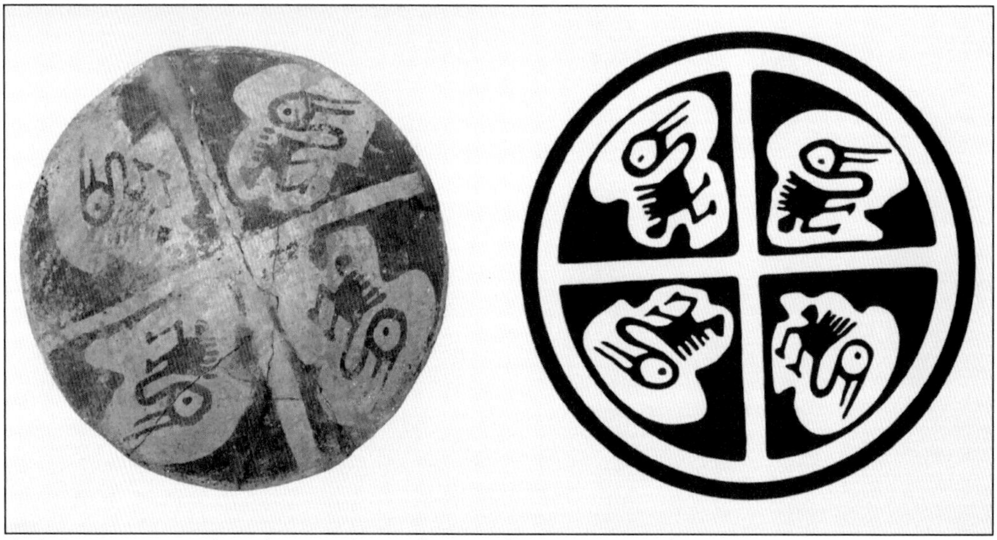

At left is a pottery plate decorated in red paint, dating to around AD 800–900. The diameter is five and five-eighths inches. At right is the logotype of the Arizona State Museum from 1940 to 2003. This plate was excavated from a human cremation during the 1934–1935 Gila Pueblo dig at the site of Snaketown. Haury worked on that dig, and it was doubtless he who decided that ASM should have a logo and selected this distinctly Hohokam design of four long-necked water birds. (L.F.H. Lowe, ASM 3823.)

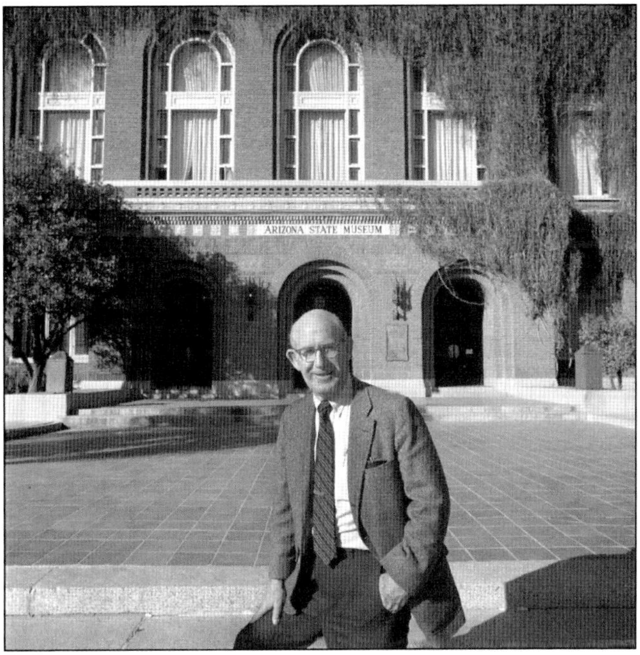

Dr. Raymond H. Thompson was ASM's longest-serving director, from 1964 to 1998. He began his archaeological career as an undergraduate at the Point of Pines Field School in 1947. Hired by the UA Department of Anthropology as a professor in 1956, in 1964, he, like Cummings and Haury before him, became both head of the Department of Anthropology and director of ASM. In 1980, he turned over Anthropology to a successor. Read Thompson's 2005 article in the *Journal of the Southwest* (see page 127) for a synopsis of his career. He is currently director emeritus and Fred A. Riecker Professor Emeritus. (H. Teiwes, ASM 57090.)

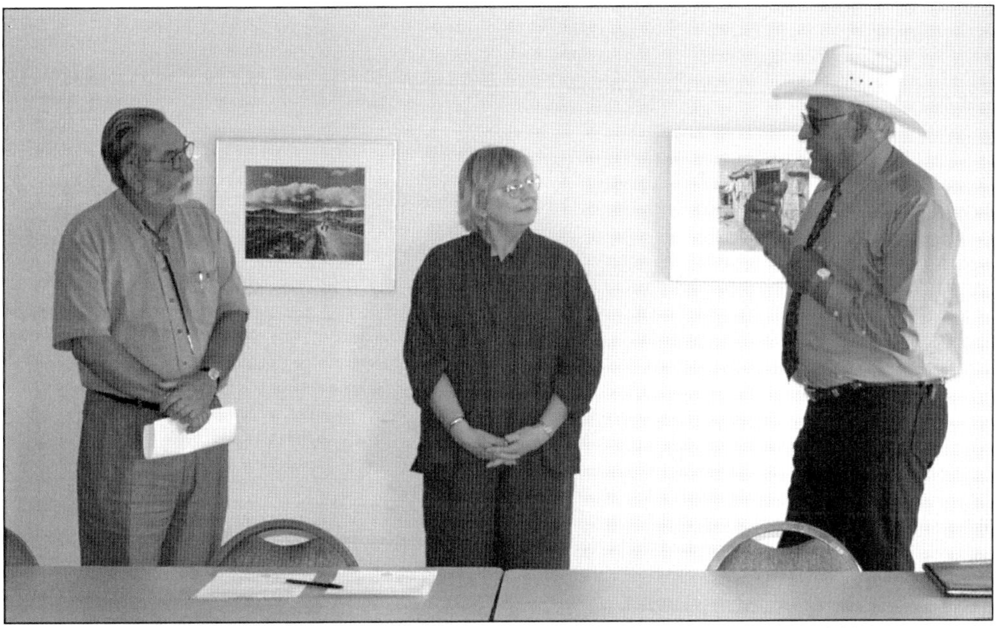

Dr. George J. Gumerman, ASM director from 1998 to 2002 (left); Lynn S. Teague, ASM repatriation coordinator from 1990 to 2002 (center); and Gila River Indian Community governor Donald R. Antone Sr. They are meeting in Room 309 of ASM North on May 18, 2001. They were signing a receipt for the first transfer of Snaketown artifacts (see page 62) from ASM to the community, repatriated under the 1990 Native American Graves Protection and Repatriation Act (NAGPRA). (Geoffrey Ashley, ASM 2003-120-6.)

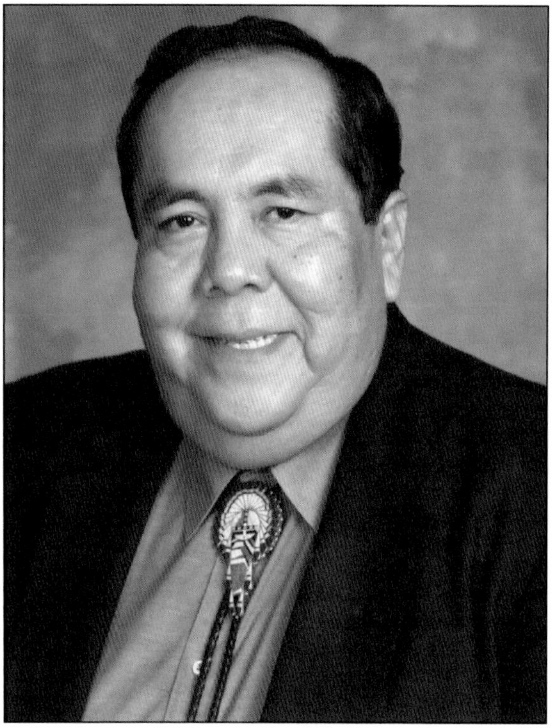

Hartman H. Lomawaima (born 1949, died 2008) was ASM director from 2002 to 2008. He was a Hopi and a member of the Honngyam (Bear Clan), born in Sipaulovi, on Second Mesa, on the Hopi Indian Reservation. Lomawaima was hired at ASM in 1994 as associate director, was also a professor in the UA American Indian Studies Department, and served on the board of trustees of the National Museum of the American Indian. He secured significant funding to complete the pottery vault (see page 36) and to rebuild the ASM North front entrance (see page 32). (J. Weakly, ASM.)

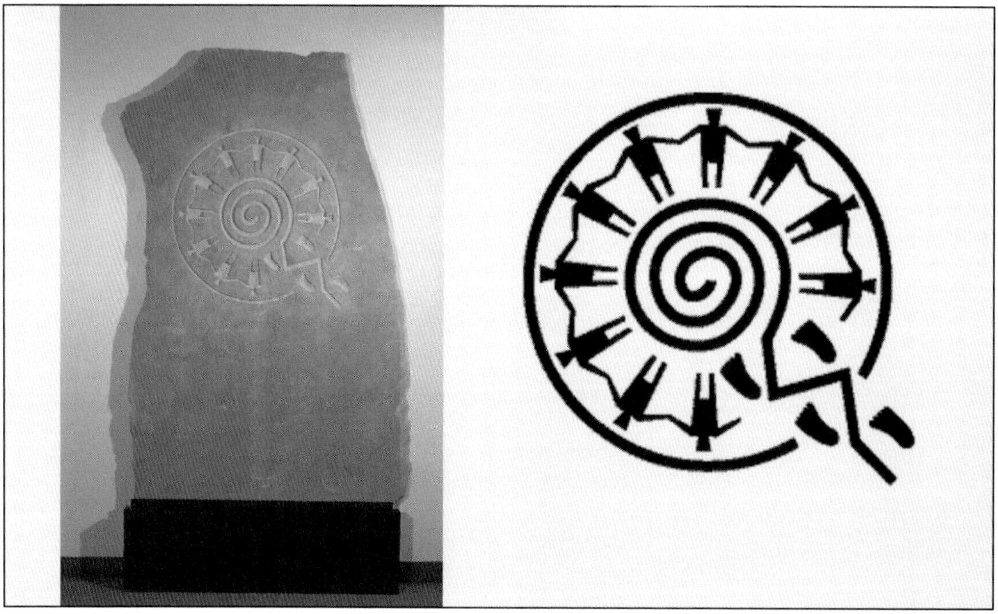

The six-foot-tall sandstone slab with a modern petroglyph seen on the left was created in 1993 by Hopi artist Gerald Dawavendewa as the *Paths of Life* exhibit logo. The footprints and spiral represent a migration of first peoples into the Southwest, and the 10 figures represent the 10 tribes featured in the exhibit and their joined lives. On the right is the logotype of ASM from 2003 to the present. The plate on which ASM's first logo was based was repatriated in 2001 (see page 115). ASM respectfully retired the old logo and adopted Dawavendewa's design as a more appropriate logo. (ASM C-29259.)

Dr. Beth Grindell was ASM director from 2008 to 2013. Her connection to ASM began as a student employee at the CAP Repository (1987–1989) (see page 105). As an assistant, and then as head of the Archaeological Records Office (1992–2003), Grindell brought ASM's site files into the computer age. As associate director (2004–2008), she coordinated ASM's involvement in the City of Tucson Rio Nuevo Project, and, as director, she oversaw planning for the perishables vault (see page 37). She is currently director emerita and a senior curator in the Archaeological Records Office. (J. Weakly, ASM.)

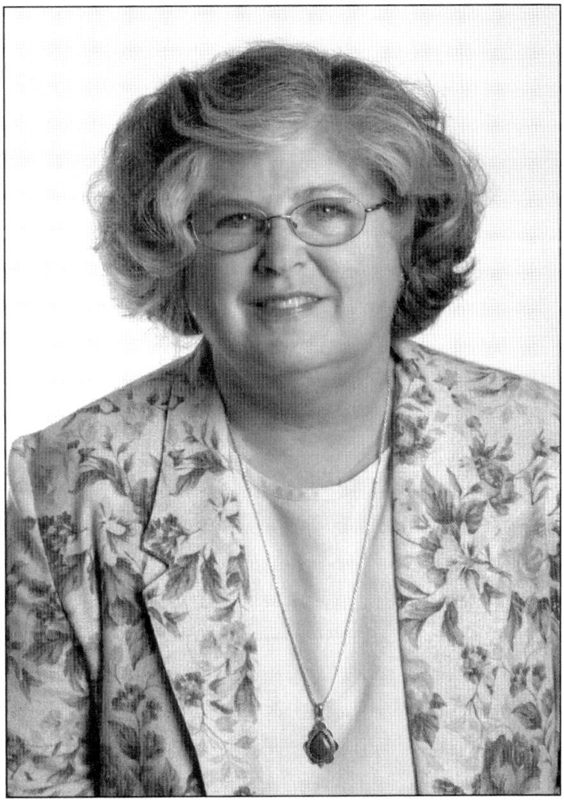

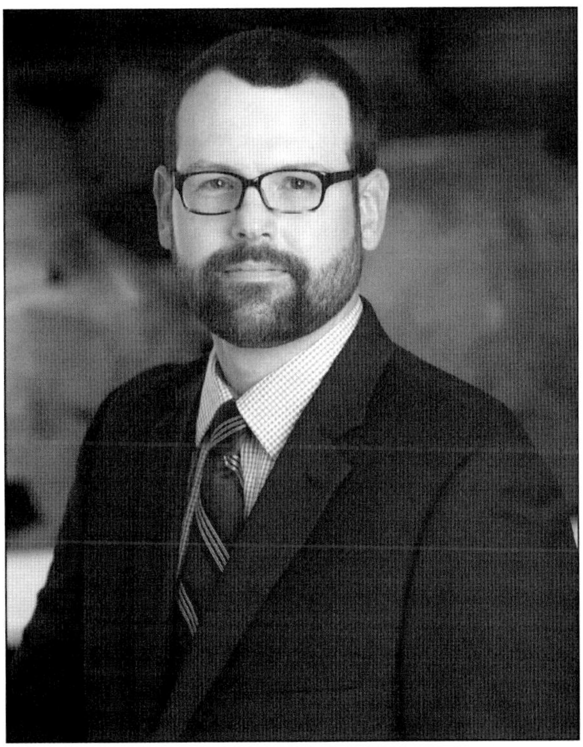

Dr. Patrick D. Lyons is the current director of ASM, as of June 1, 2013. His connection to ASM began with his 2001 dissertation based in the Homol'ovi Research Program (see page 68). Lyons was hired as ASM's head of collections (2006–2013) and additionally served as associate director starting in 2009. His goals involve fully administering Arizona's antiquities laws, fulfilling repatriation responsibilities, and solidifying ASM's financial foundation. His current research focuses on Ancestral Pueblo materials excavated by previous ASM directors at UA field schools (see pages 74, 76, and 77). (J. Weakly, ASM.)

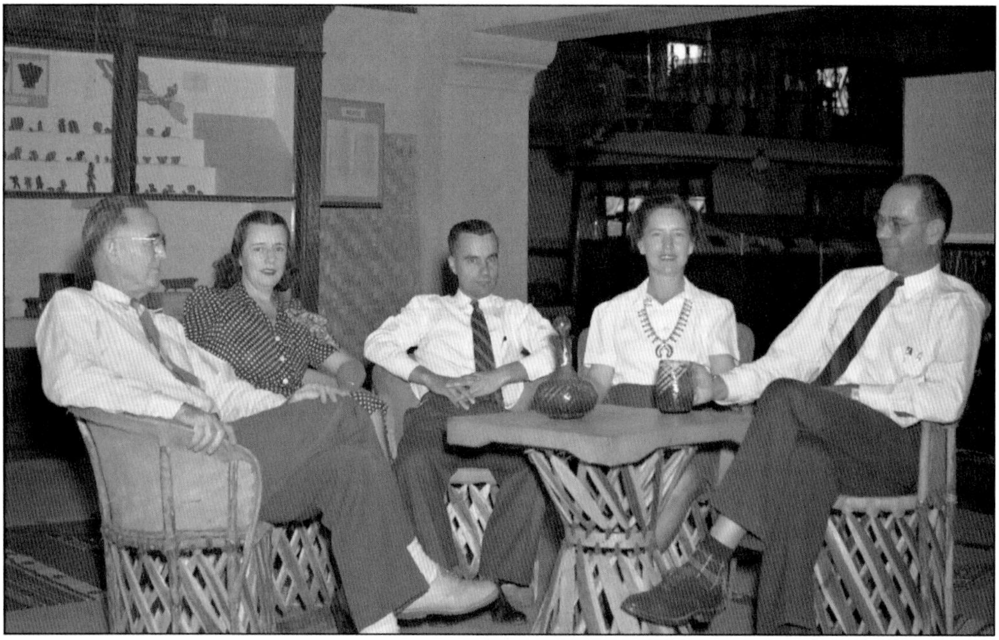

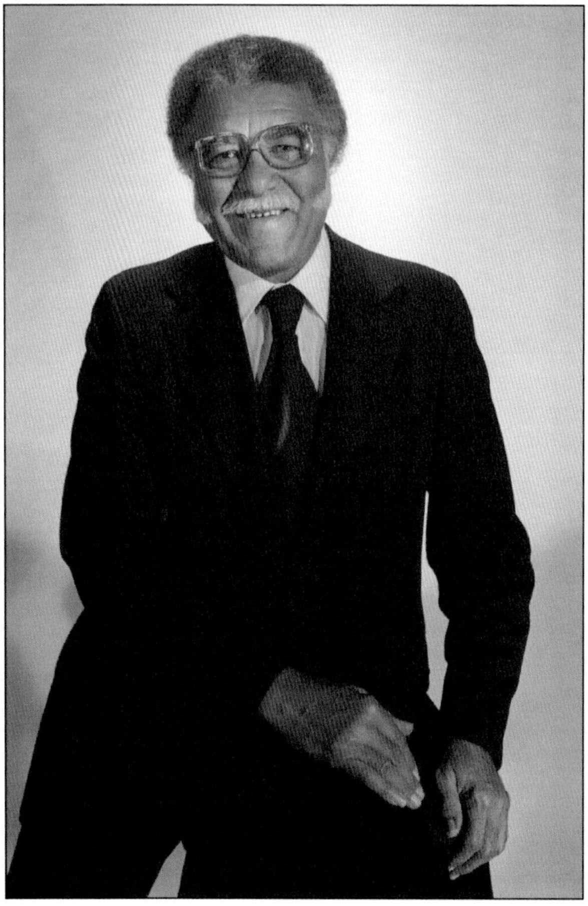

The staff of ASM and the Department of Anthropology in 1943–1944 sits in the southeast alcove of ASM's main exhibit floor. From left to right are E.B. Sayles (museum curator), Frances T. Slutes (secretary of both units), Harry T. Getty (Anthropology faculty), Clara Lee Tanner (Anthropology faculty), and Emil W. Haury (ASM director and head of Anthropology). Not present are museum assistant Carleton Wilder and faculty member Norman Gabel, who were both away on military duty in World War II. (ASM 7714.)

From 1952 to March 22, 1982, during the years of ASM's greatest expansion, Matthew "Matt" Cox was the museum's janitor in the original 1935 South Building. His job title reflected only a fraction of his contributions in being an omnipresent greeter and security presence, as well as an ever-ready assistant in the construction of exhibits. At the time of his retirement, in 1982, Cox was one of ASM's longest-serving employees. (H. Teiwes, ASM.)

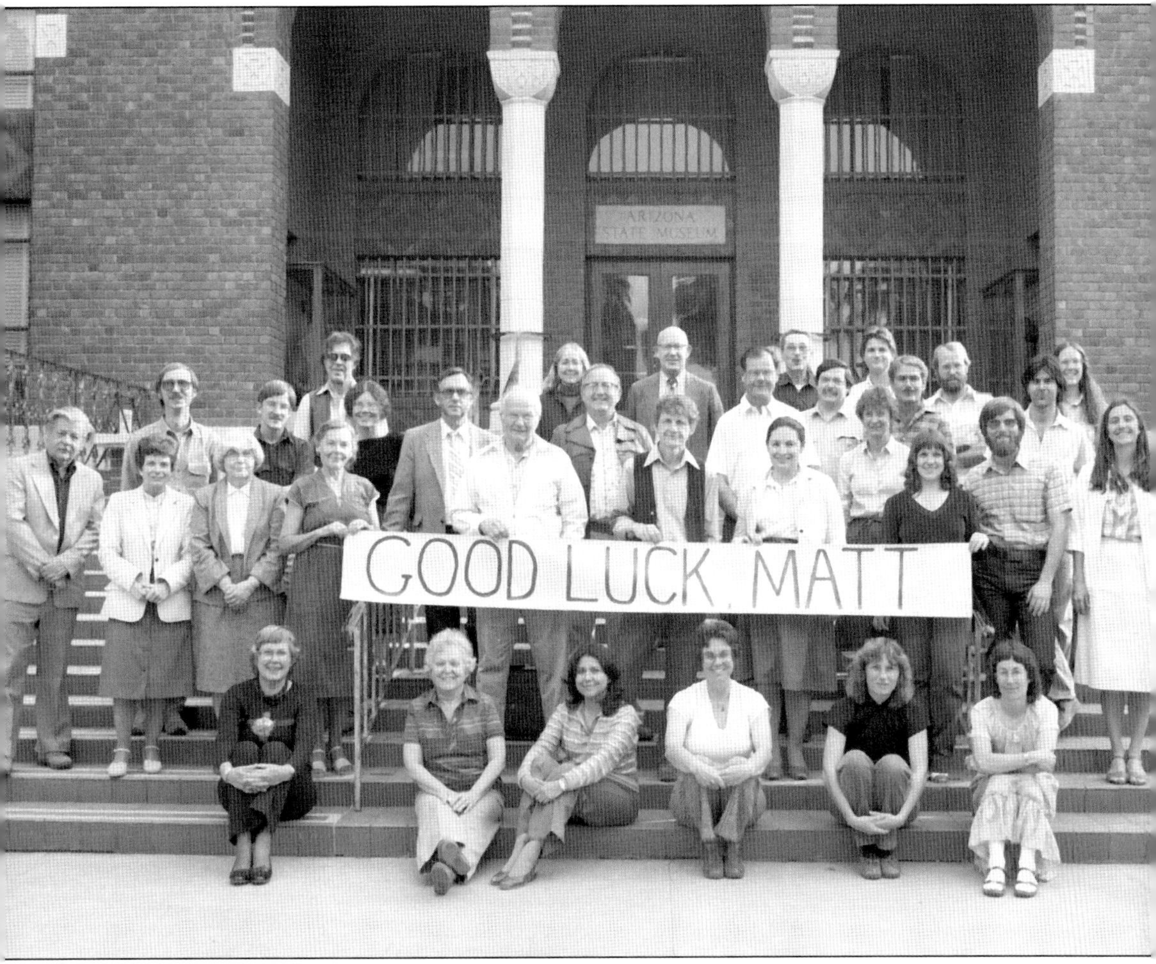

In March 1982, when janitor Matt Cox was retiring, a crowd of his friends from ASM and the Department of Anthropology posed for this photograph for him, taken on the steps of ASM South, the building he had worked in for 30 years. Pictured, from left to right, are (first row) Helga Teiwes (photographer), Harriet B. Martin (Anthropology secretary), Barbara Fregoso (Anthropology secretary), Sharon F. Urban (archaeologist), unidentified, and Ellen Horn (head of Photograph Collections); (second row) Hans Bart (librarian), Barbara Moore (conservator), Dorothy Caranchini (Anthropology secretary), Madeleine T. Rodack (OER), Ed Ferdon (ethnologist), R. Gwinn Vivian (associate director), Carmen Prezelski (Anthropology secretary), unidentified, Jon Czaplicki (archaeologist), and Diane Dittemore (Ethnological Collections curator); (third row) Richard V.N. Ahlstrom (archaeologist), David J. Eagan (Photograph Collections assistant), Donna McClure (Photograph Collections assistant), George Sample (administrative assistant), Rev. Charles W. Polzer (OER), Alexander J. Lindsay Jr. (research associate), and Jan Bell (head of Collections); (fourth row) Robert G. Baker (chief curator), Mike Jacobs (Archaeological Collections curator), Thomas H. Naylor (OER), and Stuart "Skip" Meehan (Exhibits assistant); (fifth row) Dawn Cromwell (store manager), Raymond H. Thompson (director), Walter Birkby (curator of Physical Anthropology), Thomas M. Kolaz (Ethnological Collections assistant curator), Steve Rogers (registrar), and Karen Lominac (head of Computing Services). (H. Teiwes, ASM 58148.)

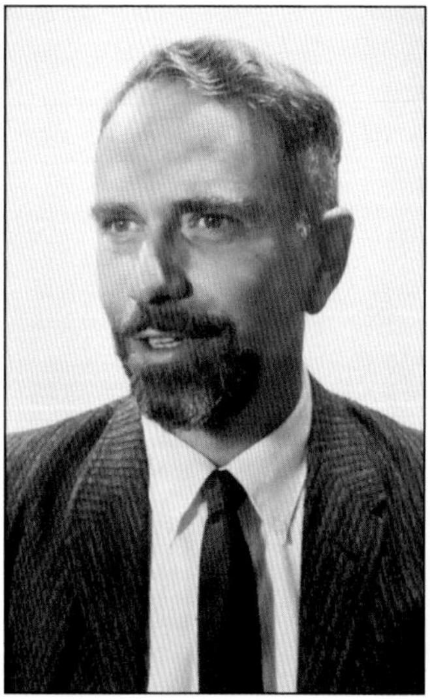 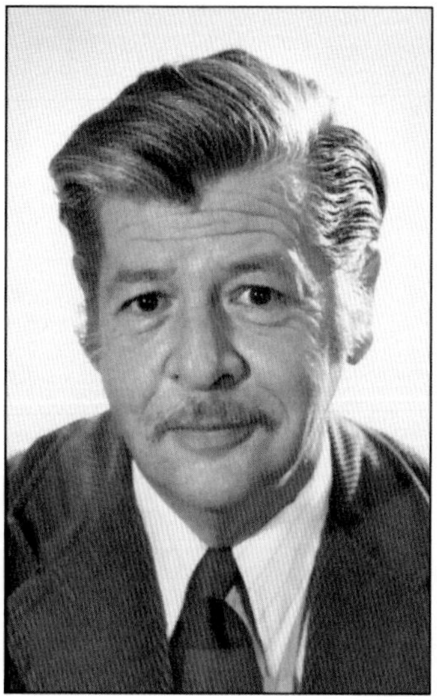 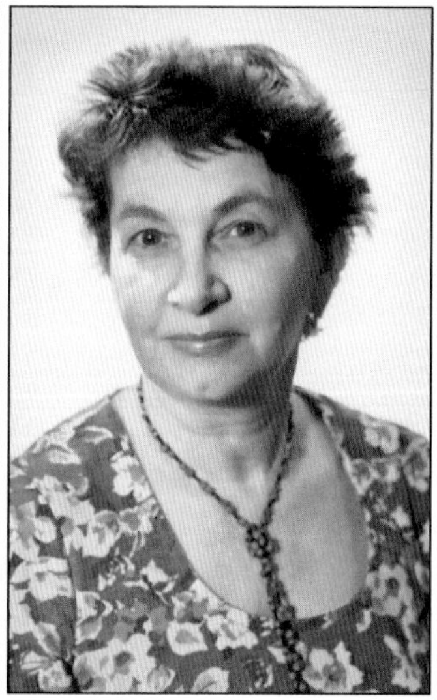

John V. Baroco (left) was head librarian from 1964 to 1974 and helped formalize the ASM Archives. Hans Bart (center) was head librarian from 1974 to 1987 and, with assistant librarian Daphne Scott (right, 1969–1987), moved the ASM Library from the Anthropology Building (see page 29) to ASM North (see page 33) in 1977. As the omniscient reference librarian, before the advent of Google, Scott was the most important ASM employee to UA anthropology students. (All, H. Teiwes; left, ASM 14918; center, 43324; right, 43332.)

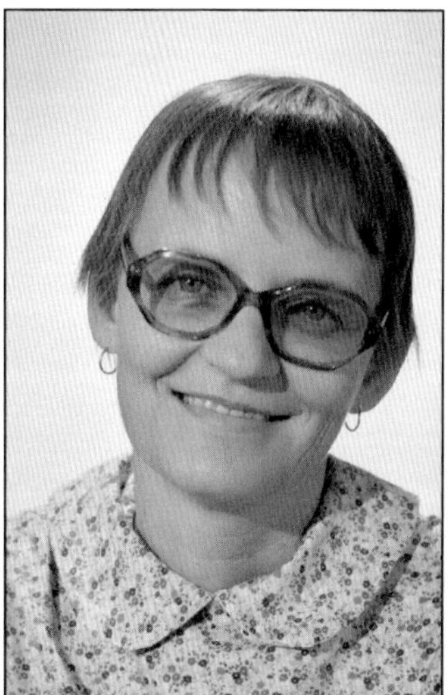 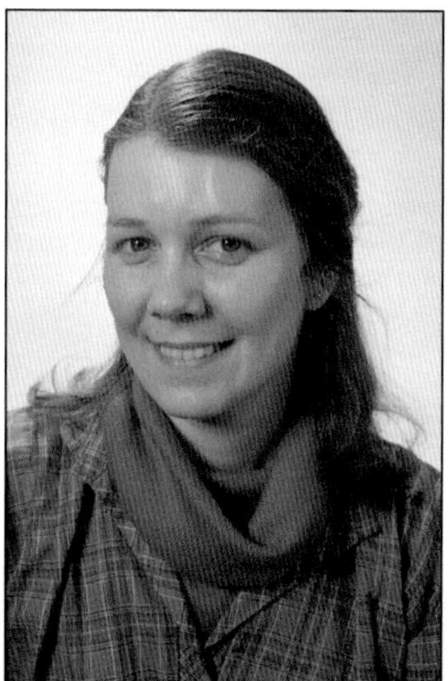 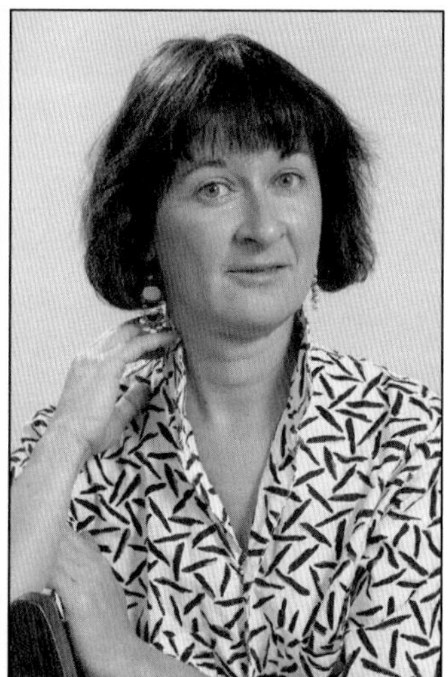

Judy D. Reis (left) helped index the archives as a student and continued that work as part of her duties as an assistant librarian (1977–1984). Madelyn Cook (center) began at ASM as a work-study student and retired as a full librarian (1978–1986, 1989–1990, and 1992–2000), working primarily as a cataloger. Jeanne Armstrong (right) was the first formal ASM archivist (1984–1992), overseeing the rising tide of reports and documentation that came to ASM as part of its permitting of contract archaeology projects. (All, H. Teiwes; left, ASM 58105; center, ASM 58084; right, ASM 67974.)

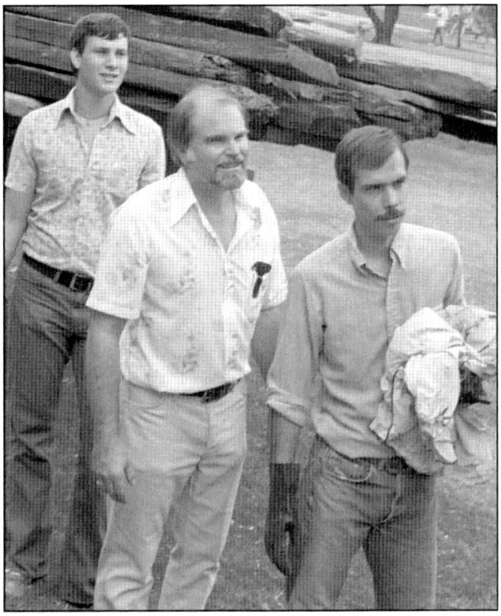

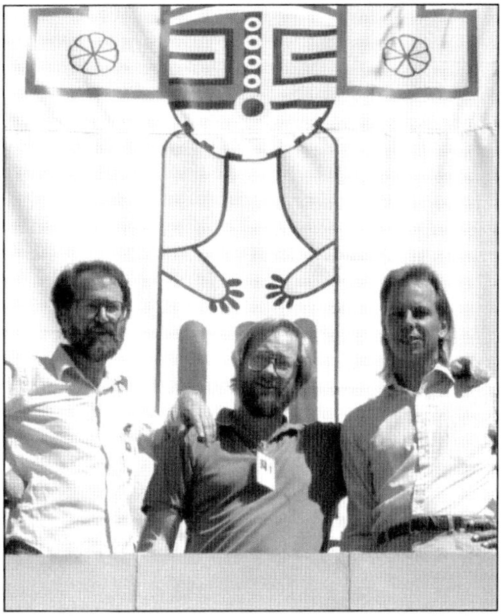

At left, from left to right, an unidentified person, Exhibits head Ernie Leavitt (1958–1987), and Exhibits assistant Arthur G. "Art" Brownlee (1974–1979) unload the Tarahumara log structures in September 1978 on the north lawn of ASM North (see pages 50 and 88). At right, from left to right, Russell Varineau (Exhibits, 1987–2003), Rhod Lauffer (Exhibits assistant, 1987–2010), and Bruce Hilpert (Exhibits and Public Programs, 1985–2003) stand on the front balcony of ASM North, having just hung the banner for the *Hopi Spirits: Contemporary Kachina Doll Carving* exhibit in September 1989. (Both, H. Teiwes; left, ASM 47745; right, ASM 83694.)

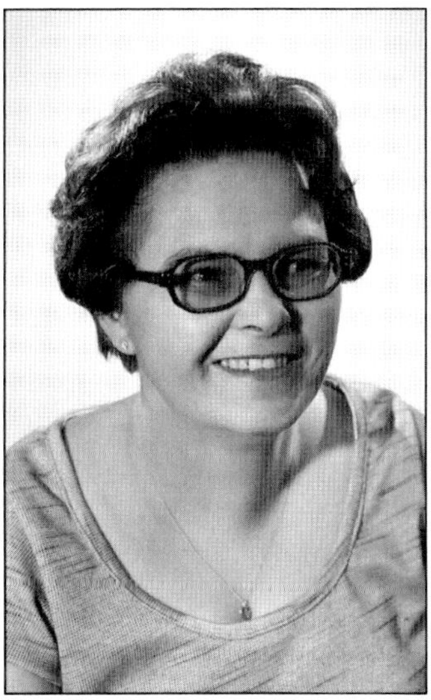

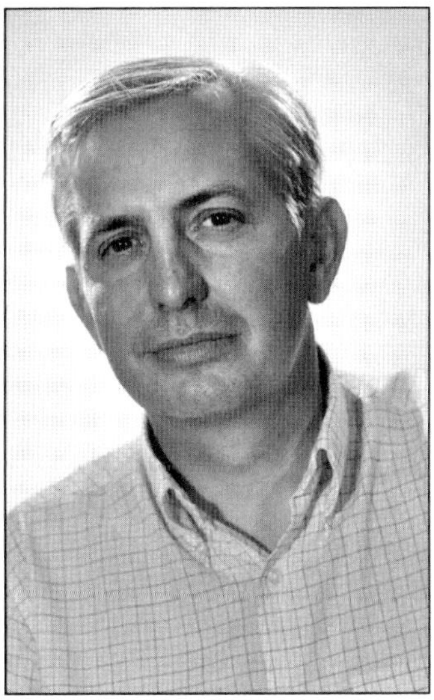

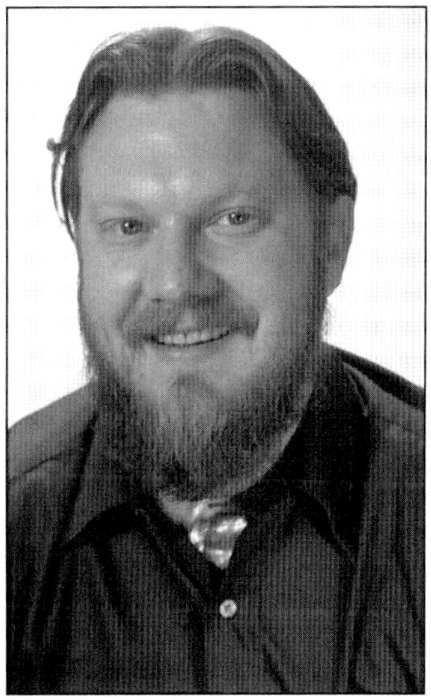

From left to right are Dola Moore, head bookkeeper from 1973 to 2000; Laurens C. Hammack, assistant Highway Salvage archaeologist and then Highway Salvage archaeologist from 1967 to 1979; and David A. Gregory, archaeologist in CRMS/CRMD from 1975 to 1977 and 1979 to 1986. (All, H. Teiwes; left, ASM 43341; center, ASM 43344; right, ASM 58092.)

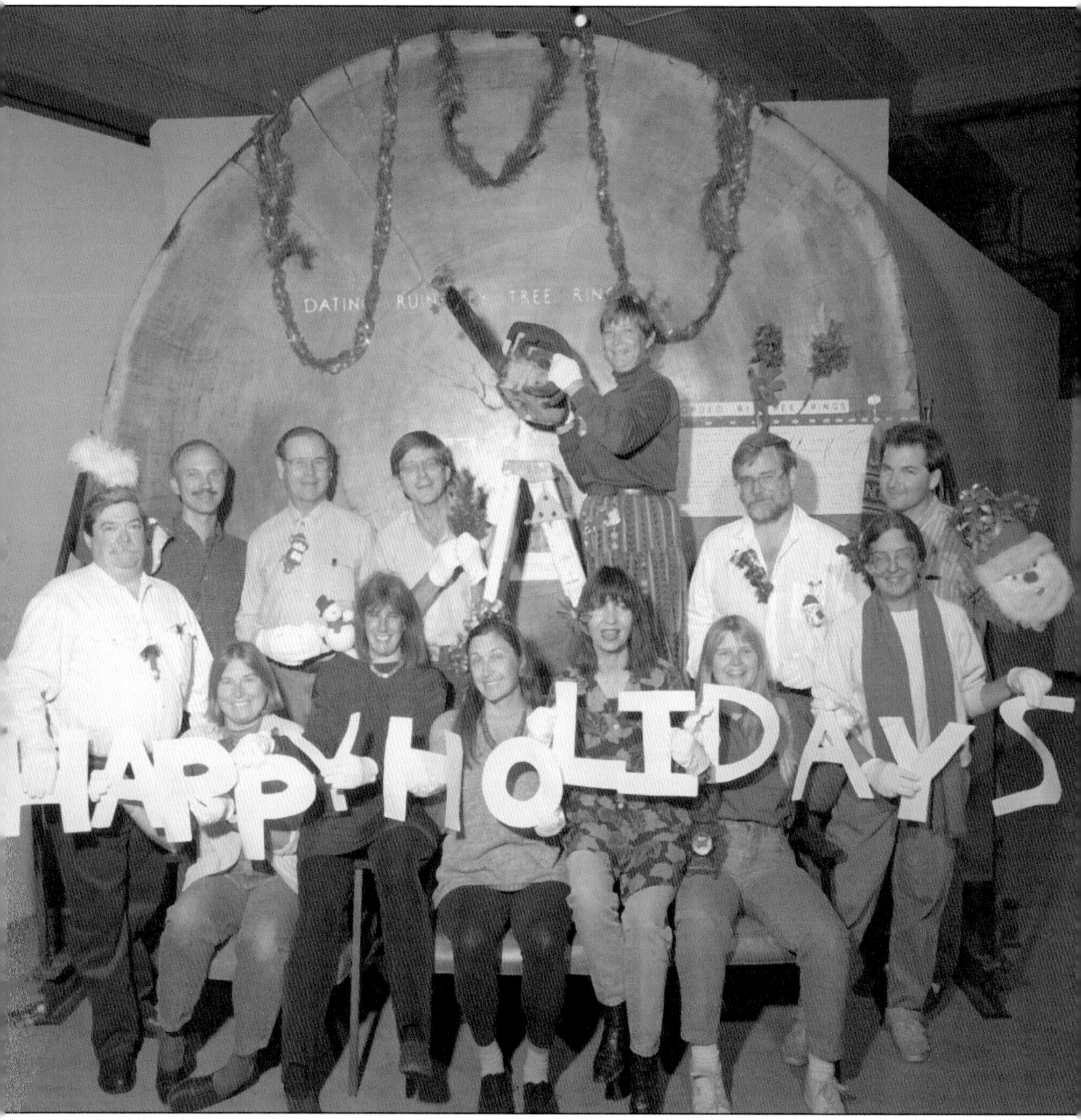

In the early 1990s, head of Collections Jan Bell made holiday cards (a photograph photocopied on color paper) for Collections Division employees to send to colleagues before winter break. The theme of this December 1993 card may have been the cutting of a Yule log, with a cameo by the sequoia section in ASM South (see page 21). Pictured, from left to right, are (first row) Nancy Odegaard (conservator), Claudine Scoville (registrar), Diane Dittemore (Ethnological Collections curator), Lisa Zimmerman (Archaeological Collections assistant curator), and Kimberly A. Swope (student employee); (second row) Mike Jacobs (Archaeological Collections curator), Ken Matesich (photographer), Alexander J. Lindsay Jr. (research associate), Alan Ferg (head of CAP Repository), Jan Bell (head of Collections), Arthur Vokes (Archaeological Repository Collections curator), Kathy Hubenschmidt (head of Photograph Collections), and Tom Kolaz (Ethnological Collections assistant curator). Note that everyone is wearing white cotton gloves, per proper curatorial procedure. (Susan Luebbermann, ASM 89434.)

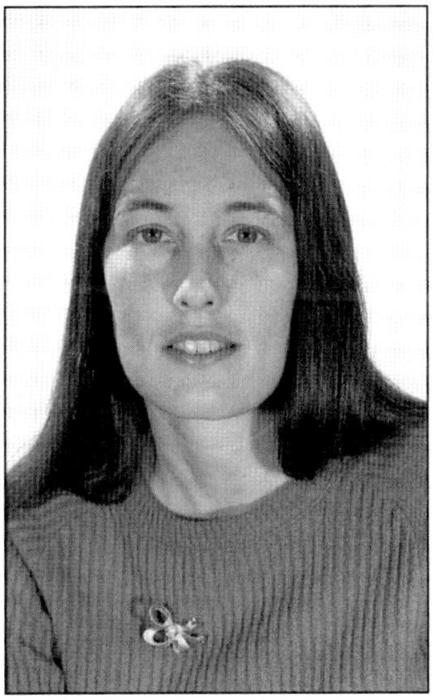
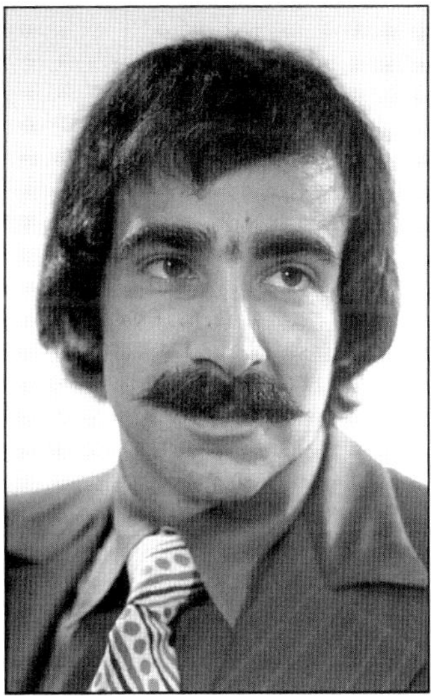
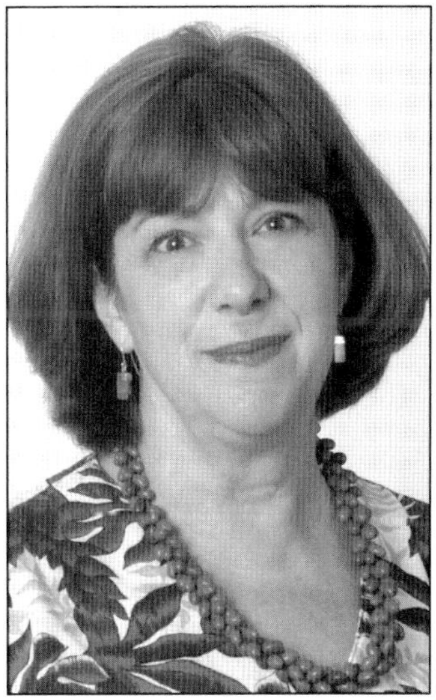

Pictured, from left to right, are Holly Chaffee, curator of Collections from 1972 to 1978; Seth Schindler, assistant curator from 1976 to 1978 and then the first curator of Ethnological Collections (1978–1979); and Suzanne Griset, head of Collections from 1999 to 2006. (Left and center, H. Teiwes, ASM; right, J. Weakly, ASM.)

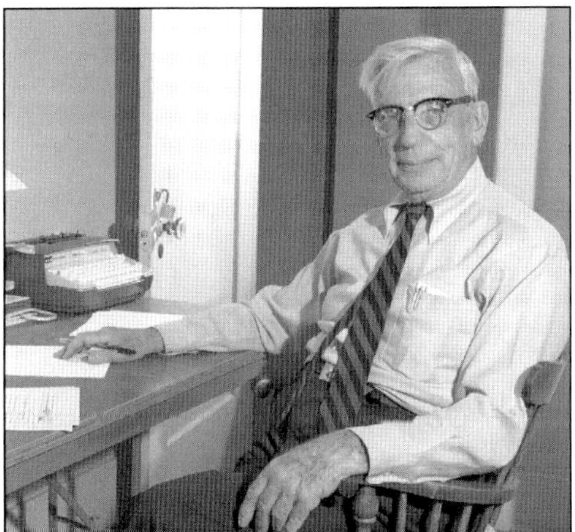
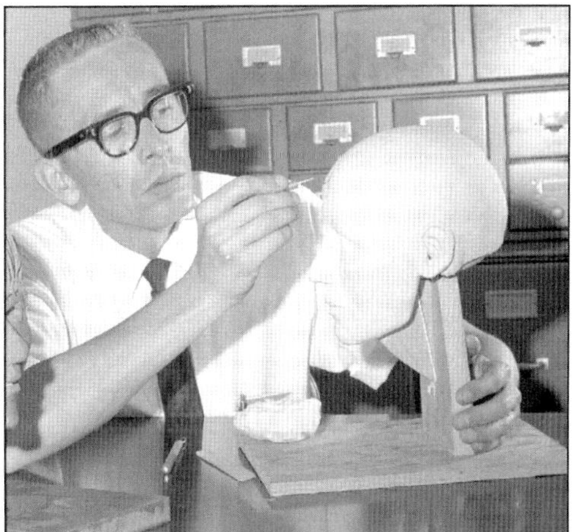

On the left is Watson Smith, a research associate from 1955 to 1978, working at his office at Casa Elizabeth Seton (see page 31) in February 1976. On the right is Walter H. Birkby, the ASM curator of Physical Anthropology from 1965 to 1996, modeling a clay facial reconstruction of a skull for a Tucson Police Department investigation in October 1968. After retiring from ASM, Birkby took his extraordinary research and teaching skills to the Pima County Office of the Medical Examiner, where he worked until 2009. (Both, H Teiwes; left, ASM 43302; right, ASM 25332.)

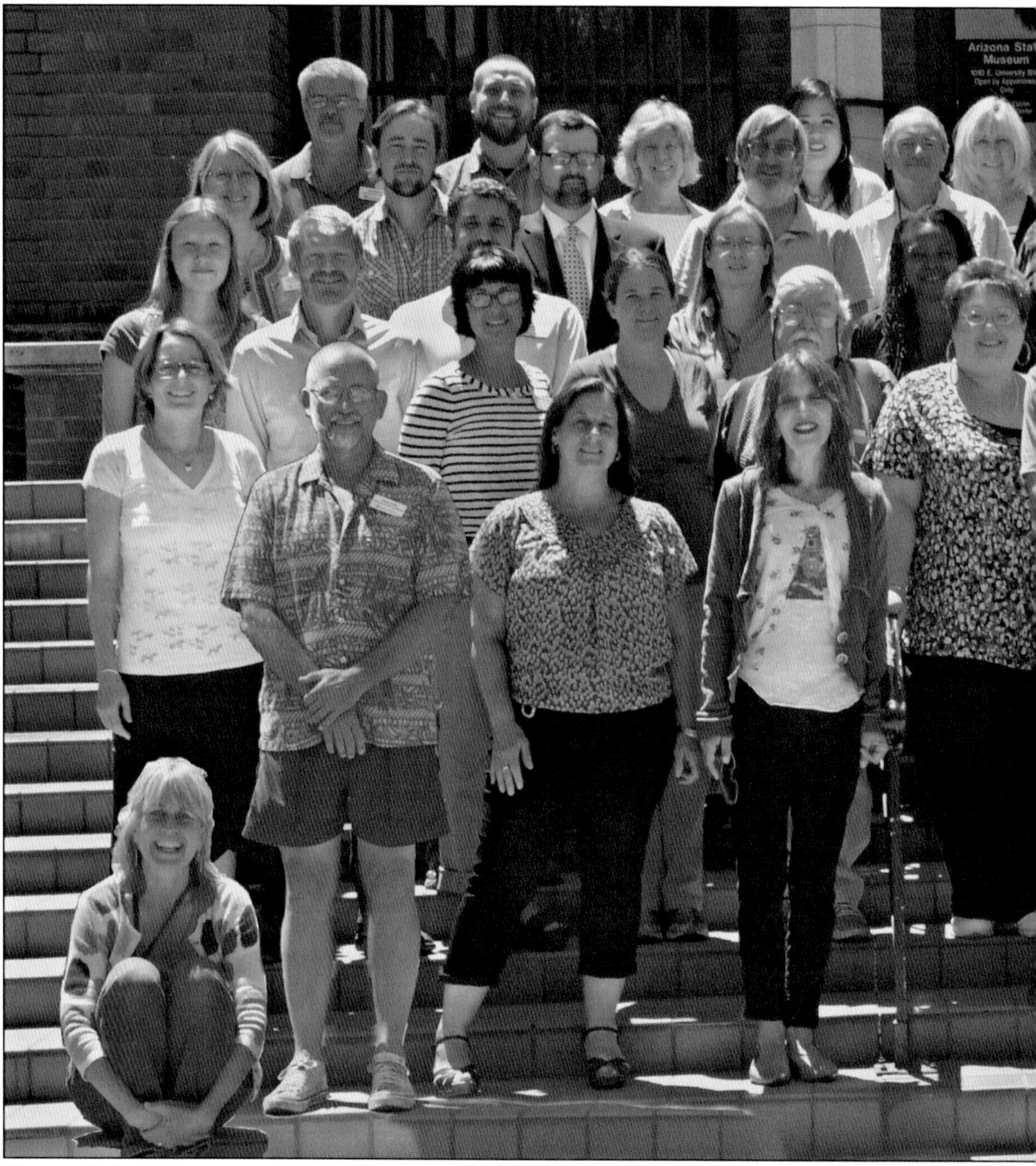

The staff of ASM poses in March 2013 on the steps of ASM South. Pictured, from left to right, are (first row) Jannelle Weakly (photographer and curator of Photographic Collections), Raphael Gill (Computing administrator), Diane Dittemore (curator of Ethnological Collections), and Dale Brenneman (Ethnohistory assistant curator); (second row) Rick Karl (AZSITE administrator), Lisa Falk (curator of Education), Lisa Zimmerman (registrar), E. Charles Adams (Archaeology curator), Beth Grindell (director), and Mary Graham (head of Library and Archives; (third row) Barnet Pavao-Zuckerman (Zooarchaeology curator), Teresa Moreno (associate conservator), Gina Watkinson (assistant conservator), Mike Jacobs (curator of Archaeological Collections), Kimberly Kepler (Business Services), Shannon Twilling (AZSITE) and daughter Sadie, Melanie Deer (Archaeological Repository), Michael M. Brescia (Ethnohistory curator), and Nancy Pearson (Archaeological Permits administrator); (fourth row) Christina Jenkins (AZSITE), Davison Koenig (curator of Exhibits), Keith Knoblock (head of Operations), Georgine Speranzo (administrative

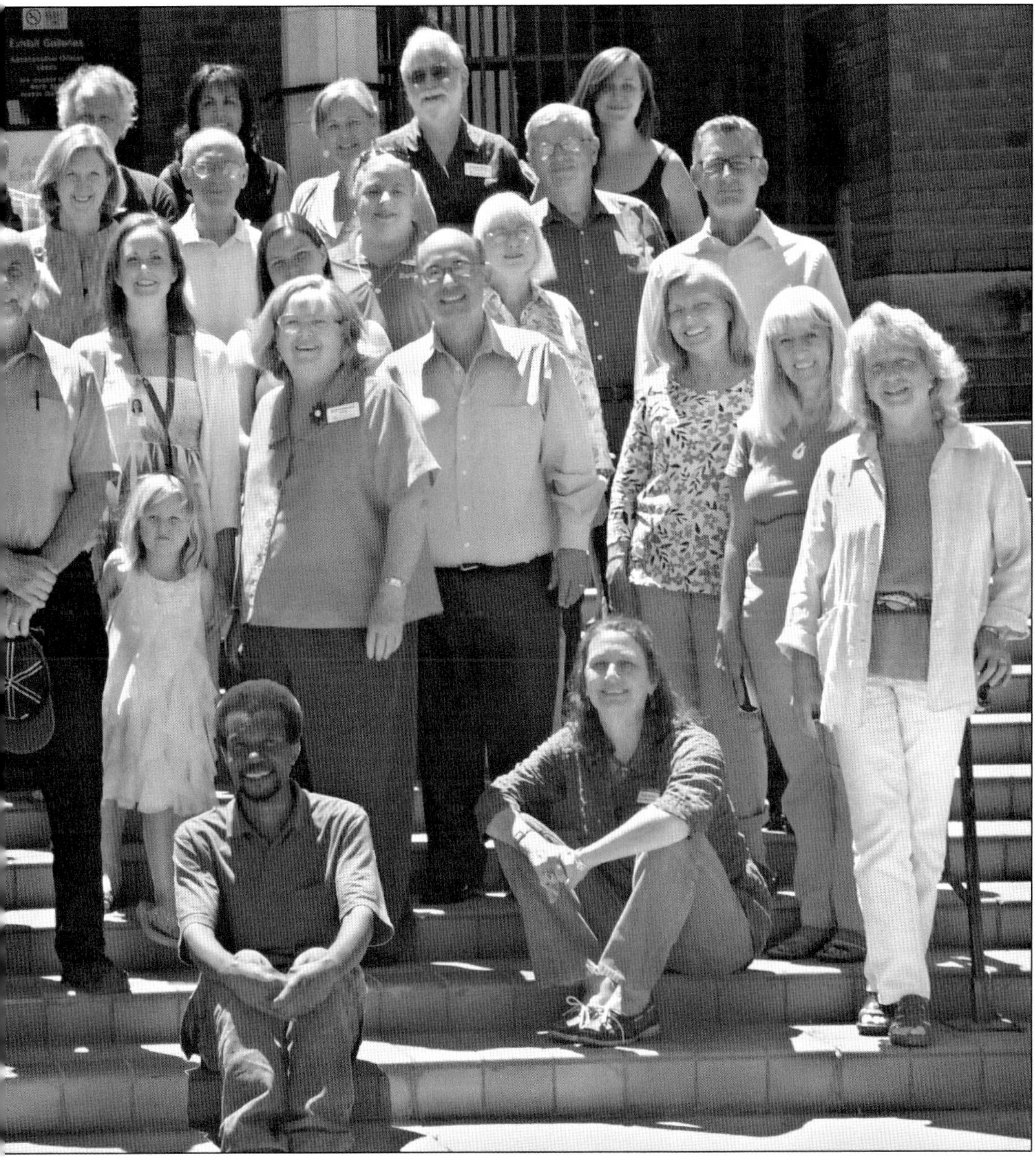

assistant), and Alegra Savage (Archives and Computing); (fifth row) Laura LePere (website administrator), Andrew Higgins (assistant curator of Ethnological Collections), Patrick Lyons (associate director), Richard Lange (archaeologist), John Madsen (archaeologist), Frank Finkenberg (website designer), Irene Bald Romano (deputy director), John McClelland (NAGPRA coordinator and Osteology Lab manager), Christina Rocha (Business Services), Suzanne Fish (Archaeology curator), Paul Fish (Archaeology curator), and Todd Pitezel (Antiquities Act and Repatriation administrator); (sixth row) Tim Price (store manager), Daniel Vander Ploeg (SWIAF coordinator), Marly Helm (associate librarian), Sandra B. Um (director of Development), Debbie Newman (assistant librarian), Jeff Bursey (Exhibits specialist), Darlene Lizarraga (director of Marketing), Beth DeWitt (Exhibits project manager), Arthur Vokes (curator of Archaeological Repository Collections), and Theah Erickson (Archaeological Repository). (J. Weakly, ASM.)

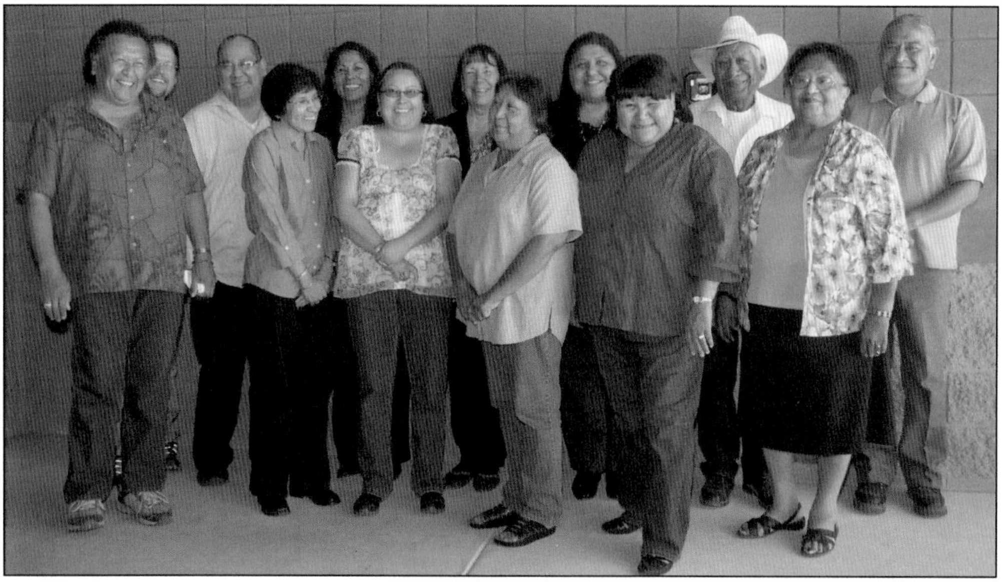

In 1992, ASM formally established a Native American Advisory Group from Arizona tribes to advise the museum. In 1999, it was renamed the Southwest Native Nations Advisory Board. Here, attendees of an April 2009 meeting pose outside the Ak-Chin Indian Community Library. They are, from left to right, Herb Stevens (San Carlos Apache tribe), Karl Hoerig (representing the White Mountain Apache tribe), Michael Tsosie (Colorado River Indian tribes), Alyce Sadongei (ASM curator for Native American Relations), Elaine F. Peters (Ak-Chin Indian Community), Valerie Epaloose (Zuni Pueblo), Judie Piner (Yavapai-Apache Nation), Willa Scott (Fort Yuma Quechan tribe), Vernelda Grant (San Carlos Apache tribe), Karen Ray (Fort McDowell Yavapai Nation), Joseph T. Joaquin (Tohono O'odham Nation), Pauline José (Fort Yuma Quechan tribe), and Barnaby V. Lewis (Gila River Indian Community). (Lisa Falk, ASM.)

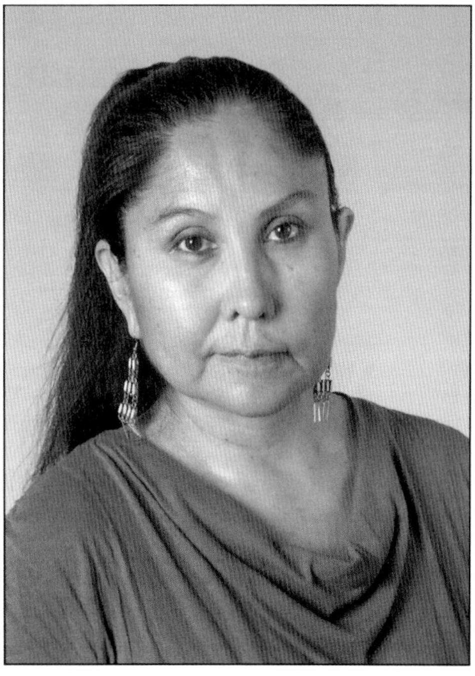

With the establishment of the tribal advisory group came the creation of a curator of American Indian Programs position, to be staffed by a Native American. The first curator was Alyce Sadongei (Kiowa/Tohono O'odham), who served from January 1999 to November 2010, intensified ASM's working relationships with tribes, and changed the title to curator for Native American Relations. After a hiatus caused by financial constraints, Martina Dawley (Hualapai/Navajo), shown here, took up the position in July 2013. (J. Weakly, ASM.)

Bibliography

Ball, Phyllis. *A Photographic History of the University of Arizona 1885–1985*. Second printing, with corrections. Tucson: University of Arizona Foundation, 1987.

Bostwick, Todd W. *Byron Cummings: Dean of Southwest Archaeology*. Tucson: University of Arizona Press. 2006.

Brace, Martha A. and Nancy J. Parezo. "The Arizona State Museum." *American Indian Art Magazine* 10(1):24–31. Winter 1984.

Burgess, Don. "Romans in Tucson? The Story of an Archaeological Hoax." *Journal of the Southwest* 51(1):3–135. Spring 2009.

Dittemore, Diane, Mike Jacobs, and Patrick Lyons. "The Southwestern Pottery Collection at the Arizona State Museum: An American Treasure." *American Indian Art Magazine* 33(4):68–77. Autumn 2008.

Gifford, Carol A. and Elizabeth A. Morris. "Digging for Credit: Early Archaeological Field Schools in the American Southwest." *American Antiquity* 50(2):395–411. April 1985.

Hartmann, Gayle Harrison and Sharon F. Urban. "The Arizona Archaeological and Historical Society: Its First Seventy-Five Years." *Kiva* 56(4):329-357. 1991.

Haury, Emil W. *Point of Pines, Arizona: A History of the University of Arizona Archaeological Field School*. Anthropological Papers of the University of Arizona 50. Tucson: University of Arizona Press. 1989.

———. "Reflections on the Arizona State Museum: 1925 and Ensuing Years." *Journal of the Southwest* 46(1):129–163. Spring 2004.

Johnston, Bernice. "Fifty Years of the Arizona Archaeological and Historical Society." *The Kiva* 32(2):42-56. December 1966.

Thompson, Raymond H. "Emil W. Haury and the Definition of Southwestern Archaeology." *American Antiquity* 60(4):640–660. October 1995.

———. "Anthropology at the University of Arizona, 1893–2005." *Journal of the Southwest* 47(3):327–374. Autumn 2005.

Welch, John R. "'A Monument to Native Civilization': Byron Cummings' Still-Unfolding Vision for Kinishba Ruins." *Journal of the Southwest* 49(1):1–94. Spring 2007.

Wilcox, David R. "Creating a Firm Foundation: The Early Years of the Arizona State Museum." *Journal of the Southwest* 47(3):375–410. Autumn 2005.

Wilder, Carleton S. "The Arizona State Museum: History." *The Kiva* 7(7–8):26–29. April–May 1942.